A Dozen Lessons for Entrepreneurs

FOREWORD BY SCOTT BELSKY

A DOZEN LESSONS

FOR

ENTREPRENEURS

TREN GRIFFIN

Columbia Business School
Publishing

Columbia University Press
Publishers Since 1893
New York Chichester, West Sussex
cup.columbia.edu
Copyright © 2017 Columbia University Press
All rights reserved

Library of Congress Cataloging-in-Publication Data
Names: Griffin, Trenholme J., author.
Title: A dozen lessons for entrepreneurs / Tren Griffin.
Description: New York : Columbia University Press, [2017] | Includes index.
Identifiers: LCCN 2017025169| ISBN 9780231184823 (cloth : alk. paper) |
ISBN 9780231545693 (e-book)
Subjects: LCSH: Businesspeople—Case studies. | Entrepreneurship—
Case studies. | New business enterprises—Case studies. | Success in
business—Case studies.
Classification: LCC HC29 .G75 2017 | DDC 658.1/1—dc23
LC record available at https://lccn.loc.gov/2017025169

Columbia University Press books are printed on permanent
and durable acid-free paper.
Printed in the United States of America

Cover design: Fifth Letter

Contents

Concept Directory   x

Foreword by Scott Belsky   xiii

Introduction   1

I. THE FOUNDER COACHES

1
Steve Blank   9

2
Bill Campbell   20

3
Eric Ries   30

II. THE VENTURE CAPITALISTS

4
Sam Altman: Y Combinator   43

Contents

5

Steve Anderson: Baseline Ventures   51

6

Marc Andreessen: Andreessen Horowitz   58

7

Rich Barton: Expedia, Glassdoor, Zillow   69

8

Roelof Botha: Sequoia Capital   78

9

Jim Breyer: Breyer Capital   85

10

Chris Dixon: Andreessen Horowitz   91

11

John Doerr: Kleiner Perkins Caufield & Byers   101

12

Peter Fenton: Benchmark   108

13

Jim Goetz: Sequoia Capital   115

14

Paul Graham: Y Combinator   124

15

Kirsten Green: Forerunner Ventures   133

Contents

16
Bill Gurley: Benchmark   143

17
Reid Hoffman: Greylock Partners   151

18
Ben Horowitz: Andreessen Horowitz   162

19
Vinod Khosla: Khosla Ventures   171

20
Josh Kopelman: First Round Capital   180

21
Jenny Lee: GGV Capital   188

22
Doug Leone: Sequoia Capital   195

23
Dan Levitan: Maveron   203

24
Jessica Livingston: Y Combinator   212

25
Mary Meeker: Kleiner Perkins Caufield & Byers   221

26
Michael Moritz: Sequoia Capital   229

Contents

27

Chamath Palihapitiya: Social Capital   236

28

Keith Rabois: Khosla Ventures   248

29

Andy Rachleff: Wealthfront   257

30

Naval Ravikant: AngelList   264

31

Heidi Roizen: Draper Fisher Jurvetson   273

32

Mark Suster: Upfront Ventures   280

33

Peter Thiel: Founders Fund   289

34

Fred Wilson: Union Square Ventures   297

35

Ann Winblad: Hummer Winblad Venture Partners   304

Conclusion   313

Glossary   315

Concept Directory

Use the chart below to understand major concepts mentioned in this book. The larger the number, the more that concept is discussed. The number after each name is the question asked in each person's chapter.

Power Law

Paul Graham #2
Bill Gurley #5
Reid Hoffman #1
Ben Horowitz #12
Vinod Khosla #1
Jenny Lee #2
Dan Levitan #10
Mary Meeker #1
Michael Moritz #11

Marc Andreessen #1   Chamath Palihapitiya
Steve Blank #12   #9
Roelof Botha #2, #12   Andy Rachleff #9
John Doerr #1   Naval Ravikant #3
Chris Dixon #1, #8   Peter Thiel #12
Jim Goetz #10   Fred Wilson #1

Contrarian

Reid Hoffman #2, #3
Ben Horowitz #5
Vinod Khosla #3
Dan Levitan #1, #11
Jessica Livingston
  #6, #12
Mary Meeker #8
Michael Mortiz #3
Andy Rachleff #11

Marc Andreessen #2   Naval Ravikant #5
Jim Breyer #1, #7   Eric Ries #10
Chris Dixon #1   Peter Thiel #11
Paul Graham #1, #4   Fred Wilson #2
Bill Gurley #12

Venture Capital

Steve Anderson #1
Kirsten Green #4
Josh Kopelman #7, #12
Doug Leone #10
Dan Levitan #7, #8
Jessica Livingston #1
Michael Moritz #5
Keith Rabois #6
Andy Rachleff #10
Heidi Roizen #7

Cycles

Jim Breyer #1, #4
Bill Gurley #2
Kirsten Green #1
Jenny Lee #5
Mary Meeker #6
Michael Moritz #10
Andy Rachleff #6
Fred Wilson #12
Mark Suster #7

Markets

9

Rich Barton #8, #9
Roelof Botha #5
Chris Dixon #8
Jim Goetz #4
Paul Graham #3
Dan Levitan #10
Andy Rachleff #1, #3
Naval Ravikant #8
Mark Suster #12

Missionary

9

Sam Altman #1
Steve Blank #5
Roelof Botha #1
John Doerr #5
Jim Goetz #1, #2
Paul Graham #9
Jenny Lee #1
Chamath Palihapitiya #12
Eric Ries #12

Recruiting

9

Sam Altman #10
Rich Barton #10
Steve Blank #9
Bill Campbell #7
Peter Fenton #1
Doug Leone #3
Dan Levitan #3
Heidi Roizen #5
Peter Thiel #9

Luck

8

Roelof Botha #7
Jim Breyer #12
Bill Gurley #3
Vinod Khosla #5
Josh Kopelman #11
Jessica Livingston #8
Michael Moritz #12
Heidi Roizen #9

Angel

7

Steve Anderson #1
Paul Graham #2
Jessica Livingston #5
Doug Leone #9
Keith Rabois #5
Naval Ravikant #3
Peter Thiel #6

Burn Rate

7

Sam Altman #10
Steve Anderson #4
Paul Graham #8
Ben Horowitz #10
Chamath Palihapitiya #10
Mark Suster #2
Fred Wilson #4

Founder

7

Chris Dixon #2
Paul Graham #5, #9
Josh Kopelman #2, #3
Jenny Lee #2
Dan Levitan #2
Chamath Palihapitiya #12
Keith Rabois #3, #4

Moat

7

Sam Altman #1, #5
Rich Barton #1
Jim Goetz #6
Bill Gurley #9
Reid Hoffman #3
Vinod Khosla #4
Peter Thiel #1

People

7

Marc Andreessen #5
Jim Breyer #9
Paul Graham #8
Vinod Khosla #5
Jenny Lee #1
Dan Levitan #1, #5
Keith Rabois #9

Humility and Hubris

6

Marc Andreessen #3
Jim Breyer #4
Bill Campbell #11
Peter Thiel #10
Doug Leone #7
Chamath Palihapitiya #5

Risk, Uncertainty and Ignorance

6

Steven Blank #4
Paul Graham #7
Jenny Lee #12
Vinod Khosla #8
Michael Moritz #1
Andy Rachleff #8

Innovation

5

Eric Ries #7
Ben Horowitz #5, #9
Jessica Livingston #10, #11
Andy Rachleff #4
Peter Thiel #2

Foreword

SCOTT BELSKY,
ENTREPRENEUR, AUTHOR, AND INVESTOR

Entrepreneurship: The Discipline of Reconciling Contradictions

"Entrepreneurship education" is a bit of a misnomer.

How can a discipline all about creating something new have a set of "best practices"? The entrepreneurs we celebrate most, from across industries, did not study the past to create the future. They may have leveraged skills in business, technology, and design, but they defied conventions, ignored the experts, and shunned the status quo all along the way.

For the budding entrepreneurs among us, there is no shortage of advice. Legendary founders write books and give talks, presenting their lessons learned the hard way—neatly tied with a bow. Investors are also not shy about sharing their wisdom, garnered from years in the boardroom and the patterns they have noticed over the course of their careers. Nevertheless, all this advice is coming from highly nuanced businesses, each with its own culture, industry, and timing. Such a myriad of perspectives yield wisdom that is both valuable and contradictory. Just a few examples . . .

We learn that experts lead industries, but we see industries transformed by neophytes.

We train to pursue industry expertise through advanced degrees and decades of experience. However, outsiders lead the boldest transformations, like Uber disrupting transportation or Airbnb disrupting hospitality. Perhaps the playbook of industry disruption requires being naïve enough at the start to question basic assumptions and then staying alive long enough to employ skills that are unique and advantageous in the industry you seek to change.

We are encouraged to be original but discouraged from reinventing the wheel.

Innovation is great, as long as we do not create something unfamiliar to customers. We learn quickly that our desire to create new terminology to differentiate our products is liable to confuse customers. Like most entrepreneurs, I learned this the hard way—naming the creative fields of Behance (the online network for creative professionals I founded in 2005) "realms" and the groups "circles," only to subsequently change their names back to the simpler "fields" and "groups." Designing new user experiences by defying normal conventions disorients users. Over time, entrepreneurs learn that innovation helps you stand out, but familiarity helps you engage.

We celebrate leaders who ruthlessly change industries while admiring leaders who build excellent teams with humility and compassion.

I have met many founders over the years who justify their arrogance with Steve Jobs anecdotes, their reality-defying confidence by comparing themselves to Elon Musk, or their culture-first orientation by citing Howard Schultz or Tony Hsieh. However, by trying to adopt the personas of leaders we admire based on their public characterizations, we fail to acknowledge the nuances of timing, circumstances, and relationships that make all the difference. You can ask for tips, but you cannot adopt someone else's approach in aggregate. More than anything else, the journey of building a company is really the construction of your own one-of-a-kind playbook for building a team, culture, and product.

We are told to listen to our customers but are reminded that customers seldom know what they need.

While big companies conduct focus groups and market research to iterate their products, small and nimble startups launch and iterate entirely new products that kill industry incumbents. The greatest new businesses create new markets or redefine old markets in ways that customers never would have imagined. How do you listen to customers and parse their unknown needs from what they claim they want? How do you discern between cynicism and criticism to seek feedback while not being deterred by scrutiny and doubt? At some point in his or her journey, every great entrepreneur learns to gain confidence from doubt. If everyone thinks you are crazy, you are either crazy or you are really onto something. Nothing extraordinary is ever achieved through ordinary means.

We are taught to plan but advised that nothing ever goes as planned.

Every seasoned entrepreneur knows that business plans are a helpful introductory exercise but nothing more. The rational and carefully planned strategy instantly falls apart on the battlefield.

It's all gut and rapid iteration as you venture into the unknown. The advice you hear from others are tactics without context. Make a plan, and edit it indefinitely.

Entrepreneurship is a business of exceptions.

Rather than selectively subscribing to whatever advice you get, perhaps the real wisdom is in the contradictions themselves. Entrepreneurship is, at its very core, a discipline of reconciling contradiction—absorbing case studies and best practices but not adopting them outright. It is an intricate balance of skill and instinct, of learning and defying.

For this reason, as an entrepreneur and investor, I have long enjoyed Tren's famous "Twelve Lessons" posts over the years. Tren captures invaluable wisdom on entrepreneurship from every angle. Tren does not proclaim to have the "right answers," nor does he subscribe to a plan for the unforeseeable. Instead, he captures and analyzes the gems from a long list of enterprising minds that break new ground in their respective fields.

The only study of entrepreneurship you need beyond your own experiential education from doing it is to reconcile the insights you get from all angles so that you can triangulate your own approach to building a team, culture, and vision—and an enduring business that is both uniquely you and bigger than you.

Scott Belsky is an entrepreneur, author, and investor. Scott founded Behance, the leading online platform for the creative industry to showcase and discover creative world, and served as CEO until Adobe acquired Behance in 2012. After the acquisition, Scott served as Adobe's vice-president of products. Scott actively advises and invests in businesses that cross the intersection of technology and design and that help empower people. He is a venture partner with Benchmark and was an early adviser to and investor in Peri-scope, Pinterest, sweetgreen, and Uber. He continues to advise and invest in early-stage startups. He is also the author of Making Ideas Happen, *and he is the founder of 99U, a publication and annual conference devoted to productivity in the creative world.*

A Dozen Lessons for Entrepreneurs

Introduction

THIS BOOK IS ABOUT entrepreneurship. The delivery mechanism for the ideas presented here is the insights of some of the most successful venture capitalists and coaches of business founders in the world.

The venture capital industry has created more new industries, as well as significantly greater wealth, than any other approach to business formation in the history of capitalism. The founder coaches and individual venture capitalists discussed here have been major facilitators of that value creation and, in the process, have obtained immeasurable insights and timeless wisdom that can be shared with any (and every) entrepreneur.

The raw material for the book are interviews I have conducted and read over the past four years with a group of incredibly talented individuals who have seen more highly successful businesses launched than any other single group on the planet. It is possible to learn from both their successes and failures. If one presumes that experience equates to wisdom when processed by people who have excellent judgment and above-average intellects, then this book could be retitled "Wisdom for Entrepreneurs."

One attribute that the individuals featured in this book share is that they are natural teachers. While the featured individuals are each unique, they do tend to share certain bedrock methods of approaching business. They are presented alphabetically.

Why the separate category of founder coaches? First, the people who coach founders deserve a unique category. A founder coach helps entrepreneurs develop as individuals, managers, and leaders. The coach mentors the founder by asking the right questions and giving advice. Many of the best venture capitalists are founder coaches, but not all founder coaches are venture capitalists. One of the venture capitalists profiled in this book said about one of the greatest founder coaches, "I know Bill Campbell wouldn't want to be called a venture capitalist. He always used to tell me he wasn't one. He said 'You make the investment decisions. I just want to work with the entrepreneurs.'" Second, by having a short, upfront section on founder coaches, the book naturally begins with an introduction to the process of helping entrepreneurs.

Six of the thirty-five people profiled in this book are women, which is more than double the industry average on a percentage basis at a senior investing level. The number of women venture capitalists at this senior level is low despite the fact that women represent 60 percent of noninvesting roles at venture firms. I am hopeful that diversity—and more importantly inclusion of all kinds—will rise in the venture capital business. Studies have shown that a diverse team produces better business and investing outcomes—diversity allows you to see more ideas, include more perspectives, and consider more products for broader consumer bases. Scott Belsky, who wrote the insightful foreword, believes, as I do, that diversity produces better outcomes:

Diversity of opinions and circumstances increases the likelihood of 'happy accidents.' Serendipity comes from differences.

Both entrepreneurs and investors must build teams that increase the odds of working at the edge of reason. The solution in one word: diversity. Diversity means different personalities, genders, backgrounds, educations, experiences, nationalities/ethnicities, etc. Diversity shouldn't be a biological checkbox since it is more nuanced than that. The best way to increase the odds that your team will see things you don't is to assemble incredibly different incredible people.

As this book was nearing final production, news broke that prominent venture capitalists were being accused of sexual harassment. This news is clear evidence that significant new efforts are needed to create a more open, transparent and welcome environment where founders and other startup employees of all genders, ethnicity, nationalities and sexual preferences can thrive.

The book includes a glossary and a concept map, which will help readers understand the principles shared by these founder coaches and venture capitalists. If you encounter an unfamiliar term in this book, such as "power-law distribution," you can refer to the glossary for a definition and then refer to the concept map to see which of the individuals reference that term. I have found that by understanding the views of several venture capitalists on a particular issue, it is possible to see whether they adopt consistent or diverse approaches and to identify patterns that can be applied to pursue similar success.

It is wise to pay careful attention when a significant number of founder coaches and venture capitalists advocate the same idea.

Three concepts appear often enough in the book that they should be defined up front. The first of these concepts is "convexity," which Jeff Bezos describes using the following baseball analogy:

Outsized returns often come from betting against conventional wisdom, and conventional wisdom is usually right. Given a 10 percent chance of a one hundred–times payoff, you should take that bet every time. But you're still going to be wrong nine times out of ten. We all know that if you swing for the fences, you're going to strike out a lot, but you're also going to hit some home runs. The difference between baseball and business, however, is that baseball has a truncated outcome distribution. When you swing, no matter how well you connect with the ball, the most runs you can get is four. In business, every once in a while, when you step up to the plate, you can score 1,000 runs. This long-tailed distribution of returns is why it's important to be bold. Big winners pay for so many experiments.

For those of you who may be unfamiliar with baseball, a home run is a hit of the ball that enables the batter to cross all four bases and score a run. The second key concept, which also comes from baseball, is the grand slam, which refers to a home run hit when all three bases are occupied by other base runners (a situation referred to as "bases loaded"), thereby scoring four runs with just one hit. A grand-slam outcome in venture capital may deliver one hundred to one thousand runs instead of just four as is in baseball. A grand slam in venture capital refers to an investment that produces a distributed spendable (liquid) return of one or more times the size of an entire venture capital fund. For example, for a firm with a $400 million fund, an investing grand slam would be a single investment that generates a return of more than $400 million. A grand slam is different from what some people call a unicorn in that a valuation is often not enough since the outcome must produce a distributed return of liquid assets to investors.

The third concept is the importance of having a "contrarian" outlook. The best venture capital investors believe that the most effective way to find convexity in their businesses is to adopt a perspective that goes against the views of most other market participants. This belief is true of all investing, not just venture capital. The hedge fund investor Ray Dalio puts it this way:

You have to be an independent thinker because you can't make money agreeing with the consensus view, which is already embedded in the price. Whenever you're betting against the consensus, there's a significant probability you're going to be wrong, so you have to be humble.

The investors profiled in this book believe that the best place to find convexity is where other investors and business founders are not looking. The first person I heard refer to the concept of a contrarian outlook in the venture capital business was Andy Rachleff, who has said he borrowed it from the famous investor Howard Marks. According to Marks, "The problem is that extraordinary performance comes only from correct nonconsensus forecasts, but nonconsensus forecasts are hard to make, hard to make correctly, and hard to act on." Airbnb is a classic example of founders thinking differently. Marc Andreessen said once that the conventional wisdom about Airbnb was "people staying in each other's houses without there being a lot of ax murders?" The book will go much more deeply into how to apply this contrarian outlook.

The famous investor Sam Zell once described the relationship among convexity, grand slams, and a contrarian approach to investing in this simple way: "Listen, business is easy. If you've got a low downside and a big upside, you do it. If you've got a big downside and a small upside, you run away. The only time you have any work to do is when you have a big downside and a big upside."

I

The Founder Coaches

1

Steve Blank

STEVE BLANK WORKED FOR eight technology companies over the course of twenty-one years before deciding to devote more of his professional life to teaching other people how to build successful startups. Andy Rachleff, a venture capitalist, has said, "Steve Blank wrote an amazing book called *The Four Steps to the Epiphany* that really started this whole idea of a Customer Development Process." Steve's contributions to what has become known as the Lean Startup movement are foundational. He was a natural choice to be the first person discussed in this book (especially since his name starts with "B"). When Steve makes a point about business, he is speaking from personal experience. He founded Epiphany in his living room in 1996; two semiconductor companies, Zilog and MIPS Computers; the workstation company Convergent Technologies; and several other startups. He is also the author of *The Startup Owner's Manual* and several other books.

1. "A startup is a temporary organization designed to search for a repeatable and scalable business model."

A business model describes how your company creates, delivers, and captures value.

There are several different approaches to defining a business model. I like the definition created by the venture capitalist Mike Maples Jr.: A business model is "the way that a business converts innovation into economic value." A capitalist economy is an evolutionary system. Innovation and best practices are discovered through the experimentation of entrepreneurs who try to establish the evolutionary fitness of their businesses. Products and services that are more fit survive, and the less fit die. Entrepreneurs run experiments when they create or alter a business. Blank and others have created ways to establish a business model by applying a trial-and-error process to a hypothesis to discover the optimal result, rather than trying to create a grand plan at once from whole cloth.

2. "A company is a permanent organization designed to execute a repeatable and scalable business model."

Large corporations are large because they found a repeatable business model, and they spend most of their energy performing—meaning doing the same thing over and over again. They figured out what the secret is to growing their business.

A business is no longer a startup once it has a repeatable and scalable business model. Blank has said that that once a business is no longer a startup, it may begin to develop "antibodies," which stifle the development of new products and services, as well as new business models. There is an inherent tension between the creation of new, repeatable, scalable business models and the optimal execution of an existing business model, because superior execution often involves eliminating anything not core to the mission of the existing model.

3. "Business plans are the tool existing companies use for execution. They are the wrong tool to search for a business model."

Startups are not smaller versions of larger companies. They are something very different. Business plans are operating programs. Startups don't even know what it is they are supposed to be operating. A business plan is the last thing you want a startup to write.

A business plan is exactly like telling you to go boil water when someone's having a baby: It's to keep you busy, but there's no correlation between success and your activity.

In a startup, no business plan survives first contact with customers.

The world is changing so quickly and there is so much risk and uncertainty that a detailed long-term business plan is essentially a work of fiction, and writing one is a waste of precious time and resources. One of the best business books on what it is like to actually run a business is *Shoe Dog*, written by Phil Knight, which chronicles the story of Nike. The book describes the long, hard slog that building a business inevitably entails. Knight says, "We had no master plan. It was totally seat of the pants. . . . There is an immutable conflict at work in life and in business, a constant battle between peace and chaos. Neither can be mastered, but both can be influenced. How you go about that is the key to success." Nassim Taleb described why business plans rob businesses of their potential value when he said, "A rigid business plan gets one locked into a preset invariant policy, like a highway without exits—hence devoid of optionality."

4. "A startup is not about executing a series of knowns.
Most startups are facing a series of unknowns:
unknown customer segments, unknown customer needs,
unknown product feature sets, etc."

A pessimist sees the danger in every opportunity, but an optimist sees opportunity in every danger.

Founders and investors harvest the biggest financial returns when uncertainty is greatest since that is when assets are most likely to be mispriced. In making decisions, founders and investors must assess three factors:

1. *Risk:* Future states of the world are known, and the probabilities of those future states are known (as in roulette).
2. *Uncertainty:* Future states of the world are known, but the probabilities of those future states are unknown (as with most things in life).
3. *Ignorance:* Future states of the world are unknown, and probabilities are therefore not computable (a state of unknown unknowns).

A founder or investor who can remain rational despite risk, uncertainty, and ignorance will be better able to capitalize on a mispriced opportunity. It is when other investors act emotionally rather than rationally that assets and opportunities may be mispriced. For example, it was precisely when the economy was at its lowest point after the financial crisis of 2008 that the greatest opportunities existed for an investor or founder. The best time to found a business is often in a downturn since employees are easier to recruit, resources are less expensive, and competition is less intense. It takes courage to found a business, especially in a recession, but that courage can pay big dividends. Optimists and people who have been through previous business cycles are much more likely to realize that the business environment will inevitably get better despite a downward phase; they understand that business cycles inevitably swing from boom to bust and back again.

5. "Products developed with senior management out in front of customers early and often win. Products handed off to a sales and marketing organization that has only been tangentially involved in the new product development process lose. It's that simple."

> The reality for most companies today is that existing product introduction methodologies are focused on activities that go on inside a company's building. While customer input may be a checkpoint or "gate" in the process, it doesn't drive it.
>
> There are no facts inside the building, so get the hell outside.

Blank has developed what he calls a Customer-Development Process, based on the idea that startups should apply the scientific method just as scientists do: Start with a hypothesis, test it, and prove it—or move on to further iterations of the hypothesis if it proves incorrect. Startups should therefore start with the product and then try to find its market, as opposed to starting with the market and then trying to find the product. Nothing drives the Customer-Development Process forward more efficiently than time spent with actual customers. The best founders, CEOs, managers, and engineers spend massive amounts of time with their customers. They do so because they love their products and want to share this love with others.

6. "This whole 'lean' stuff works best if you've failed once. If you've failed once, you appreciate the value of not just following your passion, but maybe devoting 10 percent to testing your passion before you commit three to four years of your life to it."

Good judgment tends to come from experience, which tends to come from bad judgment. So failure, while painful, can often have positive benefits. Certainly, it is less painful to learn from the mistakes of others, but personal failure is the most memorable. Few things in starting up a business are more precious than time and energy spent early in the process figuring out whether "the dogs will eat the dog food." Following your passion right off a cliff makes no sense if a relatively small effort devoted to the early testing of an idea can keep you from that fate.

7. " 'Build it and they will come' is not a strategy; it's a prayer.
Why are so many founders so reluctant to invest even five
hundred or one thousand hours upfront to be sure that, when
they're done, the business they're building will face genuine,
substantial demand or enthusiasm? Without passionate customers,
even the most passionate entrepreneur will flounder at best."

Psychological denial can be very powerful. People who want something badly often just pretend they have created something consumers will want to buy when there is no evidence that this is the case since the reality is too terrible to contemplate. For example, a team running out of seed funds and under pressure from investors may convince itself that it has created a product desired by consumers even though a child of ten knows the product isn't valuable enough for customers to pay for it. If a business has not discovered *core product value* (a solution to a valuable customer problem), no amount of growth is going to save that business.

8. "The company that consistently makes and implements
decisions rapidly gains a tremendous, often decisive,
competitive advantage."

What matters is having forward momentum and a tight, fact-based data–metrics feedback loop to help you quickly recognize and reverse any incorrect decisions. That's why startups are agile. By the time a big company gets the committee to organize the subcommittee to pick a meeting date, your startup could have made twenty decisions, reversed five of them, and implemented the fifteen that worked.

The businesses that survive in a rapidly evolving environment are those that are most agile. The lean startup movement and agile development both use a process of continuous experimentation and feedback from the results of experiments to stay on top of changes.Nassim Taleb describes a foundational principle for this type of approach in his book *Antifragile*: "Any trial and error can be seen as the expression of an option, so long as one is capable of identifying a favorable result and exploiting it."

9. "Founders see a vision, but then they manage to attract a set of world-class employees to help them create that vision."

A founder must be able to sell many things to build a successful startup. A founder's ability to recruit a team is tested early. Convincing world-class people to join something with as much uncertainty attached to it as a startup is a genuinely valuable skill and optimally the work of a person with missionary zeal. The best venture capitalists know that the first hires are critical so they will often help founders with recruiting, especially at very early stages or with first hires.

10. "You don't have to be the smartest person, but showing up is 80 percent of the game. My career has been all about just showing up and people saying, 'Who's here? Blank is here. Let's pick him.' Volunteering and showing up has been a great thing for me. But all along the way, I've always been very good

at pattern recognition and picking signal out of the noise. Not smarter than everyone else, but more competent perhaps at seeing patterns."

Basic but critical actions like being on time and developing sound judgment are the blocking and tackling of the startup and business worlds. In a letter, Woody Allen once wrote about a famous saying attributed to him:

> My observation was that once a person actually completed a play or a novel, he was well on his way to getting it produced or published, as opposed to a vast majority of people who tell me their ambition is to write, but who strike out on the very first level and indeed never write the play or book. In the midst of the conversation, as I'm now trying to recall, I did say that 80 percent of success is showing up.

To create a startup or new line of business, you must first start. As an example, the way I wrote my first book was to just start writing. I didn't know anything about book proposals, agents, or the ins and outs of the publishing world. I just wrote a book and sent it to a publisher, who accepted it. I would not recommend that process now, knowing more about the industry, but by writing that first book, I "showed up."

11. "Upper management needs to understand that a new division pursuing disruptive innovation is not the same as a division adding a new version of an established product. Rather, it is an organization searching for a business model (inside a company that's executing an existing one). When you're doing disruptive innovation in a multibillion-dollar company, a $10 million/ year new product line doesn't even move the needle. So to get new divisions launched, large optimistic forecasts are the

norm. Ironically, one of the greatest risks in large companies is high-pressure expectations to make these first-pass forecasts that subvert an honest Customer-Development Process. The temptation is to transform the vision of a large market into a reliable corporate revenue forecast—before Customer Development even begins."

Established businesses spend a lot of time coming up with optimistic market forecasts. It can also happen at many startups. These market forecasts are often created using methods pioneered by "Professor Rosy Scenario." Market-research firms make a great living supplying these supportive forecasts, some of which may leverage confirmation bias to make the firms popular with clients. Unfortunately, many of these market-research forecasts are often little more than imaginative storytelling. I like stories. Stories can be useful in motivating people and can be fun to tell. But it is important to remember that they are just stories and may not apply to reality in a significant way.

12. "I said, 'There are five hundred people in this room. The good news is, in ten years, there's two of you who are going to make $100 million. The rest of you, you might as well have been working at Walmart for how much you're going to make.' And everybody laughs. And I said, 'No, no, that's not the joke. The joke is all of you are looking at the other guys feeling sorry for those poor sons of bitches.'"

Financial success in creating and funding startups follows a power-law distribution. This phenomenon occurs because, in venture capital and entrepreneurship, feedback introduced by correlated and nonindependent decisions can produce network effects and information cascades. In contrast, so-called normal distributions arise from many independent random decisions averaging out. You will hear the term "power law" mentioned and discussed throughout this book since it is central to the venture capital business and to startups generally.

Founders, employees, consumers, and distributors take cues from previous successes in making decisions. In this way, past success feeds back on itself. The best venture capital firms and startups tend to get the best results, and the distribution of financial returns tends to reflect a power-law distribution. The researcher Duncan Watts writes about this phenomenon more generally:

> People almost never make decisions independently—in part because the world abounds with so many choices that we have little hope of ever finding what we want on our own. . . . When people tend to like what other people like, differences in popularity are subject to what is called "cumulative advantage," or the "rich get richer" effect. This means that if one object happens to be slightly more popular than another at just the right point, it will tend to become more popular still.

Overconfidence bias makes most people believe that they will be included among the winners. The inevitable failures that occur in attempts to create a new startup business are hard for the individuals involved but are the right thing for society. Nassim Taleb writes, "Most of you will fail, disrespected, impoverished, but we are grateful for the risks you are taking and the sacrifices you are making for the sake of the economic growth of the planet and pulling others out of poverty. You are the source of our antifragility. Our nation thanks you." Being a founder or early employee of a startup is not a rational act, given the odds of success. Of course, as George Bernard Shaw wrote in *Man and Superman*, "All progress depends on the unreasonable human being." The reason books like *The Hard Thing About Hard Things* by Ben Horowitz and *Shoe Dog* by Phil Knight resonate so strongly with people who have been involved in startups is that they accurately describe the terror, inevitable setbacks, and daily struggle of life in a startup business, not just the seemingly glamorous parts of the experience. Scott Belsky calls this stage of building a business "the messy middle."

2

Bill Campbell

BILL CAMPBELL, WHO PASSED away in 2016, was known as "Coach" to many of the most influential and famous people in in the world. His transition from head football coach at Columbia University to an extraordinarily successful business leader is legendary. His many business triumphs include serving as Apple's vice-president of marketing beginning in 1983 and later serving on the board of directors of businesses like Intuit and Apple. Bill Campbell coached leading business executives like Steve Jobs of Apple, Jeff Bezos of Amazon, and Larry Page of Google. Effective, insightful, hardworking, humble, trusted, and loyal are all words that apply to Bill Campbell. Benchmark's Bill Gurley points out, "When you had Bill coaching the entrepreneurs, it was like having extra wild cards in a game of five-card draw."

1. "Growth is the goal, and it comes through having innovation.
Innovation comes through having great engineers,
not great product-marketing guys."

Empowered engineers are the single most important thing that you can have in a company.

An innovative culture exists where the crazy guys have stature, where engineers are important. The Campbell School is that engineers need to have clout.

I've seen businesses dominated by a single discipline many times. Sometimes it is the sales team, sometimes it is engineering, sometimes it is scientists, sometimes it is finance, sometimes it is operations, and sometimes it is marketing. The background of the founders and CEO makes a huge difference in terms of which discipline is predominant in a given business. It is evident which discipline Campbell thinks should dominate: engineering. Marc Andreessen adds,

This view that engineering should dominate was *extremely* unusual in Silicon Valley in the '90s and early–mid-2000s when it mattered for the companies Bill worked with (Apple and Google in particular). And *particularly* extremely unusual for people with sales and marketing backgrounds like Bill himself has. It's become much more common in Silicon Valley today, but I can't tell you how unusual it was for Bill to have that view all along.

2. "When I first came out to Silicon Valley, everybody wanted to hire the IBM sales guys to be their CEO. Blue suit, white shirt, red tie. Unfortunately, these guys were all sales guys. I mean, that's all they did. And those guys all failed miserably because they didn't know the product, they didn't understand the technology; all they could do was sell."

It is no longer enough to look good in a suit, have great hair and teeth, and be a fantastic salesperson to succeed as a manager or CEO. If you don't deeply understand the products and services of the business, the competition will eat you alive. Great CEOs and managers today have many skills and are learning machines. Campbell once said, "I was very devoted to learning the businesses. I never felt I was behind technology-wise. I could learn just like everybody else. I have a consistent bias for technical stuff, and it's that hard to learn." Marc Andreessen has pointed out that while Campbell was respectful of engineers, he was not threatened by them. Campbell cracked the code for how to have a productive partnership with tech visionaries.

3. "I am a big bully about the sales process where you're the CEO and I want you to buy something, so I take you for drinks or buy your wife a gold chain. People think these guys, they're killers, they're machines, and they know how to do this stuff. They make sales this mysterious process. The jet pilot swoops in, bombs everybody up and down, and then everyone else is ready to go and clean up. I don't believe it. I want to come in there with a quantitative process and say, 'Let me tell you what our stuff does, and let me tell you based on our work what this can do for you regarding your productivity.' "

Campbell believed that sales is an essential profession. But he believed that sales is a different game now than during the days when people were selling IBM typewriters using old-school sales processes. There isn't enough remaining slack in the system to make the "schmooze the CEO, buy a gold chain" sales process effective anymore. People who sell today know that the sales process is about providing a solution to real problems and helping customers with the internal processes related to approving the sale. Andreessen agrees: "Great salespeople in the modern era are consultants to the customer and help them first justify the purchase and then succeed with the product."

4. "We have to be careful about the customer. I learned this
from Steve Jobs years ago. When I came to Apple, I brought
my Kodak research mentality, and Steve's view was, 'Stuff
your research. Nobody's ever going to give you feedback on
something that they can't conceive of.' And so we would argue
those points. And I would joke with him and say, 'A marketing
person would never have conceived of a Macintosh. But a
marketing person could have made it better.' "

Certain people are savants about new products and services. They
just seem to know instinctively what the customer wants. The best
product savant I have seen up close is cable television and wireless
pioneer Craig McCaw. He has an amazing way of putting himself
in the shoes of the customer. Watching him with a new product
is fascinating. Having a brilliant insight into products or services
is a rare thing. Accordingly, processes like lean startup have been
created to efficiently test a value hypothesis so that changes or
pivots can be made to produce something similar to what a product savant might. A foundational lean startup principle is that
the process of testing a product or service can be systematized.
The best CEOs and founders have learned that trying to predict
the future is vastly inferior to discovering what customers want by
running experiments with real customers using methods based on
the scientific method.

5. "Brilliance can't be taught, but the operational stuff can be.
Do you have operational instincts? Who cares? If you work
with me for six months, I can give you enough prowess
and process to be able to go run something,
and do something with it."

That operating shit—believe me, I fucked it up so many times.
I'm an old guy; I've made many mistakes.

23

It is encouraging to hear from someone as accomplished as Campbell that you can learn operational excellence. It has been my experience that some people are more suited to being an operator than others. For example, managers like Jim Barksdale (FedEx, McCaw Cellular, and Netscape) are natural operators who also received the right coaching and mentoring early in life. The difference between great and not-great operating executives is that the former learn from mistakes and make more new ones than old ones.

6. "People like Mark Zuckerberg, they see an application of science that hasn't been done before, and they run with it. They're founders. They're product creators."

> I don't take the company unless the founder is passionate and wants to create something durable.

At the core of any great business is an entrepreneur who creates a value hypothesis in the first place so that core product value (a real and significant solution to a valuable customer problem) can be tested and discovered. Great entrepreneurs are persistent, obsessive, and relentless, but the really great entrepreneurs also seem to have a gift for looking at the world from a customer's viewpoint. These entrepreneurs seem to know instinctively what a customer wants. Steve Blank believes "the best entrepreneurs are the ones who are passionate about solving a problem because they've had it or seen others have it, love those customers, love solving that problem, or have been domain experts. Those are authentic entrepreneurs." He believes "entrepreneurs, at their heart, are artists. What comes out from the great artists is something completely unexpected. World-class entrepreneurs are driven by passion." He believes entrepreneurship is a calling rather than a job.

7. "You need a leader. You have to go out and recruit the best person you can who knows how to create an innovation culture. He or she doesn't need to be personally the most innovative person, but he or she needs to know how to foster innovation. Then give that person license to hire. Get yourself some teams. Recruit people who have the DNA that you want."

It is all about people. If you have the right people, you will end up with the right culture.

I've fired more people for attitude and behavior than I ever have for performance.

Everyone pitches in to help with recruiting in a well-run business. Great people attract great people, and if a business gets the recruiting process right, the benefits of that attraction will grow in a nonlinear way because there is a positive feedback loop. Campbell believed that the right team, people, and systems can create multiplier effects to help scale a business and drive greater profits. But, in his view, it all starts with people.

8. "If you don't have the right product and you don't time it right, you are going to fail."

Great product and great people is the whole answer.

The number of individuals and startups focused on growing a business without a valuable product is, well, a surprisingly large number. Even if these businesses somehow do manage to create a useful product, without great people, the result will almost certainly be a disaster. The other point that Campbell made was that being too early or too late in bringing a product to market is indistinguishable from being wrong.

9. "When I work with startups, the last thing I work with them
on is marketing. I don't want to overestimate marketing.
Apple's marketing has great products."

Too many marketers believe advertising is what creates brands. The investment strategist and author Michael Mauboussin astutely points out, "Brands do not confer a competitive advantage in and of themselves. Customers hire them to do a particular job. Brands that do those jobs reliably and cost-effectively thrive." Trying to create a brand via marketing without great products is like trying to make an ice cream sundae with just a glass bowl and no ice cream. Having great products is what creates a great brand. Jeff Bezos believes,

> The balance of power is shifting toward consumers and away from companies. . . . The individual is empowered. The right way to respond to this if you are a company is to put the vast majority of your energy, attention, and dollars into building a great product or service and put a smaller amount into shouting about it, marketing it. If I build a great product or service, my customers will tell each other. . . . In the old world, you devoted 30 percent of your time to building a great service and 70 percent of your time to shouting about it. In the new world, that inverts.

Bezos has also said, "Your brand is formed primarily not by what your company says about itself but what the company does."

10. "I can't do HTML, come on. I'm just coaching them on
how to run their company better."

> I'm a third-party Jiminy Cricket. There is nothing transformative that I do. I don't have the vision of a Marc Andreessen. I am an operating guy, so I help them think about what their business

should look like, how they should organize it, and how to think about data-center management.

I believe in management. If you give people the things you want them to do. Judge them on what they accomplish. Make sure that you are bottom line about everything.

They recognize that you've got a heart. You try to help them by giving them all of that rigor. They are going to call you a leader.

There was a lot of modesty in the way Campbell presented himself. He proved that you do not need to be a great engineer to be an enabler of engineers. He worked hard to understand technology. Individuals who are highly skilled at operating a business are a rare and highly valuable asset. Operating a business requires a very different set of skills than founding a business. Some founders are great operators, whereas others are not. When people describe a great operator, they will sometimes say that she or he "makes the trains run on time," which is an excellent thing since terrible things can happen to a business if the "trains aren't running on time." Great leaders are great listeners. What changes their mind on something is facts combined with logic. Opinions are not facts, and someone like Jim Barksdale knows the difference. I have always loved a famous "Barksdaleism" on this topic: "Now I'm the president around here. So if I say a chicken can pull a tractor trailer, your job is to hitch 'em up. If we have data, let's look at data. If all we have are opinions, let's go with mine."

11. "The big brand names—Kleiner Perkins, Sequoia, Benchmark, Accel, and Andreessen Horowitz—have partners that care about growing the company, and that's the most important. They can call the right people and ask them to help get things done. It's not about the exit. I sit in board meetings and fend off the antibodies—board members who only care about the exit or the 'sales pipeline.'"

There's a reason why the same venture capital firms and venture capitalists persistently deliver the lion's share of financial returns in the venture capital industry. They have the best network of people who can help a startup, as well as a brand and talent that can attract founders, people, money, distribution, and customers. Most of the time, the startup process fails to produce a grand slam, but when it succeeds, it is a marvel to behold. The key to success is the ability of the team to establish positive feedback loops. Creating both the core from which positive feedback loops grow to massive scale and the supporting systems that enable that to happen is a rare but incredibly valuable thing.

12. "My dad was a tough bastard. We had one car when I was a kid, and my mom used to drive us down to the mill to pick him up. He had worked the midnight-to-eight shift and would come out in a jacket and tie. We would drive him to school, where he would teach all day. He would go home after teaching and sleep for a few hours and then go back to the mill."

> I enjoyed being under the radar for a long time. Under the radar. Instead of being an anonymous guy who wandered around in the Valley, I became someone people focused on.

Some of the best coaches do not feel the need to be in the spotlight. They know that a great way to get things done is to let other people take the credit. I'm not saying all coaches are this way or even most, but there are great ones, like Campbell, who are like this. Unlike when he was a head football coach at Columbia, when he was working his magic in the technology industry, Campbell was not coaching college students. His students were successful executives who needed help, often in new domains. Being humble made Bill Campbell a better coach. Not being threatened by technology or technology visionaries made him great.

When I asked someone who knew Campbell well about his personality, he said, "Make sure you talk about his loyalty. Don't leave that out." When you look at all the good things Campbell has done for his hometown of Homestead, Pennsylvania, or organizations he supported, like Columbia University, you see the loyalty. Here's a nice snippet illustrating Campbell's humility:

People have asked me in Silicon Valley, "Why are you in high tech?" I ask them, "Have you seen my football record?" The crowd laughs. Then he says that football taught him about teamwork and supporting others. But most of all, he says, he learned that he had a responsibility to "give something back."

Here's a closing story from Marc Andreessen about how humble and giving Bill Campbell was:

When he worked with us at Opsware, he refused to take stock options (or any other form of compensation). I got upset about it because he was helping us so much, and I felt like it was wrong that he wasn't getting compensated. I went to talk to him about it, and he shot me down as he had before, told me he didn't want any stock options. So I threatened him: "I'm going to find out which political party you belong to, and I'm going to donate the stock options to the other one." That finally did the trick. (And I never found out what political party he belongs to.)

3

Eric Ries

ERIC RIES IS A serial entrepreneur, teacher, and author of the *New York Times* bestseller *The Lean Startup*. Andy Rachleff has described Eric's book as "the New Testament" of the lean startup movement. Not often can you say that someone has created a movement, but Eric certainly did. Like Steve Blank, Eric teaches based on personal experience. He has founded a number of start-ups, including the social network IMVU, and has a thriving seminar and consulting business. His next book, *The Startup Way: Making Entrepreneurship a Fundamental Discipline of Every Enterprise*, will publish in the fall of 2017. Eric serves on the board of directors of Code for America and on the advisory board of a number of technology startups and venture capital firms.

1. "The minimum viable product is that product which has
just those features (and no more) that allow you to
ship a product that resonates with early adopters,

some of whom will pay you money or give you feedback.
The lesson of the MVP is that any additional work
beyond what was required to start learning is waste,
no matter how important it might have seemed
at the time."

The goal of the MVP process is to validate the hypothesis in a speedy and cost-efficient manner. The key word in this quote is "feedback," since it is through feedback that people learn. The most effective processes are feedback loops based on the scientific method: Build, measure, learn. What a startup offers as its MVP should be complete in what it does to deliver and capture value, but not a fully complete implementation of the vision. The MVP is an experiment intended to generate validated learning about what customers value enough to pay for.

An MVP approach is not the only way to go forward with a startup. Eric Ries describes two extreme alternatives:

One, which I call maximizing chance of success, says, "Look, we've only got one chance at this, so let's get it right." We're going to ship it when it's right, and that actually is perfectly rational. If you only have one shot, you want to take the best shot you can and build the most perfect product you can. The issue is, of course, that you can spend something like five years of stealth R&D building a product you think customers want and then discover to your chagrin that they don't. The other possible extreme approach is to say, "Well, let's just do 'release early, release often.'" This approach is, "Look, we'll just throw whatever crap we have out there, and then we'll hear what customers say, and we'll do whatever they say." But the issue there is if you show a product to three customers, you get thirty opinions, and now what do you do? So minimum viable product is kind of a synthesis of those two possible extremes.

2. "The question is not 'Can this product be built?' Instead, the questions are 'Should this product be built?' and 'Can we build a sustainable business around this set of products and services?' "

> Products a startup builds are experiments. Learning about how to build a sustainable business is the outcome of those experiments which should follow a three-step process: Build, measure, learn.
>
> A startup is an organization dedicated to creating something new under conditions of extreme uncertainty.
>
> As you consider building your own minimum viable product, let this simple rule suffice: Remove any feature, process, or effort that does not contribute directly to the learning you seek. If you want to do minimum viable product, you have to be prepared to iterate. And so you have to have the courage to say, "Yeah, we'll ship something, get negative feedback, and respond."

A minimum feature set in an MVP is not a goal but a tactic to create cost-effective and speedy validated learning about the hypothesis. The goal is to learn and steer based on feedback rather than try to predict and emerge with a fully formed product. The MVP process is depicted as a flywheel or loop for a reason. Most of the time, actual hypothesis testing will reveal that customers do not value the product or even the vision the product represents. If the hypothesis is not validated by the experiment, the business must iterate by revising the hypothesis or shut down.

3. "The nice thing about relying on human judgment and using the scientific method is that we develop a system for training judgment to get better over time."

Ries's point is that learning to be a better entrepreneur is a trained response. People who are paying attention while engaging in the startup creation process can learn by doing. Ries is also saying that judgment about company formation improves when it is systematized based on the scientific method. The primary cause of good judgment is experience, which often comes from bad judgment, so it is best to (1) jump into the fray and learn via making some mistakes and having some successes, and (2) engage with a community of others doing the same thing so you can learn vicariously from the successes and mistakes of others.

4. "Every action you take in product development, in marketing, every conversation you have, everything you do—is an experiment. If you can conceptualize your work not as building features, not as launching campaigns, but as running experiments, you can get radically more done with less effort."

Here, Ries is describing the process of expanding the Lean Startup concept beyond creating the product offering. Many aspects of a business, and life generally, can be turned into lean experiments. Marketing, for example, can be systematized to reduce inefficiency.

5. "The two most important assumptions entrepreneurs make are what I call the value hypothesis and the growth hypothesis. The value hypothesis tests whether a product or service delivers value to customers once they are using it. The growth hypothesis tests how new customers will discover a product or service."

A business provides core product value when it solves a genuine customer problem. Andy Rachleff (a cofounder and the current CEO of Wealthfront and a cofounder of Benchmark) created definitions of these hypotheses and the correct sequencing of them:

Eric (and I) believe to increase the likelihood of succeeding, a startup should start with a minimally viable product to test what he calls a value hypothesis. The value hypothesis should state the founder's best guess as to what value will drive customers to

33

adopt her product and indicate which customers the product is most relevant to, as well as what business model should be used to deliver the product. It's highly unlikely that a founder's initial hypothesis will prove correct, which is why an entrepreneur has to iterate on her hypothesis through a series of experiments before product–market fit is achieved.

As a consumer company, you know you have proved your value hypothesis if your business grows organically at a rapid pace with no marketing spend. Only once the value hypothesis has been proven should an entrepreneur test her *growth* hypothesis. The growth hypothesis covers the best way to cost-effectively acquire customers. Unfortunately, many founders mistakenly pursue their growth hypothesis before their value hypothesis.

Rachleff also created and named the product–market fit (PMF) concept. The core of Rachleff's idea for PMF was based on his analysis of the investing style of the pioneering venture capitalist and the founder of Sequoia Don Valentine, who stated, "Give me a giant market—always." On this topic, Valentine once said,

Arthur Rock is the representative of "You find a great entrepreneur and you back him." My position has always been "You find a great market and you build multiple companies in that market." Our view has always, preferably, been "Give us a technical problem, and then give us a big market when that technical problem is solved so we can sell lots and lots and lots of stuff." Do I like to do that with terrific people? Sure. Are we unwilling to invest in companies that don't have them? Sure. We invested in Apple when Steve Jobs was about eighteen or nineteen years old—not only didn't he go to Harvard Business School, he didn't go to any school.

Cisco provided a famous example of what can happen when you change the people involved in a business when its board of directors replaced the then-husband-and-wife team who had founded the company. In other cases, new team members are brought in to supply new skills, adding to the team instead of replacing people. Eric Schmidt's recruitment to Google is a famous example of this approach. Marc Andreessen believes,

> The life of any startup can be divided into two parts: before product–market fit (BPMF) and after product–market fit. When you are BPMF, focus obsessively on getting to product–market fit. Do whatever is required to get to product–market fit. Including changing out people, rewriting your product, moving into a different market, telling customers no when you don't want to, telling customers yes when you don't want to, raising that fourth round of highly dilutive venture capital—whatever is required.

Rachleff adds this important point: "You know you have fit if your product grows exponentially with no marketing. That is only possible if you have huge word of mouth. Word of mouth is only possible if you have delighted your customer." Tying these concepts together, Rachleff shares that entrepreneurs too often confuse product–market fit with growth in what Ries calls vanity metrics: "numbers or stats that look good on paper but don't really mean anything important."

6. "All of our process diagrams [in major corporations] are linear, boxed diagrams that go one way. But entrepreneurship is fundamentally iterative. So our diagrams need to be in circles. We have to be willing to be wrong and to fail."

The "build, measure, learn" process is one loop in a process that will often be repeated. Sometimes a failure is so significant and the blockers to success with a given direction so large that a pivot is necessary. A pivot happens when a startup pursues a new direction by leveraging what it has learned from previous iterations (pivots are not complete restarts). A decision to pivot should not be taken lightly. Some founders pivot their way right into bankruptcy. Failing is not a good thing. Instead, the ability to fail—and then recover—is a good thing.

> 7. "Innovation accounting works in three steps: (1) Use a minimum viable product to establish real data on where the company is right now. (2) Startups must attempt to tune the engine from the baseline toward the ideal. This may take many attempts. After the startup has made all the micro changes and product optimizations it can to move its baseline toward the ideal, the company reaches a decision point. That is the third step: (3) Pivot or persevere."

The most efficient way to determine if the dogs will eat the dog food is via the outcome of a trial-and-error experimentation process in the real world. In one sense, the tuning process involves many small pivots that improve the offering. The better outcome is making some great choices, having a bit of luck, and being able to stay the course and persevere. If a business ends up being forced to pivot, it often still has a shot at recovering. That a business might be able to pivot and still win is a feature of the Lean Startup process, but it is not a goal.

> 8. "The mistake isn't releasing something bad. The mistake is to launch it and get PR people involved. You don't want people to start amping up expectations for an early version of your product. The best entrepreneurship happens in low-stakes environments where no one is paying attention, like Mark Zuckerberg's dorm room at Harvard."

Some people argue that early adopters can be skeptical if a product offering from a startup is too polished. This is an interesting but unproven thesis. I look at it this way: A business that over-promises and under-delivers can quickly die. You can spend the rest of your life recovering from a bad first impression in business, and in life.

> 9. "The Lean Startup process is a method
> that can be used to create or refine
> a business model, a business strategy,
> and/or a business design."

A business model, strategy, or design is only as good as the assumptions that underlie it. I have previously defined a business model. A business strategy is the manner in which a company strives to be unique. Business design is the totality of things a business must do to be a success. Steve Blank points out that unless you have tested the assumptions in your business model strategy and design outside the building, your plans are just creative writing.

> 10. "You need the ability to ignore inconvenient facts
> and see the world as it should be and not as it is.
> This inspires people to take huge leaps of faith.
> But this blindness to facts can be a liability.
> The characteristics that help entrepreneurs
> succeed can also lead to their failure."

Convexity is most often found in places where others are not looking or where they are not seeing what is actually happening. This is why you will sometimes hear venture capitalists say they are looking for business opportunities that seem "half-crazy." Most things that are crazy are actually nuts, but once in a while, entrepreneurs find a tremendous opportunity that no one else has discovered yet. The entrepreneur's faith in his or her vision is both how new products and services are discovered and why most businesses fail. Failures vastly outnumber successes, but the impact of the successes outweighs all the failures. It is the magnitude of success, not the frequency of success, that makes the process worthwhile for society (this is the so-called Babe Ruth effect).

11. "New customers come from the actions of past customers."

Virality occurs when existing customers introduce new customers to a product they are delighted with. Virality allows a business to grow organically. The key point is simple: If customers love a product, they are going to tell their friends. If someone tells you about a product and it is not lovable, you will stop using it.

12. "Anybody can rent the means of production, which means entrepreneurship is becoming truly democratized, which means nobody is safe."

The lower cost of starting and running a business is both a key opportunity and challenge in business today. Profit is generated by a barrier to entry (otherwise, price drops to opportunity costs). Unfortunately, barriers to entry (moats) now have shorter lives than ever before. Even if a business discovers solutions to the value and growth hypotheses, without a moat the probability of the business being financially successful over time is remote. Revenue alone is not enough to sustain a business, given the inevitable competitive response. Warren Buffett writes, "All economic moats are either widening or narrowing, even though you can't see it." Moats are more important than ever, but they need to be renewed more than ever, as well. More startups than ever are being created, and this means that someone somewhere right now is thinking about disrupting your business. Factors that can create a moat are constantly in flux, because they often interrelate to create nonlinear positive and negative changes. Moat creation is incredibly difficult and rare, and maintaining one is also difficult. For every business creating disruption, some other businesses are being disrupted.

II

The Venture Capitalists

4

Sam Altman

Y *Combinator*

SAM ALTMAN IS THE thirty-two-year-old president of Y Combinator and the world's most famous startup accelerator. Altman is
a unique personality, noting about himself, "The missing circuit in
my brain, the circuit that would make me care what people think
about me, is a real gift. Most people want to be accepted, so they
won't take risks that could make them look crazy—which actually makes them wildly miscalculate risk." A *New Yorker* profile of
Altman pointed out, "Like everyone in Silicon Valley, Altman pro-
fesses to want to save the world; unlike almost everyone there, he
has a plan to do it." Altman was a cofounder and CEO of Loopt,
funded by Y Combinator in 2005, and he has personal investments in businesses like Reddit. Because Y Combinator has played
such an important role in the achievements of so many successful
startups, Altman has unique insights to share.

1. "The best companies are almost always mission oriented."

Eventually, the company needs to evolve to become a mission
to which everyone, but especially the founders, is exceptionally

dedicated. The "missionaries versus mercenaries" sound bite is overused but true.

If the founders of a startup are not passionate about solving a significant customer problem they care deeply about, the odds are small that they will be able to successfully create a business that is a grand slam. Creating a scalable, repeatable, and defensible business of this magnitude is a rare event. Venture capitalists love founders with a passion, because missionaries work harder and endure in situations where mercenaries often quit and because missionaries are less likely to sell their businesses too early.

2. "In general, it's best if you're building something that you need. You'll understand it better than if you have to understand it by talking to a customer."

Passion and a mission are more likely to exist if a business is providing solutions to problems that cause the founders personal pain. In other words, a deep understanding of a valuable customer problem and potential solutions to that problem is enhanced if the founders are themselves potential customers for the solution. Not only is this more efficient and cost-effective, but the founders will be less likely to misunderstand the needs of potential customers who have the problem in question. Yes, it is helpful to have what is referred to in Zen Buddhism as "beginner's mind" about possible new solutions. No, having deep, relevant domain expertise is not necessarily a handicap.

3. "You want an idea that not many other people are working on, and it is okay if it doesn't sound big at first."

The truly good ideas don't sound like they're worth stealing.
You want to sound crazy, but you want actually to be right.

We are the most successful when we fund things that other people don't yet think are going to be an immense deal but two years later become a big deal. And it's really hard to predict that.

A lot of the best ideas seem silly or bad initially—you want an idea at the intersection of "seems like a bad idea" and "is a good idea."

Both startup founders and venture capitalists are trying to find mispriced business opportunities that are convex. Asset prices fluctuate more than actual financial value, which is what creates the opportunity for investors. The probability of finding and successfully capitalizing on such a mispriced convex opportunity is far greater if the startup is not working on the same problem as many other businesses.

4. "No growth hack, brilliant marketing idea, or sales team can save you long term if you don't have a sufficiently good product."

Make something people want. You can screw up most other things if you get this right; if you don't, nothing else will save you.

All companies that grow really big do so in only one way: People recommend the product or service to other people. What this means is that if you want to be a great company someday, you have to eventually build something so good that people will recommend it to their friends—in fact, so good that they want to be the first one to recommend it to their friends.

Figure out a way to get users at scale (i.e., bite the bullet and learn how sales and marketing work). Incidentally, while it is currently in fashion, spending more than the lifetime value of your users to acquire them is not an acceptable strategy. Obsess about your growth rate, and never stop. The company will build what the CEO measures. If you ever catch yourself saying, "We're not focused on growth right now," think very carefully about the possibility you're focused on the wrong thing. Also, don't let yourself be deceived by vanity metrics.

In business, there is no substitute for solving a real customer problem with a product that people want to buy. Without a valuable product offering, an overly sales-driven culture will inevitably produce a customer acquisition cost so high it is fatal. With enough sales and marketing spending, almost anything can be sold at some level, but even then, customers will leave. Every aspect of a product has the potential to help make the business grow. Or not. The opportunities to create growth by making product choices are nearly endless since it is simply impossible for a product to be technically neutral. For example, you cannot design a neutral automobile, a neutral building, or neutral software. Choices must be made in creating and offering a product, and those choices can impact growth in either a positive or negative manner. Paul Graham, a cofounder of Y Combinator, points out,

> A startup is a company designed to grow fast. Being newly founded does not in itself make a company a startup. Nor is it necessary for a startup to work on technology, or take venture funding, or have some sort of "exit." The only essential thing is growth. Everything else we associate with startups follows from growth. To grow rapidly, you need to make something you can sell to a big market.

5. "It is worth some real upfront time to think through the long-term value and the defensibility of the business."

Have a strategy. Most people don't. Occasionally take a little bit of time to think about how you're executing against your strategy.

Every business must find at least some barrier to entry to generate a profit. Without a moat of some kind, competitors will increase the supply of the product offering to a point where the financial return will be equal to the opportunity cost of capital. In other words, without some limit on the supply of alternative products provided by competitors, a business will not earn an economic profit. The Harvard Business School professor Michael Porter points out, "If customers have all the power, and if the rivalry is based on price, you won't be very profitable." Moats can take many forms and have a range of contributing elements, but they must continually be refreshed since they are always under attack by competitors.

6. "Every company has a rocky beginning."

You have to have an almost crazy level of dedication to your company to succeed.

The process of creating and managing a business, most notably a startup, will never go completely according to plan. There is no manual to follow to create business success. There are no foolproof recipes or formulas. Courage, perseverance, dedication, determination, and grit will inevitably be needed to produce positive outcomes. Dr. Angela Duckworth defines grit as "perseverance and passion for long-term goals." People with grit, determination, resourcefulness, and the ability to evolve do not give up easily. The irony is that the more you focus on mission over money, the higher the odds of your being financially successful.

7. "If you're not an optimist, you make a very bad venture capitalist."

Great entrepreneurs and venture capitalists are typically optimistic, even though most of what they do results in financial failure as measured by frequency of success. Maintaining an optimistic attitude in the face of uncertainty and repeated failure is a challenge. This reminds me of a joke: An optimistic entrepreneur and a pessimistic entrepreneur are sitting in a café talking. The pessimist turns to the optimist and says, "Things can't possibly get worse." The optimist replies, "Sure, they can!"

8. "Great execution is at least ten times more important and one hundred times harder than a good idea."

Remember that you are more likely to die because you execute badly than get crushed by a competitor.

Delighting customers with magic moments is critical to creating a successful business. These magic moments are sometimes referred to as "aha" moments. A business's objective in creating magic moments is to create in its customers an emotional affinity with the product. "Delight" and "love" are strong words, but they are the right words. Andy Rachleff points to Netflix as an example of a company that is totally focused on delighting its customers instead of being paranoid about competitors. In this way, Netflix is parting ways with the Andy Grove dictum of being paranoid about competitors, instead focusing on delighting customers. Rachleff quotes Reed Hastings, the Netflix CEO, as saying, "Being paranoid about competition is the last thing you want to do because it distracts you from the primary job at hand: delighting the customer."

9. "Stay focused, and don't try to do too many things at once."

Eliminate distractions.

The hard part of running a business is that there are a hundred things that you could be doing, and only five of those matter, and only one of them matters more than all of the rest of them combined. So figuring out there is a critical path thing to focus on and ignoring everything else is really important.

Any business, but especially a startup, will face many challenges. There will always be more things that can be done than there are people and resources to do them. Great founders and entrepreneurs know the difference between what could be done and what should be done. Setting priorities and staying focused are critical. Any business must decide what *not* to do, especially since this is the essence of strategy. Distractions like industry conferences are not a way to add value, especially if the uncompleted tasks are primary ones, such as finding core product value and product–market fit. Before these two tasks are accomplished, almost everything else is a distraction since without them the business is doomed.

10. "At the beginning, you should only hire when you have a desperate need to."

Later, you should learn to hire fast and scale up the company, but in the early days, the goal should be not to hire.

Hiring is the most important thing you do; spend at least a third of your time on it.

When a business is just getting started and product–market fit has not yet been discovered, small teams are not only more efficient, but they also translate into cash burn rates that can be kept relatively low until key milestones are achieved. Low cash burn rates allow the business more time to build something customers will genuinely be delighted with and even love. If a startup's cash burn rate is high, the company can find itself under pressure to prematurely commit to an unproven value hypothesis, the result of which is often fatal. Only once product–market fit has been found and the time has come to grow the business does recruiting become a huge priority. Great founders spend far more time recruiting than people imagine, but most notably after the value hypothesis has been proven.

11. "One thing that founders always underestimate is how hard it is to recruit."

You think you have this great idea that everyone's going to come join, but that's not how it works.

A great team and a great market are both critically important—
you have to have both. The debate about which is more important
is silly.

Don't let your company be run by a sales guy. But do learn how
to sell your product.

Experienced venture capitalists are looking for evidence that founders have strong sales skills. One early test of a these skills is how
well a founder performs when making a fundraising pitch. The idea
is simple: If the entrepreneur can't sell the idea to a venture capitalist, how is he or she going to be able to recruit great people, sell the
product, and find great distribution? The ability to sell the product
to investors, sell the potential of the business to employees, and then
to sell the product to customers is core to any business. Altman is
saying that sales are only one part of what is needed for success, and
it should not be the dominant activity.

12. "Keep an eye on cash in the bank and don't run out of it."

Do reference checks on your potential investors. Ask other
founders how they are when everything goes wrong.

Good investors are worth a reasonable premium. Go for a few
highly involved investors over a lot of lightly engaged ones.

If the founders have a very good idea for a business, have a strong
team, and have targeted an attractive market, money will not be the
scarcest ingredient in creating a successful business. What will be
scarce is value-added capital (investors who can genuinely supply
the business with more than money). Even scarcer is value-added
capital that will be a big help when things are going wrong. The last
thing founders need are fair-weather investors. Taking the time necessary to research potential investors is wise since the relationship
between founder and investor will last for many years.

5

Steve Anderson

Baseline Ventures

STEVE ANDERSON IS THE founder of Baseline Ventures, a pioneering micro venture capital firm (a "micro VC"). Before starting Baseline, Anderson worked at Starbucks, eBay, Microsoft, Kleiner Perkins, and Digital Equipment Corporation. His venture capital investments have included Heroku, Instagram, Machine Zone, Social Finance, and Stitch Fix. Baseline Ventures has only one decision-maker, which makes the firm very nimble and quick to make a decision. The firm focuses on early-stage seed investing, which means Anderson has a particularly interesting viewpoint on the startup process. The differentiation has worked out very well for Anderson and Baseline.

1. "In 2006 I was starting to ruminate on the idea of founding a company. When I began to think about raising seed capital, there were few alternatives to consider."

The average exit over the last ten years . . . has been $100 million. If I own 10 percent of a $100 million outcome, that is real money for me and my cofounders. Why isn't anyone in venture capital aligned for that sort of outcome? There is an informative video on YouTube in which Anderson talks with the entrepreneur and venture capitalist Chris Dixon about how, early in their careers, they each wanted to finance their businesses and found themselves faced with the need to sell more than half the equity in their businesses at seed stage to get the cash they needed. Dixon describes the situation he encountered this way:

> When I started my first VC-backed company in 2004, there were ten to twenty firms who might consider investing in consumer Internet companies, and they were all bigger VC funds that were designed to invest in series A or later. In our seed round, we had to give up more than 50 percent of the company for $2.6 million (plus the deal was tranched, which added other challenges). It was pretty obvious that the market needed a new product. I ended up cofounding my seed fund (Founder Collective) and investing in Baseline, Lowercase, and a few other people who saw the same opportunity.

What founders should seek when their business is at seed stage is a lead professional investor who can add more than just capital. What do I mean by the professional investor? Professional investors are more than just wealthy, well-connected individuals. They can help founders solve real business problems, rather than just write checks.

2. "You have to sell at least 20 percent of your company at every financing."

Traditional venture capital firms can put a partner on only so many boards and help only so many startups at any given time. They have a high opportunity cost and in many cases can't invest without taking a significant equity stake. Compared with the period when Steve Anderson and Chris Dixon were both having a hard time raising funds for their startups without massive dilution, there are now many more professional seed-stage venture capitalists offering much more attractive terms, assistance, and valuations to founders.

Life for a business founder today is much better than it was in the past. Founders have better information and more choices.

3. "On average, I invest $500K."

If a micro VC like Anderson raises a $100 million fund, it can obviously make a lot of seed-stage investments. And, theoretically, it could make enormous seed-stage investments. But early-stage businesses should not raise too much capital since (1) too much money can be counterproductive for the business, and (2) equity must be retained to preserve incentives for founders, employees, and future investors.

4. "Ten years ago, you needed $5 million to start a business. Today, you need $70 and some coding skills."

One remarkable thing about raising funds at seed stage today is how little cash it takes to fund a company. Access to cloud services and modern software development methodology also contribute to startups needing less money and fewer people to create a successful business than ever before. However, this also means more competition among startups in many categories.

5. "My goal as an investor is to make sure there's enough financing to give companies enough cash to last a year to eighteen months."

When I invest, I want to leave enough room for pivoting or re-examining goals. Most of the time, entrepreneurs are realistic

near the end and say this isn't working. Those decisions aren't
that difficult. It gets more difficult in later stages when you've got
millions of dollars invested.

Too much money can distract a young business from focusing on
what is necessary to become a successful company. Businesses do
not die from starvation alone—they can just as easily die from
indigestion. And they often do. The cause of a business running
out of cash is often that the firm has lost focus and diverted
resources to activities that are not on the critical path toward
success.

Cash starvation or indigestion is often a symptom of bad decisions, like premature scaling, trying to do too many things at once,
or pivoting too often.

6. "Generally speaking, most of my investments are pre–product launch—they're just an idea."

There is so much risk, uncertainty, and ignorance involved in seed-
stage investing that evaluating the strength of the team is extra
important. The seed-stage venture capitalist Jason Calacanis has
said, "Startups before their A round—which is where I operate—
are a high-mortality business. Eight of ten startups angels invest
in, in my experience, are a doughnut (zero dollars returned)." In
the United States, there are typically about 1,200 seed-stage startups in a given quarter (plus or minus a couple hundred) depending upon the business climate. Of about five thousand seed-stage
startups, both reported and unreported, only eight hundred raised
a series A round in 2016, according to Mattermark. That's about
an 84 percent fatality rate just at seed stage. Mattermark calcu-
lates the odds of survival here at far less than 10 percent. This
calculation is based simply on a startup not getting to the next
phase. Other research, using different definitions, concludes,

about 75 percent of U.S. venture-backed startups fail, according to Harvard Business School senior lecturer Shikhar Ghosh. Ghosh's research estimates 30 percent to 40 percent of high-potential startups end up liquidating all assets—a failure by any definition. But if a startup failure is defined as not delivering the projected return on investment, then 95 percent of VC companies are failures according to Ghosh.

7. "With series A, B, C, or growth investments, you already know what you want to invest in."

Investing in a business before product–market fit is proven means decisions are relatively more instinct based. Anderson has even said in an interview that he tends to go with his gut on his seed investments. What underlies a venture capitalist's instinct and gut feelings about a potential investment is pattern recognition. That pattern recognition comes from experience, which takes time to develop.

8. "It's all about networks. I spend time with entrepreneurs; I meet them mostly through other entrepreneurs."

For a venture capitalist, investing at seed stage is a process that benefits from hustle but also generosity. Reaching out and helping people in advance pays big dividends owing to an aspect of human nature known as the "reciprocity principle." Doing favors for people begets favors being done for you.

9. "You will know if you like venture capital well before you know if you are any good at it."

It takes five, six, seven, eight years. . . . The cycles of feedback are long, which is difficult.

Sometimes a venture capitalist makes a mistake and does not pay the price for many years. This delayed feedback lengthens the learning period. For this reason and others, becoming a successful venture capitalist can take many years. A venture capitalist is paying the equivalent of tuition every time he or she invest in a business. Investments made early in the career of a venture capitalist tend to be more "tuition heavy" than those made later in his or her career.

10. "There is a robust seed market now."

Returns dictate everything. If the asset class has the financial returns, more money is going to come.

There are hundreds of micro-VC firms in the United States alone. The jury is still out on the right number of firms engaging in this type of venture capital. As with venture capital in general, a significant constraint on industry size is the aggregate dollar amounts of financial exits for portfolio companies. When micro VCs collectively put X dollars of capital to work, they must eventually generate enough financial exits for themselves and their investors, or they will not return enough capital to keep the category healthy. Venture capital has been, and is likely always to be, a cyclical business.

11. "Accelerators were created for people who don't have their own networks or can't grow their networks. How often do you show up to one place and see eighty companies? Of course with that scenario, you'll pay a higher price because more people are looking. That's fine. Entrepreneurs have more transparency today than ever before; they can choose the types of investors they want to work with."

It's great that investors and founders today have so many choices, including participating in accelerators. The clearer the choices are for founders, the better off everyone is, and the higher the success rate for startup businesses will be.

12. "In this business, you will have a long list of things you could have done. If I miss something, I try to learn from that."

Every venture capitalist has investments they pass on, which represent missed opportunities. That is the nature of the venture capital business. The important thing is not whether venture capitalists make these "mistakes of omission" (because they always will to some extent), but whether they learn from their mistakes. An entrepreneur should not take a rejection personally. Some of the most valuable businesses in the world were rejected repeatedly by venture capitalists.

6

Marc Andreessen

Andreessen Horowitz

MARC ANDREESSEN IS AN entrepreneur, investor, engineer, and technology activist. He was a co-creator of Mosaic, the first widely used web browser. Andreessen was also a cofounder of Netscape and Loudcloud and is a cofounder and general partner of the venture capital firm Andreessen Horowitz. A *New Yorker* profile described him as "seething with beliefs. He's an evangelist for the church of technology, afire to reorder life as we know it. He believes that Silicon Valley is mission control for mankind, which is therefore on a steep trajectory toward perfection. And when he so argues, fire-hosing you with syllogisms and data points and pre-refuting every potential rebuttal, he's very persuasive." In terms of technology, he is in my view a candidate for "most interesting person in the world." Marc serves on the board of the following Andreessen Horowitz portfolio companies: Anki, Bracket Computing, Dialpad, Honor, Lytro, Mori, OpenGov, and Samsara. He also serves on the boards of Facebook and Hewlett-Packard Enterprise. Andreessen graduated with a BS in computer science from the University of Illinois at Urbana–Champaign in December 1993.

1. "The key characteristic of venture capital is that returns are
a power-law distribution. The basic math component is that
there are thousands of startups a year that are founded
in the technology industry that would like to raise
venture capital, and we can invest in about thirty."

We see thousands of inbound referred opportunities per year.
We narrow that down to a couple hundred that are taken
particularly seriously.

Venture capitalists spend a lot of time looking at opportunities
and a lot of time saying no. Patience is a key attribute of the
most successful firms, as it is of most every investor. Success means
being very *patient* but aggressive when it's *time*.

2. "You want to have as much 'prepared mind' as you
possibly can. And learn as much as you can about as many
things, as much as you can. You want to enter as close as
you can to a Zen-like blank slate of perfect humility
at the beginning of the meeting saying 'teach me.' . . .
We try really hard to be educated by the
best entrepreneurs."

This quote from Andreessen reminds me of a famous quote from
the Sōtō Zen monk and teacher Shunryū Suzuki: "If your mind is
empty, it is always ready for anything; it is open to everything. In
the beginner's mind there are many possibilities, but in the expert's
mind there are few." If a venture capitalist attends a meeting with
a startup thinking he or she know everything, he or she will learn
nothing. The right objective is to be a "learn-it-all" rather than a
"know-it-all." Similarly, if a venture capitalist believes that he or
she can predict everything, he or she will fail. The right combination is optimistic and aggressive when the time is right and yet
humble about what you do not know.

Table 6.1

	Consensus	Nonconsensus
Success	Index fund/exchange-traded fund	Above-market return for top VCs and value investors
Failure	Poseur VC	Necessary part of success for top VCs

3. "You want to tilt into the radical ideas . . . but by their nature, you can't predict what they will be."

The entire art of venture capital in our view is the big breakthrough ideas. The nature of the big idea is that they are not that predictable.

Most of the big breakthrough technologies/companies seem crazy at first: PCs, the Internet, Bitcoin, Airbnb, Uber, 140 characters. It has to be a radical product. It has to be something where, when people look at it . . . at first they say, "I don't get it. I don't understand it. I think it's too weird; I think it's too unusual."

There will be certain points of time when everything collides together and reaches critical mass around a new concept or a new thing that ends up being hugely relevant to a high percentage of people or businesses. But it's really hard to predict those. I don't believe anyone can.

Howard Marks is famous for saying you can't predict but you can prepare. He describes the right attitude as follows:

"Hey," you might say, "that's contradictory. The best way to prepare for cycles is to predict them, and you just said it can't be done." That's true, but in my opinion by no means debilitating. All of investing consists of dealing with the future, as I've written before, and the future is something we can't know much about. But the limits on our foreknowledge needn't doom us to failure as long as we acknowledge them and act accordingly.

The best way to deal with what Marks is talking about is to purchase a portfolio composed of mispriced convexity, rather than trying to predict the unpredictable. Warren Buffett described a portfolio of bets with a convexity approach in his 1993 chairman's letter:

> You may consciously purchase a risky investment—one that indeed has a significant possibility of causing loss or injury—if you believe that your gain, weighted for probabilities, considerably exceeds your loss, comparably weighted, and if you can commit to a number of similar, but unrelated opportunities."

4. "Venture capitalists spend a lot of time talking about markets and technology and we have lots of opinions, but the decision should be around people. About 90 percent of the decision is people."

We are looking for a magic combination of courage and genius. Courage (not giving up in the face of adversity) is the one people can learn.

When you have a team of strong people, their ability to adapt and innovate gives the company and the investor valuable optionality. The ideal flywheel a founder wants to create is a phenomenon where courage becomes self-reinforcing. Courage in the right circumstances begets more courage. Once a seed is created, the feedback loop can be powerful.

5. "An awful lot of successful technology companies ended up being in a slightly different market than they started out in. Microsoft started with programming tools but came out with an operating system. Oracle started doing contracts for the CIA. AOL started out as an online video gaming network."

Because the future is not predictable with certainty, companies with convexity in the form of strong teams and research-and-development capability can often pivot into other markets. Pivoting like this can present problems if you are a venture capitalist who has decided to invest in only one company per category. But a pivot is often preferable to a shutdown and certainly preferable to staying a course that is doomed to fail.

> 6. "The great saving grace of venture capital is that our
> money is locked up. The big advantage that we have as
> a venture capital firm over a hedge fund or a mutual fund
> is we have a lock-up on our money."

> We invest in these companies with a ten-year outlook.
> Enterprise can go in and out of fashion four different times, and
> we can go and invest in one of these companies, and it is okay
> because we can stay the course.

Another investor who has figured out the value of locked-up capital from investors is Warren Buffett, who famously closed his partnership and started Berkshire Hathaway in the form of a corporation. Like a venture capital firm, Berkshire's capital is locked up, which protects the firm from people trying to redeem during a panic caused by a significant market dip. The famous investor Bruce Berkowitz said once, "That is the secret sauce: permanent capital. That is essential. I think that's the reason Buffett gave up his partnership. You need it because when push comes to shove, people run." The ability of a venture capital firm to have cash in the bank (or at least the capacity to call on cash contractually promised by limited partners) allows it to invest through downturns, which are often excellent times to start a company and make investments.

> 7. "The thing all the venture firms have in common is they did
> not invest in most of the great successful technology companies."

The mistakes that we make in a field like venture capital aren't investing in something that turns out not to work. It's the big hit that you missed. And so every venture capitalist who had the opportunity to invest in Google and didn't just feels like an idiot. Every venture capitalist who had the opportunity to invest in Facebook and didn't feels like an idiot. The challenge in the field is all of the great VCs over the last fifty years, the thing that they all have in common, is they all failed to invest in most of the big winners. And so this again is part of the humility in the profession.

Buffett and Charlie Munger call this type of mistake an "error of omission" (i.e., what you don't do can hurt you more than what you do). Every investor makes errors of omission whether he or she is aware of it or not. Munger points out, "The most extreme mistakes in Berkshire's history have been mistakes of omission. We saw it but didn't act on it. They're huge mistakes—we've lost billions. And we keep doing it. We're getting better at it. We never get over it." You cannot be in the venture capital business for long without passing on or not pursuing a startup that will eventually become a great financial success.

8. "With tech—and you see this with a lot of these new entrepreneurs—they're twenty-five, thirty, or thirty-five years old, and they're working to the limit of their physical capability. And from the outside, these companies look like they're huge successes. On the inside, when you're running one of these things, it always feels like you're on the verge of failure; it always feels like it's so close to slipping away. And people are quitting, and competitors are attacking, and the press is writing all these nasty articles about you, and you're kind of on the ragged edge all the time."

Starting a business is not easy or for the faint of heart. Working for a startup is something that some people might want to put on a personal bucket list, but wanting is not doing. Lots of people talk a good game about wanting to leave a big company for a startup, but when the time comes, most don't do it.

> 9. "There's a new generation of entrepreneurs in the Valley who have arrived since 2000, after the dotcom bust. They're completely fearless."

> Founders today are very technical, very product centric, they are building great technology, and they just don't have a clue about sales and marketing. It's almost like they have an aversion to learning about it.

> Many entrepreneurs who build great products simply don't have a good distribution strategy. Even worse is when they insist that they don't need one, or call no distribution strategy a "viral marketing strategy." a16z is a sucker for people who have sales and marketing figured out.

Entrepreneurs who appear to have no fear are common today. It is good to be optimistic, but an absence of fear may lead to problems caused by hubris and blind spots. To illustrate one such problem, a major issue with the dot-com bubble of the late 1990s was that too many companies were being driven by sales and marketing people who forgot or failed to appreciate that the business needed to deliver core product value (i.e., products that solve real customer problems) in very large markets. Too much capital delivered to too many businesses driven by the fear of missing out caused people to make very significant mistakes. However, just because sales and marketing can be taken too far too early does not mean that sales, marketing, and distribution are not essential to the success of a business. For example, the serial entrepreneur and investor Rich Barton believes,

> Search engine optimization (SEO) and natural search results are in decline. And, as alternative search paradigms (mobile, Alexa,

App Store) grow, and as Facebook/YouTube/Snapchat radically increase the volume and diversity of "avails," I would argue that we are entering a new golden age of marketing and branding. The future is a diverse and modern marketing team, made up of the clever analytical marketer who uses big data to make smarter decisions, the public relations expert who finds ways to help the brand tell great stories, the social media guru who knows how to stay on top of the latest channels and engage directly with consumers, and, yes, the artist/storyteller who can move people to tears. Marketing is back.

10. "You spend most of your time dealing with your companies who are struggling and trying to help them. It's the companies that are struggling or failing that need the most help. The enterprises that are succeeding are doing just fine without you. The companies that are failing are the ones that need help and support. And so a lot of what you end up doing at the job is helping struggling entrepreneurs. It's kind of continuously humbling. You are a troubleshooter. There's always something going wrong. Psychologically—we talk about this with our partners—you have to be psychologically prepared for the opposite. It seems like it's going to be a life of glamor and excitement. It's more of a life of struggle and misery. And if you are okay with that—because it's part of the package—then the overall deal is pretty good."

Venture capital is a service business. Venture capital is not sitting in expensive chairs picking winners and speaking at conferences, but rather working day in and day out in the trenches helping entrepreneurs succeed. An effective venture capitalist spends time on things like trying to recruit engineers and other talented people for portfolio companies, closing early big sales, and finding new sources of distribution. Andreessen is saying that while both an entrepreneur and a venture capitalist should expect the journey to sometimes be a struggle, the process is worthwhile. Almost everything important in life involves tradeoffs, and venture capital is no exception.

11. "Software is eating the world."

"Everybody's going to have a computer. Everybody's going to be on the Internet. And that's a new world. That's a world that we've never lived in before. We have no idea what that world is going to look like. It's brand new. One of the things that you know is that all of a sudden if you can conceive of a way to make a product or a service, and if you can conceive of a way to deliver it, through software, you can now actually do that.

When you apply software you can do it in a very cost-effective way. . . . We now for the first time can go field by field, category by category, industry by industry, product by product, and we can say, 'what would they be like if they were all software?' "

Andreessen's "software is eating the world" thesis has always reminded me of what Bill Gates once said about why he decided not to build a PC in the early days of Microsoft:

When you have the microprocessor doubling in power every two years, in a sense you can think of computer power as almost free. So you ask, why be in the business of making something that's almost free? What is the scarce resource? What is it that limits being able to get value out of that infinite computing power? Software.

What is new today, and what Andreessen is talking about when he says software is eating the world, is that the hardware is already in place and is waiting for the software at global scale. There is no longer a requirement for software businesses to also manufacture the hardware systems needed to implement the system. Smartphones are increasingly ubiquitous. Computers and storage can be bought on demand. The power of software to enable change drives Andreessen's infectious optimism:

> This is sort of where I disagree so much with people who are worried about innovation slowing down, which is that I think the opposite is happening. I think innovation is accelerating. Because the minute you can take something that was not software and make it software, you can change it much faster in the future. It's much easier to change software than it is to change something with a big, physical, real-world footprint.

12. "It's honestly hard to not be an optimist in this job, because we get 2,000 founders a year who come in here, sit in that chair right there, and they just tell us everything. They unspool the future to us, and they're optimistic or they wouldn't be here. Then all the new ideas. I wonder whether people outside a firm like this would be more optimistic if they could see and hear all of that stuff."

There are two very different parts of the economy. There's the part where there's rapid technological change and very rapid productivity improvement. You've got this other, second part of the economy that's the exact opposite — where quality is not improving and prices are rising.

The economy has bifurcated. In high-productivity sectors, prices are crashing. The sectors where prices are crashing are shrinking as a percentage of the economy. TVs are going to cost ten dollars and health care is going to cost a million dollars.

The rising cost of a modern college education is just staggering. In the industries where there's rapid productivity growth, everybody is freaked out, because what are people going to do after everything gets automated? In the other part of the economy, that second part, health care and education, people are freaked out about, "Oh my God, it's going to eat the entire budget! It's going to eat my personal budget. Health care and education is going to be every dollar I make as income, and it's going to eat the national budget and drive the United States bankrupt!" And everybody in the economy is going to become either a nurse or teacher. It's really funny, both sides of the economy get polar opposite emotional reactions.

Today's technology advances often produce efficiency improvements which in turn produce lower costs, which translates into lower spending and measured GDP. More is being done with less and yet traditional measurements say that productivity is decreasing since less money is being spent in more productive sectors. In addition, many people assume that innovation always creates more producer surplus and profit. Charlie Munger describes the reality:

The great lesson in microeconomics is to discriminate between when technology is going to help you and when it's going to kill you. And most people do not get this straight in their heads. There are all kinds of wonderful new inventions that give you nothing as owners except the opportunity to spend a lot more money in a business that's still going to be lousy. The money still won't come to you. All of the advantages from great improvements are going to flow through to the customers.

These are confusing times, but that is no reason to adopt a pessimistic outlook on the potential of innovation to create enormously beneficial impacts. There is no question that today's economy and the technological changes that power the economy have created a significant number of new problems like worker retraining that we must solve. We must discover new solutions to these new problems and this will require innovations of many kinds.

7

Rich Barton

Expedia, Glassdoor, Zillow

RICH BARTON IS AN entrepreneur and investor. He started Expedia from within Microsoft in the mid-1990s, spun it out as a public company, and was CEO until 2003. Nick Hanauer, a Seattle venture capitalist who was an early investor in Amazon and is a close friend of Barton's says, "You can name people who are richer than Rich, but you can't name very many people who have his track record. You will find very few people in this country who have as many times created something from nothing." Barton's "power to the people" thesis is at the core of many of his investments. He believes that "giving consumers access to information and databases that they knew existed because they either saw or heard professionals over the phone clacking away on a keyboard accessing that information" can be the foundation of very valuable business. He is a cofounder and the chair of Zillow and Glassdoor and is a venture partner at Benchmark. He is also on the board of directors of Artsy, Avvo, Liberty Interactive, Netflix, Nextdoor, and RealSelf. He graduated from Stanford University in 1989 with a degree in engineering.

1. "'Marketplace' is an important word.
It takes two sides to make a marketplace."

> User-generated content models are magic. And they are magic because the more reviews you have of hotels, for instance, the more it attracts users to the site. And the more users you have, of course, the more reviews you get. This is a very simple, elegant example of a positive feedback system. This flywheel spins faster and faster, and what happens is the competitive moat—the defense, the competitive differentiator or the moat around the castle—gets wider and deeper every day with every review that is done.

Barton is saying that a user-generated content system can be made to feed back on itself in a positive way to create more and more success. To illustrate, if Side A of a marketplace values the platform more if there are more customers on Side B, positive network effects are created. Marketplaces like Expedia, Glassdoor, and Zillow have multiple "sides," which interact directly through a "platform," which generates network effects, which can act as a barrier to entry for competitors as more and more user-generated content appears in the system. The venture capitalist Yuri Milner believes, "From a margin standpoint user-generated content is very magical." A new media business that is able to get its users to create content will have far lower costs than a traditional media firm.

2. "If you do have a flywheel, it is OK to spend money to get it spinning. It is OK to do un-economic things to hand-crank stuff, so long as once it is spinning, you can take your hand away."

The first step in getting to critical mass with a marketplace platform is sometimes called overcoming the "chicken and egg" problem. This challenge can be described simply: how to get one side interested in a platform before the other side exists, and vice versa. Part of the challenge is to get enough customers on both sides so that critical mass can be achieved. Critical mass is tricky to obtain, particularly if the two sides need to show up simultaneously. Businesses that are slow to get to critical mass can run out of cash and momentum. How do you get one side on board? Well, one crucial task is to acquire market participants in a cost-effective way. What you want is a low customer-acquisition cost. Barton is saying that investing money to get the flywheel spinning from a standing start is an important part of the process. But even if money is spent in the beginning to get the flywheel spinning, the goal is to be able to reduce spending once the positive feedback loop is operating. At that point, it is hoped that customers are being acquired organically at very low cost. Barton uses his experience at Zillow to illustrate:

> We didn't have much money and we couldn't invest in advertising, but we knew the most important "P" of the marketing mix "five Ps" is "product." So, we built a highly provocative product (with the Zestimate), and married that to a brilliant PR plan conceived by our head of communications, Amy Bohutinsky (now our COO). On day one, so many millions of users showed up that Zillow.com tipped over for a day and a half. For years after that, product and PR were our bread and butter. Only after we had fifty million users per month and a business model did we layer on traditional brand advertising, including TV.

3. "My tendency has been to focus on big vertical industry categories where there has historically been database information that's been locked up behind walls by the industry. I want to empower users to access that info. I like those verticals that involve real people, real decisions, and real money because it is easier to monetize. It's not a stretch to sell ads in the industry because they want to be there when people are making decisions."

Expedia, Glassdoor, and Zillow are prime examples of Barton's "power to the people" thesis. Simply put, this thesis states, "If we're doing things for regular folks that make their lives better and save them money and give them transparency, we're on the side of the angels." Barton told a great story about this investment thesis in a *Wired* article:

> I wanted to give consumers access to information and databases that they knew existed because they either saw or heard professionals over the phone clacking away on a keyboard accessing that information. I remember I wanted to jump through the phone and look at the screen myself, turn it towards me and just take control. And I knew that I would spend more time and do a better job searching than this person who was doing something on my behalf, and who didn't know my preferences but was just trying to approximate them.

Part of Barton's thesis is that certain vertical industries involve a lot of real-money transactions and often high customer-acquisition costs. Barton has shown that a user-generated content marketplace in a vertical market in which businesses pay significant amounts of cash for effective advertising can be an attractive business.

4. "What I tell people is, if it can be rated it will be rated. If it can be free it will be free, and if it can be known it will be known."

Here, Barton is saying that digital information is increasingly not going to be located behind firewalls, inaccessible to the public. The model of giving away information to create a marketplace is so valuable in creating a platform business that it is likely that someone will decide to make it free. Similarly, the value of a user-generated content-based business model is so alluring that everything will also be rated since ratings can be used to sell advertising or to power other market-based business models.

5. "Find me a provocative topic, and I'll show you something you don't have to spend a lot of marketing dollars to launch. People like to be provoked, and if you are provoking with information that is on the side of the angels, on the side of the consumer, the louder the industry reacts. And they just can't win. It's the greatest way to market."

We now see businesses that are transforming controversy (e.g., Uber) or valued information (e.g., Glassdoor, Zillow) into free brand impressions, which leads to more usage, which translates into more controversy or information (and on and on). Postive feedback loops are a hallmark of business today, and the best entrepreneurs know how to use them to create a sustainable advantage for their businesses.

6. "Ideas are cheap. Execution is dear."

Great leaders need three key attributes to successfully execute: brains, courage, and heart.

Ideas are necessary but not sufficient for success with a startup. The idea itself will inevitably evolve as time passes and the environment changes. Barton is saying that executing is more difficult than generating a good idea. Establishing a team to build the product, finding the correct product–market fit, and scaling the business are all challenging tasks.

7. "It is much more powerful long-term to make up a new word than it is to use a literal word. I also like high-point Scrabble letters in my brands if I can work them in. They are high point because they are rarely used. A letter that is rarely used is very memorable. 'Z' and 'Q' are all worth ten points in Scrabble.

'X' is 8. They jump off the page when you read them, and they stick in your memory as interesting."

> When you successfully make up a new word and introduce it into everyday language, you own it. It becomes a major differentiating asset that cannot be confused with anything else or encroached upon by competitors. At the very best, you end up defining a whole new category: Kleenex, Levis, Polaroid, Nike, eBay. The downside to creating your brand is that it is hard, and most of the time, very expensive and time-consuming to hammer a new word into the consumer vocabulary.

People willing to make an effort to try to transform a made-up word into a powerful brand are thinking big, which is attractive to a venture capitalist since they need grand slams to make their business models work. That an entrepreneur thinks he or she can turn a startup into a verb is a "tell" that they have the right mindset and DNA for an entrepreneur who should be seeking venture capital.

8. "If you want to have a growing and vibrant organization, you want to have big, new opportunities opening in front of you."

It is much more interesting to work on a team and for a business that is growing and vibrant. Barton was fortunate to work at Microsoft early in his career in an era when the company was growing incredibly quickly and the opportunities to advance and learn were unlimited. During this period, Microsoft was growing so fast that people's responsibilities and opportunities were constantly expanding. The environment was far from a zero-sum game. During Barton's tenure at Microsoft, there were many battlefield promotions. Barton has the same high-growth situation for employees at his portfolio companies, including Glassdoor and Zillow. This is in contrast to a business in decline where the employee count is shrinking. Shrinking opportunities mean employees face a less-than-zero-sum game, which too often creates toxic internal politics and a divisive culture.

9. "You can have a great team of people, but if they're fishing in the wrong spot, they're not going to catch any fish."

Tech startups are not capital intensive. It takes money to build the first version of the software, but it's very inexpensive to deliver that to millions of people. They're high-margin businesses if you can get scale.

A big dream and a clear vision, and a little bit of nuttiness are required to take something from an idea stage all the way to creating something that realizes that dream.

Dreams are largely self-fulfilling. There is almost as much blood, sweat, and tears in building something small as there is in building something big.

Venture capitalists are focused on finding audacious entrepreneurs who are trying to create value in enormous markets. If the plan is not just a little bit nutty when the entrepreneur first starts working on it, competitors will inevitably be working on something similar. If you are devoting years of your life to this effort, why not try to accomplish something great? And if the founders' goal is a genuine mission, that provides extra motivation beyond financial returns. If you can do great things for society and do well financially at the same time, that combination is a very powerful thing.

10. "It's key to hire the best and sharpest folks in the beginning so that you can build an organizationally wise company."

Surround yourself with superstars. And not just the people you choose to work with. That's really important. But the people you raise money from as well. Surround yourself with superstars, and everything else takes care of itself. Whenever in my career

I've compromised because I've had a short-term itch I needed to scratch—and I just had to hire somebody—it's been a mistake. And I've regretted it. It's hard to get rid of the (poor) performers. Surround yourself with superstars. They hire superstars.

Being around smart people who love to get things done makes you smarter and more able to get things done. Barton is making the point that the early hires are of particular importance as they are the core around which culture, values, and best practices are built. Fixing a bad hire is way more costly and time-consuming than most people imagine. In short, bad hires can be toxic. Smart people who are secure about themselves love to hire and be around other smart people. Individuals who are easily threatened hire nonthreatening individuals who add less value to the business as a result.

11. "Get the highest-octane fuel in the tank when choosing a venture capitalist."

Rather than just raising cash as they grow their businesses, the smartest entrepreneurs select venture capitalists who can deliver valuable services. The best venture capitalists have access to the best networks, which further amplifies their value. Money is not the scarcest resource when you have an attractive business idea and a strong team in a huge market or potential market.

12. "The whole idea of building a career these days is much different from, say, when my dad did. My father graduated from Duke University with an engineering degree—I don't know what the year was, it was probably like 1956 or something—and he went to work for a large chemical company, which was the computer company of his age. Plastics. Like in *The Graduate*. My dad always said, 'What you are doing on the Internet, I was in plastics, and that was the thing.' Anyway, he went to work

for that company, and he retired from that company thirty-four years later. And he worked there the whole time, and that was his era's idea of work. The company man. The gray suit, and the briefcase. And the martini on Friday and the hat and the whole thing. I love and admire my dad, and I love that he was always supportive and tickled by how I built my career and my views on the modern career path. From my perspective, making a career is trying something fascinating, getting some skills, putting tools into your toolkit, going to the next place and putting a few more tools in, until finally, you have all of the tools to build your own house."

Here, Barton is making a point about the importance of accumulating skills over the course of a career and being opportunistic in acquiring those skills. In today's world, this means taking a path that is often nonlinear. The "jungle gym" replaces the "ladder" as the metaphor for a career. A person's actual skills, work product, and personal network have become more important than formal credentials. The ability to demonstrate one's competence to a potential employer via a work product is replacing the traditional résumé.

8

Roelof Botha

Sequoia Capital

ROELOF BOTHA IS A partner at the venture capital firm Sequoia
Capital, where he is responsible for strategy, team composition,
and fundraising. Botha grew up in Pretoria and Cape Town, South
Africa. Botha started his career working for McKinsey in Johan-
nesburg from August 1996 through June 1998. He then moved to
the United States where he completed an MBA at Stanford University. He is also a trained actuary. After serving in a number of
roles at PayPal, including CFO, he joined Sequoia in 2003. His
portfolio companies have included Instagram, Stripe, Tumblr, and
YouTube. Botha believes "it's very hard to be in venture capital if
you haven't walked in the shoes of a founder or entrepreneur, or
been involved in building a company."

1. "The key characteristic of a founder is the desire to solve a
problem for the customer. That is the driving passion, not
'I think this is going to be a billion-dollar company
and I want to hop in because I can get rich.' "

> I look for the personal passion of the entrepreneur, their ability to describe the problem articulately, and the clarity with which they can explain why they have a unique and compelling solution to the problem.

> The most successful entrepreneurs tend to start with a desire to solve an interesting problem—one that's often driven by personal frustration.

If a business is not solving a genuinely valuable problem for customers, nothing else matters and failure is inevitable. Founders who are thinking about growth models, term sheets, and lots of peripheral issues when the business is unable to provide core product value are missing the boat. In making these statements, Botha is expressing a desire for missionary founders over mercenary founders. Brian Chesky of Airbnb once said, "In a war, missionaries outlast and endure mercenaries."

> 2. "There is a 50 percent mortality rate for venture-funded businesses. Think about that curve. Half of it goes to zero. Some people try for 3X returns with a very low mortality rate. But even that VC model is still subject to a power law. The curve is just not as steep."

This fact of life in the venture business means focusing on big markets and businesses with the potential to grow revenues and profits at nonlinear rates. Most companies formed by entrepreneurs are not candidates for venture capital. That's okay. The best way forward for most businesses is bootstrapping with internally generated cash, business loans, or investments from friends and family.

> 3. "Entrepreneurship is much more than what VCs participate in."

Many businesses described by founders as needing venture capital are just small businesses that should be looking for what amounts to small-business finance. The businesses and markets created by these entrepreneurs are a key part of building a healthy economy and creating jobs. But they are not the sort of companies suitable for venture investing. Again, that's okay. The amount of venture financing overall is a relatively small part of an economy. Because of its impact on innovation and productivity, venture capital punches far above its weight in terms of impact, but the absolute dollar amount invested per year by venture capitalists is relatively small when put into the context of the overall economy.

4. "Think of yourself as the central point of a network."

The best way to scale a business quickly is to create flywheels; that is, self-reinforcing phenomena. In the center of the flywheels benefiting a startup are the founders and their team. To get a flywheel going, the founders must create a seed that will jump-start a process that will reinforce itself. The tricky part of setting up any flywheel is overcoming the "chicken-and-egg" problem. How does the business generate initial momentum before all the pieces are in place? Usually, the jump-start takes the form of a free "chicken" or "egg." While sometimes it does not matter which one is free, there is usually an optimal side of the market to become the seed and another that is the source of profit.

5. "The answer to creating a flywheel lies in two essential variables: the size of the market and the strength of the value proposition. Growth goes through an exponential curve, then flattens with saturation. If the ceiling of the market opportunity is $200 million, even if you get a flywheel, it will take you from twenty to sixty or seventy million, then peter out because you saturated the available space."

The bigger the market, the more runway you have—so if you hit that knee of the curve, you can grow exponentially and keep going for a long time. Doubling a business of material size for three to four years leads to a vast company. That's a fundamental element in the flywheel idea.

To achieve the growth needed by venture capitalists to make their business model work, it is best to be surfing on a nonlinear phenomenon. Moore's law as broadly considered is one such phenomenon, especially when the business also benefits from network effects. Sometimes a flywheel is created in a small market, and that is not as interesting to a venture capitalist.

6. "Companies can end up with too much cash. They might have a fifteen-month runway. They get complacent and there's not enough critical thinking. Things go bump at nine months, and it turns into a crisis. And then no one wants to invest more."

One suggested rule of thumb is that a startup with twelve months of cash should be thinking about raising more cash, should start raising capital by the time they have nine months of cash, and should be nervous if they only have six months of cash on hand. It is much harder to raise a series A round of financing than seed-stage capital. Compared with the past, there is not much more series A capital available today, but there are more seed-funded startups competing for that money.

7. "To achieve a big success, many things must come together. In some cases, what looked like smooth sailing from the outside was more like a near-death experience; a few small changes and the outcome would have been dramatically different. There is always a mixture of skill and luck involved."

When considering the difference between luck and skill, it is always best to refer to the work of Michael Mauboussin who has said, "There's a quick and easy way to test whether an activity involves skill: ask whether you can lose on purpose. In games of skill, it is clear that you can lose intentionally but when playing roulette or the lottery you can't lose on purpose." If you can influence the outcome by working harder, that is skill and not luck.

8. "Problem companies can take up more of your time than the successful ones."

Time is the scarcest resource for a founder or venture capitalist. And the biggest time sink of all is a business with lots of problems. It is when problems arise that the value of a great board of directors, advisers, and mentors kicks in. And it is because of the inevitability of problems that, when given a choice, a startup should always want to raise more than money. Investors who bring hustle, good judgment, expertise, and significant relationships to the business are preferable to purely financial investors.

9. "It's important to choose initial investors who are not twitchy and rushing for an exit."

Who are you getting in business with? You have to get to know the venture capitalists you might be working with. You're essentially entering a long-term relationship.

Consider a simple two-by-two matrix: On one axis you have "easy to get along with the founder" and "not." On the other, you have "an exceptional founder" and "not." It's easy to figure out which quadrant VCs make money backing.

When you are potentially entering into a relationship with people who will be in your life in a significant way for many years, why would you want to include anyone who is hard to get along with? Not only do poor relationships with key people in your life substantially lower your chances of success, they will also make you miserable. Why be miserable? Life is short. Being happy is highly underrated.

10. "Think about private investing. It's very different from hedge-fund investing or public investing; you can take advantage of market psychology and short-term mismatches because you can exit. We don't have that luxury in venture capital. We can't bet this trend will be fashionable for the next three years. By definition, we need to have a long-term stance. Maybe the company goes public or is acquired in three years, five years, ten years—who knows? We like long runways."

The length of time it takes for a venture capital investment to pay off financially drives many aspects of the industry. Sequoia is rather famous for saying to its portfolio companies, "If you don't have cash for a long runway, you better have a revenue model that gets you to cash flow–positive quickly." The better option is to have enough cash and cash flow to last a long time.

11. "You cannot . . . expect to make money by simply cutting checks. That is, you cannot simply offer a commodity. You have to be able to help portfolio companies in a differentiated way, such as leveraging your network on their behalf or advising them well."

Every startup and its founders, employees, business model, and markets are unique. Startups need hands-on help with finding product–market fit, recruiting, finance, team building, and other aspects of building a business. If the venture capitalists involved in a startup are not assisting with things like raising funds, hiring key employees, and even closing big sales, the startup has the wrong venture capitalists.

12. "There is a subtle benefit of actuarial science, which I didn't appreciate when I joined the profession. Actuaries are trained to think thirty years into the future, and accountants are trained to think a year in arrears. Part of what actuarial science enforces in you is long-term thinking, and that frame of mind influences the work that I do today. We invest in companies that employ three people, and we have to imagine what the company might turn out to be in ten or fifteen years."

Botha trained as an actuary. He points out that a successful venture capitalist must be able to imagine what a startup might look like in ten to fifteen years. In imagining the potential outcome, a venture capitalist needs to think about "what can go right." Extrapolating the past out fifteen years, as an accountant might do, is not the key to success in the venture capital business.

9

Jim Breyer

Breyer Capital

JIM BREYER IS THE founder and CEO of Breyer Capital, an investment and venture philanthropy firm. He is also a partner at the venture capital firm Accel. His most famous investment has been Facebook, but he has also been involved in many other successful businesses, including Etsy and Spotify. Breyer's parents arrived in the United States as refugees from Hungary in 1956. He started his career as a summer and part-time employee at Apple while he was an undergraduate at Stanford. Breyer and the Chinese venture capital firm IDG Capital have raised one of the largest venture capital funds in China. Breyer has served on the boards of Dell, Marvel Entertainment, and Walmart. He meditates each morning to clear his mind.

1. "I've learned that when the pessimism is high, dial up the investment pace. When the optimism is high, take a breather."

It is easy to advise being fearful when others are greedy and greedy when others are fearful, but it is hard to do. People's desire to run with the crowd can be unyielding at times. Most investment mistakes are based on emotional and psychological errors, but so are most investment opportunities since it is when others make mistakes that mispriced assets become available. In short, being contrarian based on the bipolar actions of the mob can generate market-beating investment returns. As an example, Jim Breyer was very cautionary before the Internet bubble burst and took a lot of heat as a result. He was wrong in the timing of his prediction—until he was eventually right.

2. "Investing is very psychological. Whether you're Warren Buffett or early-stage technology venture capitalists, psychology plays such a central role."

The hardest aspect of investing is keeping control of your emotions. As Buffett has said, "Investing is simple, but not easy. The most important quality to do well is temperament." Like Buffett, Jim Breyer is saying that what is not easy is the investor psychology needed in venture capital. Keeping control of your emotions is a never-ending struggle since most mistakes are emotionally or psychologically based.

3. "There's a pattern recognition and real-time knowledge that comes with investing and building companies from the earliest stages over an extended period of time."

Becoming a successful venture capitalist takes time since pattern recognition comes from making a range of mistakes that help one acquire good judgment. One key to this process is avoiding certain errors that fall into what the Nobel Prize–winning psychologist Daniel Kahneman calls "System 1." Michael Mauboussin describes the two types of thinking as follows: "System 1 is your experiential system. It's fast. It's quick. It's automatic and difficult to control. System 2 is your analytical system: slow, purposeful, deliberate, but malleable." Mauboussin provides the right cautionary note: "For System 1 to work efficiently, you need to deal with situations that are linear and consistent. If you're dealing with decisions in a realm where the outcomes are nonlinear, or the statistical properties change over time, intuition will fail, because your System 1 doesn't know what's going on." Investing decisions are best made as System 2 decisions since the business world is nonlinear. When you use System 2 the right way, the power of counter-intuition can be a source of investing opportunities since others will make valuation mistakes by using System 1 thinking. Using System 2 correctly requires training so that investors develop the right outlook when making decisions.

4. "We like to think that we will make a mistake only once and learn from it. We also are humbled every day by a new mistake."

If you are repeatedly making the same mistakes, something in your investment process is broken. To acquire the right decision-making outlook it is a useful habit to rub your nose in mistakes shortly after you make them. The natural human tendency is to gloss over mistakes with psychological denial. But by celebrating, rather than burying, your mistakes, you learn faster.

5. "The investment and venture capital cycle is continuously changing, and one of the most fascinating internal discussions is often around where we are in the cycle."

We will have many booms and busts forever in Silicon Valley.

All markets are cyclical. People do not make decisions independently, and when one person makes a decision and acts, other people tend to follow until they unpredictably stop. The idea that the sequence of behaviors that make up a business cycle is precisely predictable is a triumph of hope over experience. Venture capital is more cyclical than other markets, not less. One of the most talked about "tells" that a change may be coming in the business cycle is when people start talking about there being no cycle anymore.

6. "The dangers of over-capitalization are, in many cases, even higher and graver than under-capitalization."

We've always said that risk reduction is all about, in the first twelve months, take out the technical risk; in year two, take out sales and marketing risk; in year three, build for working capital and international distribution; year four, take the company public. That's a classic venture model regarding how we stage investment. But, in fact during the Internet bubble, there was no staging. No risk reduction was occurring because the capital was so free; the companies could raise it all at once and were simultaneously trying to address all these issues.

Too much money at a startup can lead to a range of problems, including a lack of focus and a failure to innovate. A business that attempts to solve problems with money rather than doing things that do not require much money, like changing broken processes or culture, is making a terrible mistake. Too much money can also wreck a capitalization table, make later financing rounds hard to achieve, and make a painful "down round" of funding inevitable.

7. "We look for a business that demonstrates differential insight."

If you are not searching for ways to be contrarian and to be right about that contrarian view, you are not going to outperform markets as an investor. This applies to many levels and domains in investing, including the process of defining a target market for a startup. Startups that chase the tailpipes of other startups and companies are far less likely to be a success. The essence of strategy is intelligently deciding to be different in significant and enduring ways.

8. "Most of the best businesses in Silicon Valley started with a very simple concept and extended into adjacent market segments as well as into global markets."

Focus matters. The most successful companies tend to concentrate on serving a market where there is not a lot of competition or on inventing a new market. This allows the business to grow faster and to possibly generate a strong base from which to expand into adjacent markets. This is a variant of a "land-and-expand" strategy.

9. "We are always looking for a fit between people, opportunity, ideas."

The balance between optimism, candidness, intellectual honesty, and integrity results in a virtuous set of characteristics that are shared by all exceptional entrepreneurs.

The Harvard Business School professor Michael Porter is an advocate of including "fit" as an objective in creating a company strategy and in assembling a moat for a business. He writes, "Fit drives both competitive advantage and sustainability: When activities mutually reinforce each other, competitors can't easily imitate them. Fit is leveraging what is different to be more different." This focus on fitness is in some cases enhanced by what Charlie Munger calls a "lollapalooza." The impact of a lollapalooza involves vastly more than a simple addition of the interacting components. In other words, the right fit in a business can have nonlinear benefits.

10. "The history of technology businesses, as well as many others, suggests that it's very often the case that the second or third mover ends up winning. Sometimes it pays to let someone else create a market and be the second or third entrant. That was true in the spreadsheet business with Lotus. That was true in the personal computing business with Dell, true in the router business with Cisco; and true in the operating system business with Microsoft."

What wins in the market is being first to product–market fit rather than first to market. What seems like sustainable competitive advantage can be far more brittle than people imagine. The cable television and wireless pioneer Craig McCaw has said to me several times, "Sometimes pioneers get an arrow in the back for their efforts."

11. "In every deal I can think of there's a dark day when board members sit around the table and simply wonder how we can dig ourselves out of the hole we're in."

Many very successful startups nearly expire in the early months and years of building the business. Successful venture capitalists know this and do not give up easily. Knowing when it is time to fold up the tent versus when it is worth continuing to fight is a skill acquired only with time and experience.

12. "Some people get real lucky. But that's no way over an extended period of time to operate a venture capital firm or an investment business. It sure helps to get lucky, but you can't count on it."

To rely on luck to bring you success is just plain dumb, as it is to discount the role of luck in your success. If you are not thankful for your luck, you have not been paying attention. As one gets older, one should become more humble.

10

Chris Dixon

Andreessen Horowitz

CHRIS DIXON IS AN entrepreneur, programmer, and investor. He is a general partner at Andreessen Horowitz, before which he cofounded Founder Collective, a seed-stage venture capital fund. He is a polymath who writes clearly and thoughtfully about technology and business. Dixon cofounded SiteAdvisor (now WebAdvisor), a security startup purchased by McAfee, and Hunch, where he was CEO for a time. He has also worked for eBay and as a programmer at a hedge fund specializing in high-frequency trading. He has invested in companies like Airware, BuzzFeed, Coinbase, Comma.ai, Dispatch.ai, Envoy, iCracked, Improbable, Keybase, Nootrobox, Oculus, OpenBazaar, Ringly, Shapeways, Skydio, Soylent, Stack Overflow, and Wit.ai. Dixon earned a BA and an MA in philosophy from Columbia University and an MBA from Harvard Business School. He has also been an active angel investor, making personal investments in technology companies including Behance, Foursquare, Kickstarter, OMGPop, Pinterest, Stripe, Warby Parker, and others.

1. "If everyone loves your idea, I might be worried
that it's not forward thinking enough."

The best opportunities for startups tend to be in areas that are overlooked and less well known by others. What Dixon is saying is that if everyone loves your idea, it may be a "tell" that there will not be opportunities for extraordinary profit. Dixon also believes "you shouldn't keep your startup idea secret." He identifies a range of positive benefits that flow from sharing ideas and getting feedback and points out that "there are at best a handful of people in the world who might drop everything and copy your idea."

2. "How do you develop a good idea that looks like a bad idea?
You need to know a secret in the Peter Thiel sense: something
you believe that most other people don't find. How do you
develop a secret? (a) Know the tools better than anyone else;
(b) know the problems better than anyone else;
and (c) draw from unique life experience."

> Founders have to choose a market long before they have any idea whether they will reach product–market fit. In my opinion, the best predictor of success is whether there is what David Lee calls "founder–market fit." Founder–market fit means the founders have a deep understanding of the market they are entering, and are people who personify their product, business, and ultimately their company.

Dixon is saying that the people most likely to know a "secret" about a business opportunity are individuals with deep domain expertise. In other words, it is not nearly as likely that someone without deep domain expertise will be successful, as they will not have a solid understanding of the technology, the best methods to create the product, the best ways to bring products to market, or the needs of the customer. People who work for a startup who have in-depth domain knowledge are a likely source of convexity. When a team working on a startup has what Dixon and Thiel call "secrets" as a result of deep domain expertise, their ability to adapt and innovate gives the investment greater convexity.

3. "The business of seed investing, and frankly, early-stage entrepreneurship, is so much about getting useful information. And almost all of that information, unfortunately, is not published."

Great venture capitalists are always trying to find great sources of information, particularly unpublished information. If information about a business is hard to obtain, that is a great thing for a startup since that information can help create a mispriced opportunity. In other words, uncertainty and ignorance in the early stages of a startup are friends of the entrepreneur. As the team pushes forward to reduce technology and market risk, find product–market fit, and discover methods to scale the business, it has an opportunity to retire uncertainty and ignorance and create value. One part a great venture capitalist's job is to provide entrepreneurs with an entry into networks that will allow them to quickly and cost-effectively find the private information that will help them achieve their goals.

4. "Ideas matter, just not in the narrow sense in which startup ideas are popularly defined. Good startup ideas are well developed, multiyear plans that contemplate many possible paths according to how the world changes."

Characteristics of the best ideas: (a) Powerful people dismiss them as toys; (b) They unbundle functions done by others; (c) They often start off as hobbies; and (d) They often challenge social norms.

> The best ideas come from direct experience. When you differentiate
> your direct experience from conventional wisdom, that's where
> the best startup ideas come from.

What Dixon is talking about here is perhaps best explained by an example. I spent much of my career working for Craig McCaw, who is a savant when it comes to developing ideas into great businesses. In the very early days of what is now referred to as the mobile industry, the cellphone offered enough value to be a commercial success for only a minuscule number of users. McCaw was an avid user of the product and had deep domain expertise. The consumer device was so big that it required a suitcase or a car installation to be useful. Real estate agents and construction workers were among the most avid users, but costs were high. Eventually, genuinely portable mobile phones appeared, but they were still quite cumbersome and expensive—and they were still analog. During that period, McKinsey famously predicted that no one would ever use a mobile phone if a landline phone were available. McKinsey placed little or no value on what McCaw called the ability of people to be "nomadic." But McCaw appreciated the freedom of working out of his "mobile office," meaning in a car, plane, or yachts and was therefore a natural enthusiast for the product. When the time came to sell his cable TV business to double-down on the mobile phone market, the choice was made easier by his love of being nomadic.

5. "There is a widespread myth that the most important part of building a great company is coming up with a great idea."

> A great way to show you can build stuff is to build a prototype
> of the product for which you are raising money. That's why so
> many VCs tell entrepreneurs to "come back when you have a
> demo." They don't wonder whether your product can be built—
> they wonder whether you can build it.

The ability of a team to execute is more important than a bright idea. Most everyone has said more than once "I thought of that idea first" when they see a new business. The best idea in the world will not amount to a hill of beans without a team with the will to make it happen. Dixon is saying that one of the best pieces of evidence a team can execute on a plan is a successful demo. The best proof that you are able to create fully functional software, for example, is a software demo.

6. "What the smartest people do on the weekend is what everyone else will do during the week in ten years."

Hobbies are what the most intelligent people spend their time on when near-term financial goals don't constrain them.

Dixon is not referring to smart people who play ping-pong in their garage or fantasy baseball in their dorm rooms on weekends. He is talking about the sort of people who founded the Homebrew Computer Club, an early hobbyist group in Silicon Valley that had it first meeting on March 5, 1975. The critical element Dixon seeks is an advanced technology that is useful to very smart hobbyists but does not yet have clear financial returns associated with its use. Over time, the cost and performance of such a hobby often rise to a point that enables the hobby to become a thriving business.

7. "In this era of technology, it seems that the core theme is about moving beyond bits to atoms. Meaning technology that affects the real world, transportation and housing and health care and all these other things, as opposed to just moving bits around. And those areas tend to be more heavily regulated. This issue is only beginning to be significant and will probably be the defining issue of the next decade in technology."

The intersection of technology and regulation is certainly going to be a challenge in the future. Dixon is making a statement about where future opportunity may exist. Too many venture capitalists are camp followers who move into a trend when others have long since moved on to other opportunities. Deviating from a consensus view for its own sake is suicidal, but doing it occasionally and being very right in doing so is what makes a great venture capitalist like Dixon.

8. "Anyone who has pitched VCs knows they are obsessed with market size."

If you can't make the case that you're addressing a possible billion-dollar market, you'll have difficulty getting VCs to invest.

If you are arguing market size with a VC using a spreadsheet, you've already lost the debate.

For early-stage companies, you should never rely on quantitative analysis to estimate market size. Venture-style startups are bets on broad, secular trends. Good VCs understand this.

Startups that fill white spaces aren't usually world-changing companies, but they often have stable exits. They force incumbents to see an application they had missed, and those incumbents often respond with an acquisition.

It is impossible to make a silk purse out of a pig's ear. For a startup to generate the necessary grand-slam financial return for a venture capitalist, the potential market for the product must be massive. The entrepreneur who pulls out a spreadsheet and tries to make the case that the market is large enough based on fake assumptions and guesses does little but destroy his or her credibility. Venture capitalists hate to see hockey stick–shaped distribution curves based on unrealistic assumptions that do not map to reality. Yes, they want to see as many facts as possible that support the narrative. No, they do not want to hear wild, optimistic guesses presented as facts.

9. "There are two kinds of investors: the Ron Conways who try to create value by finding good people and helping them build something great, and others, who want a piece of someone else's things. The builders and the extractors. Avoid the extractors."

> Founders too often view raising capital as a transaction, when it is a very deep relationship. They think of money as money, when there is smart money, dumb money, high-integrity money, and low-integrity money.

A startup's success is increasingly being determined by its access to networks of people and resources. If a startup has a choice between (1) just money and (2) money plus access to these networks, why not choose the latter? Perhaps some founders are made less fearful by a venture capitalist who is mostly a cheerleader, but the smartest entrepreneurs want someone who can directly help with tasks like fundraising, recruiting, pricing, and distribution.

10. "VCs have a portfolio and they want to have big wins. They'd rather have a few more lottery tickets, while for the entrepreneurs it's their whole life. Let's say you raised $5 million and you have a $50 million offer. The entrepreneurs are saying, 'Look, I can get paid millions of dollars. I'll be able to start another company.' Usually that is where the tension comes."

Dixon has been both a founder and a venture capitalist, so he has empathy for both on this set of issues. He is most certainly correct that this type of situation creates tension. The question is, what is the best way to resolve the tension in ways that are mutually beneficial? The answer is complex and involves some give and take. The wisest outcome on founder and employee liquidity issues will depend on the facts and circumstances of each case. In other words, there is no connect-the-dots formula that works for all situations. Fred Wilson points out that there is an incentive to create some liquidity: "Providing some founder liquidity, at the appropriate time, will incentivize the founders to have a longer-term focus, and that will result in exits at much larger valuations because, contrary to popular belief, the founders drive the timing of exit way more than VCs do." Of course, it is one thing to concentrate your investments if you have a net worth measured in millions of dollars and quite another if you have just a small financial cushion if the business fails. The important point Dixon raises is that a significant conflict can exist between founders and venture capitalists, and it can create tension if not dealt with intelligently.

11. "If you aren't getting rejected on a daily basis, your goals are not ambitious enough. The most valuable lesson I had starting out in my career was when I was trying to break into the tech world, and I applied to jobs at big companies, startups, and VC firms. I got rejected everywhere. I had sort of an unusual background. I was a philosophy major, a self-taught programmer. It turned out to be the most valuable experience of my career because I eventually developed such thick skin that I just didn't care anymore about getting rejected. And, in fact, I turned it around and started embracing it. Eventually that rejection emboldened me. Through those sort of bolder tactics, I eventually landed a job that got my first startup funded. So every day to this day I try to make sure I get rejected."

The ability of some salespeople to handle nearly constant rejection is something that has always fascinated me. Why can some people knock on door after door and suffer rejection after rejection and still maintain a positive attitude long enough to generate an eventual sale? For some people, a single rejection turns them into a nervous wreck, whereas others power through to close the sale. Perhaps this resilience can be explained by a combination of innate personality and learned skill. In any event, starting a business, and building a successful career, involve way more selling than most people imagine. Entrepreneurs are always selling themselves, their business, and their products to potential employees, suppliers, distributors, investors, and customers. If you cannot or do not want to sell, starting a business is probably an unwise decision for you.

> 12. "Before I started my first company, an experienced entrepreneur I know said, 'Get ready to feel sick to your stomach for the next five years.' And I was, 'Eh, whatever.' Then later, I was, 'Shoot, I should listen to the guy.'"

You've either started a company, or you haven't. "Started" doesn't mean joining as an early employee, or investing or advising or helping out. It means starting with no money, no help, no one who believes in you (except perhaps your closest friends and family), and building an organization from a borrowed cubicle with credit card debt and nowhere to sleep except the office. It almost invariably means being dismissed by arrogant investors who show up a half-hour late, totally unprepared, and then instead of saying no give you noncommittal rejections like "We invest in later-stage companies." It means looking prospective employees in the eyes and convincing them to leave secure jobs, quit everything, and throw their lot in with you. It means having pundits in the press and blogs who've never built anything criticize you and armchair quarterback your every mistake. It means lying awake at night worrying about running out of cash and having a constant knot in your stomach during the day fearing you'll disappoint the few people who believed in you and validate your smug doubters.

Illustrating this point is best done with another example. I was the fourth employee of a business founded by Craig McCaw and Bill Gates known as Teledesic. At one point, the company raised funds at a valuation of $3 billion, which made it a triple unicorn. Although I wasn't a founder of the business, it was nevertheless a life-changing experience. I decided to take the job because I believed the business had a compelling mission. Unlike the situation described by Dixon, we were not short of cash to keep the lights on, but we needed to raise and spend $9 billion before we generated any revenue. The need to raise that much capital and make other scary decisions at Teledesic made me feel sick to my stomach plenty of times. It was a frightening but thrilling roller-coaster ride.

11

John Doerr

Kleiner Perkins Caufield & Byers

JOHN DOERR IS A partner and the chair of the venture capital firm Kleiner Perkins Caufield & Byers. His record as a venture capitalist is outstanding and includes backing businesses such as Amazon, Compaq, Google, Intuit, Macromedia, Netscape, Sun Microsystems, Symantec, and Twitter. Doerr began his professional career at Intel in 1974, the year the company introduced the pioneering 8080 microprocessor. His time at Intel in engineering, marketing, management, and sales roles allowed him to develop into a well-rounded startup investor and adviser. Doerr has said, "My advice for people who want to be a venture capitalist is to forget about it. Try to be a successful entrepreneur instead." His advice echoes Buffett's that being in business makes you a better investor and vice versa. Doerr earned bachelor's and master's degrees in electrical engineering from Rice University and an MBA from Harvard Business School.

1. "Swing for the fences when your time is right."

What Doerr is talking about is the so-called Babe Ruth effect. Michael Mauboussin writes that there is "a lesson inherent in any probabilistic exercise: The frequency of correctness does not matter; it is the magnitude of correctness that matters." When you find a clear bet with a big upside and a relatively small downside (i.e., convexity), bet big! That will not happen very often, but when it does, you must be ready to act aggressively. The wise investor is patient but aggressive when the time is right. Venture capital, like all forms of investing, is an activity in which a knowledge of probability and statistics is essential. Charlie Munger said once, "If you don't get elementary probability into your repertoire, you go through life as a one-legged man in an ass-kicking contest." What Munger said applies very much to venture capital.

2. "We believe that ideas are easy; execution is everything."

A good idea or invention is necessary but far from sufficient to achieve success in business. It takes an entrepreneur to take an idea and turn it into a genuinely scalable business. A "roll up your sleeves" and a "make the trains run on time" effort from a team of people is essential. On this topic, Bill Gates once said,

> Being a visionary is trivial. Being a CEO is hard. All you have to do to be a visionary is to give the old 'MIPS to the moon' speech. Everything will be everywhere, and everything will be converged. Everybody knows that. Which is different from being the CEO of a company and seeing where the profits are.

3. "Believe me; selling is honorable work—particularly in a startup, where it's the difference between life and death."

How could someone describe the importance of sales to a startup more starkly? Poor sales results mean inevitable death for a startup. When it comes to sales success, I have seen just about everything from nonexistent to excellent. At one end of the spectrum, I have seen startups composed entirely of engineers, none of whom knew how to sell. The result in a situation like that is not attractive. I have also seen sales teams able to sell products and services at superhuman levels given competition and the nature of the product. But in such cases, the customers eventually wise up and stop using the product, which means the company dies. Staging is important. A compelling product that solves a real customer problem must be created before the business devotes resources to sales and marketing.

4. "The best entrepreneurs don't know what they don't know, so they attempt to do the impossible. They often succeed."

Convexity is often found in what at first seems impossible. If a new business does not at first seem a little impossible, there would inevitably be many people already pursuing the opportunity. Many entrepreneurs fail as they attempt the impossible and are forgotten by history as survivor bias kicks in. Failure is an essential part of human progress. Capitalism without failure is like heaven without hell. It does not work.

5. "The best entrepreneurs don't focus on success. They concentrate on building a company that can be a leader in the global economy. They know success will follow. If you focus on success, you won't get there. If you focus on contribution and customer value, then you can win."

Mercenaries are driven by paranoia; missionaries are driven by passion. Mercenaries think opportunistically; missionaries think strategically. Mercenaries go for the sprint; missionaries go for the marathon. Mercenaries focus on their competitors and financial statements; missionaries focus on their customers and value statements. Mercenaries are bosses of wolf packs; missionaries are mentors or coaches of teams. Mercenaries worry about entitlements; missionaries are obsessed with making a contribution. Mercenaries are motivated by the lust for making money; missionaries, while recognizing the importance of money, are fundamentally driven by the desire to make meaning.

A venture capitalist I know recalls Doerr using the "missionary-versus-mercenary" metaphor as early as 1998 at a Stewart Alsop Agenda conference. Doerr has repeated this idea often over the years, and it has essentially become a meme in the venture capital industry. In short, mercenaries are motivated primarily by money. Missionaries are driven by a cause. Doerr prefers a missionary approach to starting a business but realizes that mercenaries can sometimes succeed. Missionaries tend to hang in there longer since they are pursuing a cause and not just wealth. They have greater grit and determination and will not be as likely to sell out too early. Elon Musk is an example of a missionary founder who is more interested in changing the world and creating enduring businesses than just the financial rewards that may flow to him. Mercenaries may sometimes succeed financially, but they do not bring as much lasting value to their communities. What a city or nation wants in terms of economic development are businesses that produce jobs, innovative products and services, and a better quality of life, and that add to the tax base over the long term.

6. "The best entrepreneurs are the ones who go the distance with their companies, who are always learning."

Great leaders are great communicators. They have incredible integrity: They're usually the first to recognize problems. They're ruthless, entirely intellectually honest. They are great recruiters: They're always building their network of talented people. And they're great sales executives: They're always selling the value proposition of the enterprise.

Great leaders and entrepreneurs have a big bag of skills. Having just one skill, or even a few, is not enough. The best way to create a big bag of competence is to be a learning machine. A corollary to this point is that a diverse team in the broadest possible sense is a stronger team. Great founders and CEOs hire people who complement their skills and are multipliers of what the CEO can do on his or her own.

7. "In anything worth doing, it takes a team to win."

In the world today, there's plenty of technology, lots of entrepreneurs, plenty of money, plenty of venture capital. What's in short supply is great teams. Your biggest challenge will be building a great team.

Recruiting is such a huge part of a startup's success that it is hardly possible to emphasize it enough. Great people attract other great people. As Bill Gates has said, "There's an essential human factor in every business endeavor. It doesn't matter if you have a perfect product, production plan, and marketing pitch; you'll still need the right people to lead and implement those plans."

8. "If you can't invent the future, the next best thing is to fund it."

Doerr is saying that funding innovation is a noble second choice to being a founder. Of course, many founders go on to be successful venture capitalists. Being a founder definitely requires more courage.

9. "No conflict, no interest."

This quotation may be apocryphal since no one seems to be able to cite a source. Whether Doerr said this or not, it is certainly true that in private markets investors can look for a proprietary edge that would be unacceptable in public markets since the same disclosure requirements do not exist.

10. "The old economy was about people acquiring a single skill for life; the new economy is about life-long learning."

> Choose your first job based on the experience, not how much money you will make. Carry a bag (sell something), launch a product, manage a dozen people, learn from great companies. You will be judged on your ability to listen and think critically. Confront problems, not people. Learn. You'll get extra points for a sense of humor. Always network. That means, learn about people and what they do. Also, develop a couple of mentors.

People with access to better networks have better information, which they can turn into achievement, which gives them better information. Success feeds back on itself.

11. "Everyone who is a practitioner of the venture business knows most of the returns accrue to a small group of firms. And I don't think that's ever going to change."

Returns in the venture capital business are not spread evenly like peanut butter. Because other aspects of life have outcomes that reflect a bell curve distribution, people may underestimate how extreme outcomes can be. Venture capital is part of what Nassim Taleb calls "Extremistan."

12. "Stanford is the germplasm for innovation. I can't imagine Silicon Valley without Stanford University."

To illustrate Doerr's point, I like to tell a story about how the spoils were politically distributed when Washington Territory joined the United States as a state in 1889. Tacoma was the terminus for the railroad, not Seattle. Olympia was awarded the state capital. Walla Walla received the penitentiary. And Port Townsend, which had a thriving port, received a customs house. What Seattle won

in the political process that resulted in statehood was more funding and support for the University of Washington, which had been
founded in 1861. In terms of economic development, having the
university in Seattle made all the difference. Great cities get built
around great colleges and universities. Seattle without the University of Washington would not be Seattle. Doerr is saying that
Silicon Valley without Stanford would not be Silicon Valley.

12

Peter Fenton

Benchmark

PETER FENTON IS A partner at the venture capital firm Benchmark, before which, he spent seven years as a partner with Accel. The list of businesses he has invested in includes Hortonworks, New Relic, Polyvore, Quip, Twitter, Yelp, Zendesk, and Zuora. He is also a helicopter pilot and serves on the boards of the San Francisco Opera and the California Academy of Sciences. What is most interesting to me about Benchmark is that it has a very explicit strategy of being what Fenton has called "more of a guild than a corporation." Fenton has a BA in philosophy from Stanford University and an MBA from the Stanford Graduate School of Business.

1. "The principal question that we focus on before an investment is the quality of the person we're going to work with. There are three attributes that I try to be reductionist about that define the greatness that we see in our world. First, I think there's just a profound, deep, innate motivation. Second,

I think there's a common trait that I would call the ability to learn. The third thing is perhaps the most obvious, which is the ability to attract great people."

Fenton efficiently conveys three key points here: (1) Motivated people are far more likely to persevere through inevitable adversity and do the necessary hard work; (2) the ability to be a learning machine means a business can adapt and grow in an uncertain world; and (3) the ability to recruit people to a mission or cause rather than just a business is essential. One commonality in what Fenton says is a strong focus on building the business rather than finance or deal terms. Grounded in business fundamentals, his advice applies to a new bakery, a grocery store, or a startup. Without a sound underlying business, a startup will not be successful. When an entrepreneur is building a business, he or she should not seek a cheerleader as their venture capitalist—they should find someone who has extensive relevant business skills and is willing to work alongside the entrepreneur to build the business.

2. "The great entrepreneurs have found they need to find complements. If you look at yourself and reflect on your skills and your talents and your unique abilities, you'll find that everybody has their gaps."

Everyone has strengths and weaknesses. Having the right partners and colleagues is a way to create a force multiplier by filling in gaps in your skills and talents. As an example, Warren Buffett has said, "One plus one with Charlie Munger and me certainly adds up to more than two. CEOs get into trouble by surrounding themselves with sycophants. It's beneficial to have a partner who will say, 'You're not thinking straight.'" The Harvard professor and expert bridge player Richard Zeckhauser similarly describes why one plus one equals more than two: "Most big investment payouts come when money is combined with complementary skills, such as knowing how to develop new technologies." The lesson is simple: If your strength is technical, find people who have other skills, and vice versa. If you like novelty, find someone with complementary skills and talents that will "make the trains run on time." Additional skills and abilities are not only a key to great partnerships, but better investing results.

3. "Some venture capitalists aren't in touch with the human realities of running a company, and they have a false sense of the ability to predict things and be certain about the future. When you are running a company, you don't know much of anything about the next six, twelve months; you're working through a lot of ambiguity."

Strong teams that can adapt when conditions and opportunities change create tremendous optionality for a business given the reality of an uncertain and unknown business environment. Since venture capital is a search for rare but massive financial payoffs that can be harvested by finding mispriced convexity, it should surprise no one that Fenton focuses on solving challenges associated with ambiguity and being humble about the ability to predict the future. Staying humble and agile is the best way to deal with risk, uncertainty, and ignorance.

4. "The term we like to use is 'shoulder to shoulder,' where there's a real depth of engagement, and we don't know how to create more time in the day for that. So the business model we have doesn't scale. And the core premise of the Benchmark model has always been optimizing for the depth of the relationship with the specific companies we're working with."

Every Benchmark partner I have known loves to actively participate in the creation of a new and valuable business. These partners want to work alongside the team running the business. This approach is just part of who they are. It engenders fun, and increases their competence. If you like novelty, uncertainty, solving puzzles, and making a positive difference, what could be more fun?

> 5. "There's no substitute for creating the magic of the product
> in capturing our attention. And if that doesn't occur,
> and it's more about getting money from a venture firm to
> enable that, I challenge the assumption that you need us.
> We want to do company-building and to do that we need
> to be committed exclusively in a matrimonial kind of way
> where we can give our heart, and our souls,
> and our energies to a company."

Startup founders who want only to raise money from investors are shortchanging themselves. Money is not scarce if you have the right opportunity and the right team. Fenton is saying that if all you want is money, Benchmark is not the right firm for you. What the best founders want is value-added capital. The most successful venture capitalists deliver superior financial results again and again for a reason: They add business value, not just capital, to the startups in their portfolios.

> 6. "We love the day-to-day work with the entrepreneurs,
> which prevents us from scaling. We don't have an ability to
> offload any part of our relationship in the way we practice it
> to anyone other than ourselves. So, there are no associates,
> no principals; there is nothing beyond the group of people here
> and our assistants who keep our lives sane. That's a strategy.
> Another perfectly sensible strategy is to try and build a
> particular set of services that you use to differentiate."

There are different ways to be successful in the venture capital business. Benchmark's approach works very well for them. It suits the personalities of the partners and makes them happier. Other venture capitalists have adopted a platform approach that involves more people than just the partners providing a greater range of services.

7. "The attributes of the great board meetings that
I can point to are focused on asking tough questions and
applying critical thinking, as opposed to just updates. A lot of
the entrepreneurs I work with, I encourage to get rid of the
PowerPoint. A typical board meeting will have thirty to sixty
PowerPoint slides. So, I ask entrepreneurs I work with to think
about that as a Word document, and can you reduce it down
to something we can read before the board meeting, so we
don't sit there looking at slides for three hours."

If you cannot describe what you want to do in simple declarative sentences in a written document, you have not thought it through. I am a fan of Amazon's "write a Word document describing the purpose of the meeting if you are the one who called it" approach.

8. "There is a ten-year-plus learning curve for being
any good at the venture business."

No one is born with all the skills needed to be a successful investor. You learn these skills on the job over a period of years. What makes it difficult to apply these skills is the fact that we all have biases and dysfunctional heuristics that cause us to make emotionally and psychologically based mistakes. The best way to learn how to invest is to invest. If you have the right process in place, making mistakes can make you smarter. Or not, if you are not paying attention or willing to change.

9. "Be a learn-it-all, not a know-it-all."

This quote is a version of a simple Charlie Munger philosophy: Be a learning machine. A "know-it-all" approach to both investing and life is a great way to experience big falls as a result of hubris. If you never encounter situations in which your decisions are wrong, it is strong evidence that there is far less learning taking place than is optimal. If you have not destroyed a cherished idea at least once a year (Charlie Munger's standard), you probably have a broken learning process.

10. "The saying that we like to have at Benchmark is that good judgment comes from experience, which comes from bad judgment. So, we get it wrong a lot, but what's interesting is when you get it right."

Munger's approach to investing is again applicable here: Pay attention to your mistakes and the mistakes of others. Learn and adapt. Make new mistakes. All these methods will help you deal with the fact that life and the investing environment require people to make decisions in an environment typified by risk, uncertainty, and ignorance. Individuals who do best with uncertainty are those who know how to adapt to change. If you think you can stop learning and that you "know it all," you are in big trouble.

11. "What we discovered is you can take product-driven entrepreneurs and back them in the enterprise market and achieve orders of magnitude more scale than you could with a sales-driven model."

When the dogs love eating the dog food and tell other dogs how good the dog food tastes, any business will scale better. As a bonus, a product-driven business involves more creativity and is more fun.

When products and services drive founders instead of sales, businesses make better products and services. In an age when it is so easy to get information on which products and services work well and which do not, better products and services mean better scaling, because information about the quality of those products and services will spread by word of mouth, and customers will be acquired organically.

12. "What you hope for is that the product model and the business model play off of one another, and so that's what we look for . . . can you get resonance where if I use the product in a certain way, it'll open up the economic opportunity? Google is the best example of that, of course, where the product model is the business model."

The biggest successes in the venture business all involve feedback. You cannot deliver the scaling qualities needed to generate grand-slam financial returns without creating at least one nonlinear phenomenon that comes from positive feedback. What is most desired in a startup is a phenomenon in which several types of mutually reinforcing positive feedback loops are present. Creating and sustaining virtuous cycles is both powerful and rare; Facebook's outcomes are an example of this. But when you create the right network of positive feedback loops, it can be almost magical. Alignment of the product model, the business model, and the growth is particularly magical. Fenton has generated far more than his share of magic. Repeated success in the venture business is truly unique.

13

Jim Goetz

Sequoia Capital

JIM GOETZ IS A venture capitalist at Sequoia Capital. Prior to joining Sequoia, Jim served as a general partner at Accel. He has been the venture capital backer of many successful firms, including Nimble Storage, Palo Alto Networks, Ruckus Wireless, and WhatsApp. He says he is really interested in new investing categories where there is no existing market. Of his current investments, Goetz says he is "most interested in mobile and the post-PC transition, and in disrupting the enterprise IT stack." Goetz received a BS in electrical and computer engineering from the University of Cincinnati from 1983 to 1988 and an MS in electrical engineering and computer systems from Stanford University from 1988 to 1990.

1. "I am looking for unknowns, who are passionate and mission-based."

One of the most attractive things about the venture capital world is that someone without credential X or Y can still become a success.

Some of the most famous founders did not graduate from college. That is not to say that credentials are irrelevant or unhelpful, especially early in a person's career. But history has shown that they are not absolutely required. One of the very best credentials, of course, is previously scoring a very big financial return, most importantly for the person considering your proposal. Increasingly what people are looking for in a potential team member is skills-based credentials that can be witnessed in real-world achievements.

Mercenaries are motivated primarily by money. Missionaries are driven by a cause. Missionaries are not only more likely to persevere during challenging times, they are also more liable to work to keep the business independent—characteristics that tend to produce the most grand slams. Underdogs with huge ambition for their businesses are rarer than most people imagine.

2. "Many of the entrepreneurs that we back are attacking a personal pain."

Passion for the customer pain point is what creates the desired missionary quality. Personal pain also inevitably means that the founder understands the problem deeply. If a business is not solving a genuine customer problem in a unique and compelling way, the business will not succeed. Steve Blank has made the same point when he said,

> The best entrepreneurs are the ones who are passionate about solving a problem because they've had it or seen others have it, love those customers, love solving that problem, or have been domain experts. Those are authentic entrepreneurs. Entrepreneurs, at their heart, are artists. What comes out from the great artists is something completely unexpected. World-class entrepreneurs understand something that is driven by passion.

In this way, entrepreneurship is a calling rather than a job. Steve Jobs said once,

I'm convinced that about half of what separates the successful entrepreneurs from the non-successful ones is pure perseverance. Unless you have a lot of passion about this, you're not going to survive. You're going to give it up. So you've got to have an idea, or a problem or a wrong that you want to right that you're passionate about; otherwise, you're not going to have the perseverance to stick it through.

3. "We're looking for clarity and focus."

One in fifteen entrepreneurs that come through our doors can convey their initial market position in literally five minutes.

Goetz recommends that entrepreneurs spend significant time developing a concise and compelling story. Can an entrepreneur convey his or her pitch in only five minutes? How about in just two minutes? Can the idea for the business be conveyed with clarity and focus in two or three sentences?

When you are in a business driven by optionality, like the venture capital business, investing a lot of resources in creating spreadsheets is a waste of time since the assumptions in it are in many cases just guesses. The best way to quantify an uncertain opportunity is actually with a story. Chris Sacca puts it this way: "Good stories always beat good spreadsheets. Before drawing a single slide of your pitch deck, tell the story out loud to anyone who will listen. Again and again." The more you tell stories, the better you get at telling them. Referring to notes while telling your story is vastly less effective. If you speak from the heart in telling your story, you can say a tenth as much but have twice or more as much impact. Many entrepreneurs have an investable idea, but they cannot express it well enough to get funded and attract the necessary team. In such a case, the entrepreneur may need to find a cofounder who can tell the story well. But the better approach is to learn to be a storyteller. Some may consider Dale Carnegie and Toastmasters training to be corny, but it works for many people who have not yet learned how to tell a story.

4. "Most interesting to us are new categories."

When you are in a new category, there is less competition. Having breathing room at a startup is an underrated attribute for a business. The most successful startups are often the creators of new categories. They typically create an innovative new technology and a market to go with it. This is hard to do, but also very valuable if it can be accomplished.

5. "Think big, start small."

A great deal of passion and energy around a specific pain point for a very specific customer. Focus, focus, focus.

Our view is that, early on, if you're solving a meaningful problem, even if it's for a small group of people, there is an opportunity to expand beyond that over time.

It is easy for a startup to lose focus. There are lots of shiny new pennies that people like journalists like to talk about, which can cause distraction. Paying attention to what is actually going on in a business and avoiding distractions are essential.

Creating a minimum feature set in a business that has not yet found product–market fit is not a goal but a tactic that can be used to create cost-effective, speedy, validated learning about the value hypothesis. The goal is to learn and then steer based on feedback, rather than try to predict and emerge with a killer, fully formed product. The most effective processes are based on feedback loops, which are in turn based on the scientific method: Build, measure, learn. What the startup offers as its minimum viable product should be complete in what it does to deliver and capture value, but not a fully complete implementation of the vision. The minimum viable product is an experiment intended to generate validated learning about what customers value enough to pay for.

Goetz has told the founding stories of Apple, Cisco, and other companies to make this point. In each case, the founders discovered a solution to a particular customer pain point before they moved on to bigger ambitions. If a business can generate adoption and credibility in solving a single customer problem through applying greater focus, it can then more easily move to cross-sell and up-sell additional services. Product and service extensions will arise naturally.

6. "What are your unfair advantages?"

You need to be able to break into a market and dominate.

This point of Goetz's describes where strategy kicks in the hardest. Among key strategy questions that every business should ask are the following: (1) What will the businesses do differently than its competitors? (2) What sustainable advantage can the business create versus competitors? and (3) Is that differentiation sustainable in the face of competition? These strategy questions focus on matters quite different from what Professor Michael Porter calls "operational effectiveness." Without a moat, competition among suppliers will inevitably cause increases in supply, which will cause the price to drop to a point at which there is no long-term industry profit greater than the cost of capital. When Buffett says, "Microeconomics is business," this is what he means. Too much supply is bad for profits. It is that simple. Founders will lower their credibility if they are not realistic about existing competitors. Pretending competitors do not exist in presentations to investors and potential employees is unwise.

7. "Business models can be a weapon against incumbents."

The subscription and cloud-based business model, thanks to Marc Benioff, is now a weapon for all of you.

The process of taking innovation and turning it into value is the essence of a business model. The objective of a startup in creating a business model is to build a scalable business that delivers unique sustainable customer value. Goetz is saying that the innovation that drives the success of a business is often the business model. Goetz uses the business model of software as a service (SaaS) as an example of this phenomenon. One of the key elements of the SaaS business model is that it is so extraordinarily beneficial to customers. Paying only for what you need just in time is a huge customer benefit. This model creates new challenges for the provider, of course. In a SaaS model, capital and operating expenditures are transferred to the service provider, and the customers pay only as they need the service. But these challenges can be barriers to entry against the competition for a SaaS provider. Netflix is an example of a company with a business model that acts as a weapon against incumbents in a consumer setting.

8. "We are looking for depth and substance of passion for the pain and experience."

We are very interested in your expertise in the domain.

When you know what you are doing, it is amazing how much you can accomplish. Having a Zen-style "beginner's mind" toward creating solutions to new problems is helpful, but this does not mean that it is ideal to be clueless about the domain itself. Domain expertise relevant to the business is treasured, as is humility about what you do not know. In the case of WhatsApp, Goetz says the founders' domain expertise came "from their lives and frustrations from working at Yahoo [where both founders had worked] and seeing what happened when the company shifted its focus to advertising and away from the user."

9. "We talk about 'times-ten' productivity. That's where you assemble a small group of elite engineers and get them amped up. It happens because they're genuinely excited to their core."

Engineers who are in an enabling and challenging environment feel empowered, and that empowerment translates into extreme levels of productivity. WhatsApp (backed by Goetz) is a famous example of an empowered team doing amazing things with a tiny number of engineers/employees. Pioneering venture capitalist Franklin "Pitch" Johnson once said that part of what you must offer to be a successful venture capitalist is commitment. To be committed you can't help but get somewhat emotionally involved and that means being available. Johnson also once said, "We invest stomach lining in those companies because any venture capitalist with his or her salt gets emotionally involved. You can't be that detached because the entrepreneurs are very emotional people who want to succeed."

10. "Do the numbers make sense?"

A company that raises more money than needed may lose some discipline in the culture, and you may start to see some behavior that may not be the foundation for a long-term enduring business.

There are a range of key performance indicators that are relevant to any business and a few that are particularly important. These metrics are not always the same since business models vary, but they should be designed to enable a business to get to the right place. Everyone on the team should know the metrics that will drive success. Having a single metric that the entire company can rally around can be particularly valuable.

One vitally important number is the amount of available cash. You can be forgiven for a lot of things in business—except running out of cash. Many accounting problems can eventually be overcome as long as the business has access to cash, which is the oxygen of business. Having said that, even famously frugal managers are not opposed to spending money as long as it creates value. One thing that people often underestimate is the need to acquire customers in a cost-effective way. Acquiring customers cheaply is such a beautiful way to make generating a profit easier. Conversely, paying too much to acquire a customer is an unsolvable problem. The cost of acquiring a customer and the cost of serving a customer can be stone-cold killers for a business. One aspect of a startup that makes life far easier is high gross margins. Life is so much better for a business if gross margins approach 80 to 90 percent. Sales and marketing, research and development, and general and administrative expenses come after gross margin, and if they are collectively too high, they can kill a business.

11. "If it begins to work, it will wildly exceed everyone's expectations. We desperately try to convince the founders to remain independent."

As the world becomes more digital, positive feedback is increasingly becoming what determines the financial result in a business. When the right network effects can be created, the payoff in a digital world can be nonlinear. And when network effects disappear, the speed at which that happens may be nonlinear. In other words, network effects are a double-edged sword: Success can disappear just as quickly as it was created. The loss of network benefits can be even more spectacular since it is often something very visible that transforms into nothing in such cases. When network effects create benefits, the early success is unseen and more surprising since the phenomenon involves "emergence." Something suddenly appearing in a way that is far greater than the sum of its parts can be surprising.

12. "I don't try to tout the next great thing I want to get in front of because I don't set that course. The entrepreneurs do that."

If all a founder needs is capital, then they are quite lucky indeed—and probably delusional. Goetz is saying that a board's primary role should be advising the founders and management, not trying to run the business. Someone like Goetz has seen many different boards and knows how important a good board is in terms of increasing the probability of a business's success. Being humble and a life-long learner can pay big dividends for both the venture capitalist and the entrepreneur; as Warren Buffett says, "Risk comes from not knowing what you are doing." The pioneering venture capitalist Bill Draper believes, "Venture capital is not all about money, it's really mostly about building a company with the entrepreneurs who do the heavy lifting." Implicit in this statement is that the best venture capitalists help with "light lifting." Different venture capitalists and firms have different models for how much support they provide to portfolio companies. Venture capitalist support can range from (1) extensive support from so-called platform approaches that offer end-to-end support (e.g., public relations, marketing, finance, recruiting, sales, distribution) to (2) lighter-touch support, where the venture capitalists get involved in only a few issues, like recruiting or scaling growth, in addition to their board duties. No venture capitalist can be an expert in all domains of knowledge. It is the venture capitalist's job to learn from the entrepreneur and to substitute his or her vision for that of the entrepreneur.

14

Paul Graham

Y *Combinator*

PAUL GRAHAM WAS A cofounder of Y Combinator, the most famous and most successful startup accelerator in the world. Y Combinator provides seed funding, advice, and access to its network of startups in two batches each year. A profile of Graham in *Forbes* described the accelerator as "a startup-rearing juggernaut that's part incubator, part drill sergeant and part liaison to the investor class." Y Combinator invests $120,000 in return for 7 percent of a company's equity. Graham is also a computer scientist known for, among other things, his work on the Lisp programming languages. Graham has written three books and numerous essays on a wide range of topics, including "Why Nerds Are Unpopular" and "Startup Equals Growth." He cofounded Viaweb, which was acquired by Yahoo in 1998 and became Yahoo Stores. He has broad interests and at one time studied painting, attending both the Accademia di Belle Arti in Florence and the Rhode Island School of Design.

1. "Y Combinator is a minor league farm club.
We send people on up to VCs."

Graham and his cofounders successfully found a unique place for Y Combinator in the startup ecosystem that has allowed it to thrive. Y Combinator partners with other investors to provide growth capital to its graduates. This symbiotic relationship has produced remarkable success. The *New Yorker* described what Graham and his cofounders have created in the following way: "Thirteen thousand fledgling software companies applied to Y Combinator this year, and two hundred and forty were accepted, making it more than twice as hard to get into as Stanford University. After graduating thirteen hundred startups, YC now boasts the power—and the peculiarities—of an island nation."

2. "One of the two most important things to understand about startup investing as a business, is that effectively all the returns are concentrated in a few big winners. I knew this intellectually, but didn't grasp it until it happened to us. The total value of the companies we've funded is around $10 billion, give or take a few. But just two companies, Dropbox and Airbnb, account for about three-quarters of it."

> What investors are looking for when they invest in a startup is the possibility that it could become a giant. It may be a small possibility, but it has to be nonzero. They're not interested in funding companies that will top out at a certain point.

The most interesting part of this quote is Graham's admission that even though he understood the power-law phenomenon in venture capital intellectually, he was still surprised when he experienced it. For most of human history, people's life experiences have been overwhelmingly linear. Humans are accustomed to encountering situations that reflect a simple proportional relationship between cause and effect. People expect that when they do X, Y will happen if Y is what happened in the past. This type of linear thinking is comforting to people since it is familiar. The famous inventor Ray Kurzweil believes, "Our intuition about the future is linear because that is the way the world worked for most of history. Prey animals did not get exponentially faster for example." Except for a virus or bacterial infection multiplying inside your body, few things in ordinary life are nonlinear.

The rise of modern science combined with modern distribution and other processes developed by businesses has resulted in people increasingly encountering nonlinear change. The economist Paul Romer explains one common reaction: "People are reasonably good at estimating how things add up, but for compounding, which involves repeated multiplication, we fail to appreciate how quickly things grow. As a result, we often lose sight of how important even small changes in the average rate of growth can be." When something is sufficiently nonlinear, a phenomenon can seem almost magical. Especially when the outcome of a nonlinear change is negative, tendencies like loss aversion can kick in, and people can have a strong tendency to react in highly emotional ways. Even people who are otherwise rational may not think clearly in such situations.

Most entrepreneurs do not raise venture capital. They grow their business from savings, internally generated cash flow, bank loans, or equity capital supplied by investors seeking financial returns that do not reflect the skewed distribution that exists in venture capital. In the United States, the number of new restaurants alone is ten times the number of new startups that seek venture funding each year. There is less failure overall among new nonventure-backed businesses, but fewer of those firms will have the huge financial returns produced by a venture capitalist harvesting convexity.

3. "If you want to start a startup, you're probably going to have to think of something fairly novel. A startup has to make something it can deliver to a large market, and ideas of that type are so valuable that all the obvious ones are taken.

Usually, successful startups happen because the founders are
sufficiently different from other people—ideas few others
can see seem obvious to them."

Finding a business opportunity that competitors have not fully discovered and developed and that is capable of generating grand-slam
financial returns is unlikely to happen with traditional approaches.
By seeking novelty, a startup can sometimes find hidden convexity. In other words, convexity is most likely to be found in places
where there is a lot of uncertainty and ignorance. Similarly, financial bets on a startup business that operates in areas with not a lot
of uncertainty and ignorance are not as likely to have mispriced
convexity. Unique people with unique interests often find value that
others do not see.

4. "The very best ideas usually seem like bad ideas at first.
Google looked like a bad idea. There were already several other
search engines, some of which were operated by public companies.
Who needed another? And Facebook? When I first heard about
Facebook, it was for college students, who don't have any money.
And what do they do there? Waste time looking at one another's
profiles. That seemed like the stupidest company ever. I'm glad
no one gave me an opportunity to turn it down."

Convexity is everywhere if you know how to find it. Sometimes it
is looking you right in the face. The challenge is to see the world in
a different way. You won't always be right, but being right all the
time is not required to be a successful venture capitalist or entrepreneur. Since so few investments result in a grand-slam financial outcome, making just one contrarian bet is not a workable
approach for a venture capitalist. So venture capitalists create a
portfolio of bets. But entrepreneurs are not nearly as diversified.
They can make a few bets in their lifetime, but that number is
limited. Being an entrepreneur requires more courage.

5. "We thought Airbnb was a bad idea. We funded it because we liked the founders. They were so determined and so imaginative. Focusing on them saved us from our stupidity."

Great venture capitalists put a large emphasis on a great team since great teams give investors additional optionality. Great teams not only adapt better to change, but they know when to adapt. Great people also attract other great people—who also attract money, partners, distribution, and customers in ways that are mutually reinforcing. The ability to successfully adapt to change is part of what makes a great founder and, in and of itself, adds to the convexity of an investment. In other words, a great team of people gives a business valuable added optionality, which is often essential to success given the need to adapt. Striking the right balance on this set of issues is key since it is important to maintain a founder's motivation and persistence. Sometimes a founder's dogged persistence sends a business right off a cliff, whereas at other times it is the key to success.

6. "For a product or service to surprise me, it must be satisfying expectations I didn't know I had. No focus group is going to discover those. Only a great designer can."

The greatest founders are savants and artists. They essentially perform alchemy and make something that people could not imagine before they first saw it. Steve Blank puts it this way: "The best entrepreneurs are the ones who are passionate about solving a problem because they've had it or seen others have it, love those customers, love solving that problem, or have been domain experts. Those are authentic entrepreneurs." He believes, "Entrepreneurs, at their heart, are artists. What comes out from the great artists is something completely unexpected. World-class entrepreneurs understand something that is driven by passion."

7. "I never say, 'These guys are going to be great.' All I ever say is, 'These guys are doing great so far,' because some percentage of the time, it turns out there's some explosion around the corner. Not just founder disputes, there are all kinds of explosions. Startups are very, very uncertain."

Since startups and the markets they target are complex systems, changes can be nonlinear in both a positive and negative way. In the life of a startup, it is "never over until it is over." Some successful startups will almost fail, and some failures will almost succeed. The world has been fundamentally changed by digital networks and software. Businesses and customers connected by networked digital systems create amplified network effects, which means the velocity of business and the level of competition and innovation are higher than they have ever been. Increasing the ability of a business to adapt to a changing world has never been more important. Virtually every niche in the business world is constantly being explored by challengers. This constant experimentation by entrepreneurs makes profit harder than ever to sustain, especially if its source was traditionally information asymmetry (i.e., the seller knew more about something than the customer). Unless a business has a moat based on something like network effects, there is nowhere to hide from the constant onslaught of competition.

Even if a business is fortunate enough to have a moat based on network effects, the life of a business can still be nasty, brutish, and short. In other words, since network effects are brittle and work in both directions, a moat can be destroyed just as quickly or more quickly than the time it took to create it in the first place.

8. "You need three things to create a successful startup:
to start with good people, to make something customers want,
and to spend as little money as possible."

We have discussed the importance of a great team and the need to make dog food that dogs like to eat more than other dog food sold by competitors. The new point illustrated by Graham's quote here is that acquiring customers while spending as little money as possible is essential. Bill Gates said once, "Take sales, take costs, and try to get this big positive number at the bottom." Waiting many months or even years for a *big-bang* product or service launch that is the result of a focus group–driven process may leave a business with insufficient resources to survive a mistake since feedback has come so late in the process. Steve Blank puts it this way:

> Why are so many founders so reluctant to invest even five hundred or one thousand hours up front to be sure that, when they're done, the business they're building will face genuine, substantial demand or enthusiasm? Without passionate customers, even the most passionate entrepreneur will flounder at best.

9. "The reason startups do better when they turn down acquisition offers is not necessarily that all such offers undervalue startups. More likely the reason is that the kind of founders who have the balls to turn down a big offer also tend to be very successful. That spirit is exactly what you want in a startup."

Founders who go "all in" because the startup is more about the mission than the money are more likely to generate grand-slam financial outcomes. Some of these missionary founders will fail due to an overreach, but that is a positive for society overall since the successful outcomes are often spectacular. Mercenary founders succeed less often, and even when they do succeed, they do so in less spectacular ways.

10. "The exciting thing about market economies is that stupidity equals opportunity."

To earn above-market financial returns, assets must be mispriced. Graham is saying that assets are often mispriced when people are "stupid." This happens when people participating in a market become overly optimistic or pessimistic. The swing between these two states (greed and fear) is a "Mr. Market" phenomenon. By being greedy when others are fearful and fearful when others are greedy, positive things can happen since an investor can buy at a bargain and sell at a premium if they are disciplined and can control their emotions. Warren Buffett believes,

> The true investor welcomes volatility. Ben Graham explained why in chapter 8 of *The Intelligent Investor*. In that classic book on investing, he introduced "Mr. Market," an obliging fellow who shows up every day to either buy from you or sell to you, whichever you wish. The more manic-depressive this chap is, the greater the opportunities available to the investor. That's true because a wildly fluctuating market means that irrationally low prices will periodically be attached to solid businesses.

11. "It's better to make a few people really happy than to make a lot of people semi-happy."

Focus matters in a startup, as does finding core product value. When creating a minimum viable product with product–market fit, it is preferable to start with a solution to a real problem that customers really care about instead of a solution to a vague and broadly defined problem that customers are lukewarm about. It is easier to expand from genuine customer delight about a solution than a solution that generates an attitude of "It's okay."

12. "It's hard to do a really good job on anything you don't think about in the shower."

What Graham is talking about here is the idea that you are so passionate about your work that you are thinking about it all the time (including in the shower). If you are thinking about your business even in the shower, you are more likely to be focused on making your business better than someone who is less passionate. Steve Blank agrees:

Founders fit the definition of a composer: They see something no one else does. And to help them create it from nothing, they surround themselves with world-class performers. This concept of creating something that few others see—and the reality-distortion field necessary to recruit the team to build it—is at the heart of what startup founders do. It is a very different skill than science, engineering, or management. Entrepreneurial employees are the talented performers who hear the siren song of a founder's vision. Joining a startup while it is still searching for a business model, they too see the promise of what can be and join the founder to bring the vision to life.

15

Kirsten Green

Forerunner Ventures

KIRSTEN GREEN IS THE founder of the San Francisco–based Forerunner Ventures. Green has led efforts to raise over $250 million from leading investors and has invested in more than forty early-stage companies. Forerunner Ventures portfolio companies include or have included Birchbox, Bonobos, Dollar Shave Club, Glossier, Hotel Tonight, Jet.com, Warby Parker, and Zola. She currently serves on the board of directors of several Forerunner portfolio companies, including Glossier, INTURN, Outdoor Voices, Ritual, and Rockets of Awesome. Before founding Forerunner, Green was an equity research analyst and investor at Bank of America Securities (formerly Montgomery Securities), covering publicly traded retail and consumer stocks. She graduated from the University of California, Los Angeles, with a BA in business economics. She is also a certified public accountant and certified financial analyst.

1. "I'm always looking for things that are addressing a real need . . . high-margin products, real revenues, businesses that can scale."

Green looks for certain attributes when evaluating an investment. The classic trilogy is product, market, and team. Core product value represents a solution to a real problem or need that is valuable enough to make people to want to pay for a product. This may seem an obvious attribute to look for, but the number of times venture capitalists have funded businesses that are trying to grow before having a valuable product is not small. A customer first recognizes core product value when they connect with the product in what is known as an "aha" moment.

Green also says that she looks for high-margin products. Businesses come in all varieties, and the gross margins generated by different activities vary significantly as well. Software companies and pharmaceutical firms typically have high gross margins. A company like Costco has low gross margins. Some companies make up for relatively low gross margins by selling a lot of products, and some do not. Some companies have high operating costs below the gross-margin line on the income statement, and some do not. If a business does have low gross margins, it does not have a lot of elbow room for operating expenses. Green is saying that life for a business is just better if it has high gross margins. Like many things in life, high profit margins can be a double-edged sword since it is much easier for a disruptive new business to attack an incumbent with high margins. Jeff Bezos has famously said, "Your margin is my opportunity." In other words, Bezos sees a competitor's love of margins and other financial ratios as an opportunity for Amazon: The competitor will cling to them while Bezos focuses on absolute-dollar free cash flow and slices through them like a hot knife through butter. If a business does not have a moat, its margins are at risk. Finally, Green looks for revenue and scalability in the businesses in which she invests. She wants more than an idea, and that idea should be capable of growing quickly into a large market.

2. "It is important for every founding team to be thinking about how to market in efficient, low-cost ways, as it is incredibly challenging to build a long-term sustainable business on paid marketing alone."

Every business has a customer acquisition cost (CAC). A company that does not know its CAC is like a blindfolded poker player. Customer acquisition cost is a particularly important part of customer lifetime value since it is paid up front, which means cash going out the door in month one of the customer relationship. That cash going out the door may not be recovered for some time, creating a painful negative cash flow. If a business is able to grow revenue organically by word of mouth via direct customer-to-customer interaction, the customer acquisition cost drops. Customers acquired organically without paid advertising also remain customers longer, pay their bills on a more regular basis, and convert from free offerings to paid at a much higher rate.

3. "If you build an outstanding service or product, people will use it, they will talk, and others will come."

A product that generates so much customer delight that experience with it produces positive customer word of mouth is hugely valuable for a business. The idea is a simple one (if a client loves a product, they will tell their friends) but not an easy one to realize. Conversely, if someone tells you about a product and it is not lovable, you will stop using it. Venture capitalists and entrepreneurs, like Andy Rachleff, point to Netflix as an example of a company that focuses on delighting its customers instead of being paranoid about competitors. In this way, Netflix is parting ways with the Andy Grove dictum of being paranoid about competitors, instead focusing on delighting customers. Rachleff quotes Reed Hastings as saying, "Being paranoid about competition is the last thing you want to do because it distracts you from the primary job at hand: delighting the customer." Green is focused on adding companies to her portfolio that sell products that consumers genuinely love.

4. "It's the entrepreneurs who have to give you permission to do this job."

If I weren't doing this, I would have gone to school for psychology and been a therapist. I am the friend that people want to tell their problems to.

The financial performance of a venture capitalist depends on his or her reputation with founders. To enhance that relationship, many venture capitalists act as mentors to their founders. Michael Bloomberg said once, "Over the course of one's life, there are a few people who have a major influence on the way you look at the world and define what is most important." He has described much of what a mentor can be in that sentence. The correct definition of a mentor is very broad and not limited to a formal relationship as some might imagine. Anyone who has a significant influence on your worldview can be a mentor. The venture capitalist Aileen Lee strives not only to be a mentor to founders, but also to "become a critical part of the life cycle of these companies." Lee says, "I like to be part of the trusted pit crew they are looking to for guidance."

5. " 'E-commerce' is a bit of a dated word. I think it is part of the way in which we shop. You've got that huge new population

of consumers that behave extraordinarily differently than any other population we've had before."

Customers today have many choices and loads of information about their options. They do not need to accept an inferior offering. Technology and customer access to information have also made markets far more winner-take-all. If a CEO fails to see a shift in the market, his or her company can quickly find itself dead. Jeff Bezos understands this new environment well:

> The balance of power is shifting toward consumers and away from companies. . . . The individual is empowered. . . . The right way to respond to this if you are a company is to put the vast majority of your energy, attention, and dollars into building a great product or service and put a smaller amount into shouting about it, marketing it. If I build a great product or service, my customers will tell each other. In the old world, you devoted 30 percent of your time to building an excellent service and 70 percent of your time to shouting about it. In the new world, that inverts.

Almost every customer is "showrooming" (comparing provider prices and quality) using tools made ubiquitously available by the Internet and a range of modern hardware devices. The days when a business could take advantage of an extensive information asymmetry to earn a higher profit on the sale of a good or service are either rapidly disappearing or already gone. The showrooming phenomenon has resulted in lower gross profit margins and an increasing focus on customer retention, which often takes the form of a subscription business model and a membership mentality. The theory behind this new approach is simple: By delighting customers on a more regular basis, treating customers as if they are members of a club, and tracking their engagement via a range of metrics, you reduce the risk of churn. Amazon Prime and

Netflix are examples of businesses with a membership mentality. Another less obvious example is Costco, which makes the bulk of its profit on membership fees. The minimally marked-up merchandise in Costco stores (about 14 percent), the cheap hot dogs, and the free samples are all about delighting customers enough to renew their memberships.

6. "Now that people are bombarded with information, we are in a golden age where brands matter."

The good news is that because of the Internet, we now have access to a great deal of information. And the bad news is that because of the Internet, there is sometimes too much information. People still need to make choices, and brands are helpful in that process.

An entrepreneur like Howard Schultz understood from Starbucks's beginning that nothing created brand value and shareholder value more than strong customer word of mouth. Yes, Starbucks eventually invested in brand advertising in the mass media, but that was late in its history. As another example, Rich Barton's company Zillow did not buy mass-market brand advertising until it had fifty million unique users.

7. "You increasingly cannot compete just on the product. To have a product that the consumer is willing to exchange money for is table stakes. So the thing to compete on is delivering a great experience."

As products become more of a commodity because best practices and technology now spread so quickly, many businesses have discovered that market competition is increasingly based on price. Price-based competition can be ruinous. Green understands that one crucial way to escape price-based competition is to offer consumers a better experience since experience is harder to replicate than product. This better approach requires that a business create a regular series of "aha" moments during which the customer reconnects with core product value.

> 8. "Today consumers have access to so much more information than ever before; they have so many things influencing their decisions about their lives and about what they choose to engage in and spend their money on. . . . It's a time when you can enter the market, and if you have the right proposition, you can be just as compelling, or more compelling, than something that has been around for a long time that doesn't speak to the consumer in the same way."

One reason why Green is so effective is that she has unique skills and experience that apply to retail and brands. What has been a graveyard for other investors has been a happy hunting ground for her. Some very prominent hedge-fund investors have been punished brutally by venturing into retail, via companies like J. C. Penney and Sears. Retail is hard. For example, Warren Buffett has said that many of his investment mistakes have been in retail because he strayed outside of his circle of competence. When hedge funds are losing to disruptive competitors in consumer markets, it is often a business backed by Green that is doing the disrupting.

> 9. "Birchbox and Warby Parker were the culmination of an 'aha' moment that was all of these things I had been looking for. The path to purchase is so different."

A time of great change usually creates a tremendous opportunity for disruptive challengers of incumbents. It is volatility in valuations, risk, and uncertainty that create the potential for investors to outperform a market average. Keeping a customer in today's hyper-competitive business world is often more profitable than paying to acquire a new customer. This increased focus on customer retention in no small part explains why so many businesses are shifting to a "lifetime-value" approach to valuing customers. Having to reacquire customers again and again for every transaction is not an ideal way to run a business today when customer acquisition costs are so high and customer switching costs so low. As a result, businesses are focused on delivering nearly constant value for their clients and keeping them engaged and happy.

Diagrams of a service development process must increasingly look like flywheels. Failure is an essential part of the process, which is a feedback loop. The model is "build, measure, learn, repeat." Here is the scientific method at work but systematized with telemetry allowing for timely, accurate measurements like never before and cloud computing radically lowering the cost of the experiments.

10. "The way I stay out of the fray is to have a point of view, and to stand for something."

We think we bring an edge in understanding the consumer and what will resonate with them.

With the way Amazon and eBay had become big companies and with the way people were embracing technology, I was like, it is so obvious that this is going to be a huge game changer in this space. The combination of these things is going to change what it means to retail, what it's like to launch brands, what it means to connect with your consumer. That was the spark I jumped after very early on.

Venture capital investors can often be more successful if they find areas of specialization. This approach can enable the individual investor or firm to concentrate work, time, and talent in fewer areas and put more wood on a smaller number of arrow heads.

Some venture capital firms like Maveron are consumer only. Other venture capitalists are primarily or even exclusively focused on enterprise startups. And other venture capital firms have prospered by being opportunistic generalists.

11. "Thinking about the acquirers, the state of the public markets, how a business is being valued—that's an essential way to understand the overall ecosystem."

Being a retail analyst at an investment bank in public markets, a certified financial analyst, and certified public accountant has provided Green with a broad background in business that is very helpful in her current role as a venture capitalist. Investors like Howard Marks believes that almost everything is cyclical. And it is clear that venture capital is no exception to this rule. People like Green who have seen business cycles inevitably turn know that sometimes growth is valued more than profitability by markets, and sometimes it is not. Sometimes cash is relatively easy to raise when you have a good business, and sometimes you can't raise five cents even with a great business. Howard Marks likes to say that you cannot predict, but you can prepare. Having enough cash on hand to survive an inability to raise new money for a significant period helps prepare a company for adverse turns in unpredictable cycles. As Green says, it is "essential to understanding the ecosystem."

12. "I think I rightfully thought Bonobos was in jeopardy several times."

There is a stage in the life of a business that is the least glamorous but often the most important. Many companies particularly struggle for survival during the time between the launch of a startup and a financial exit. Scott Belsky calls this period "the messy middle."

Ben Horowitz refers to what happens during this time as "the Struggle." Many companies almost fail before they succeed during this period. The venture capitalist often must perform triage and determine which companies to help and which have little hope. Aileen Lee notes,

> Most successful startups take a lot of time and commitment to break out. While vesting periods are usually four years, the most valuable startups will take at least eight years before a 'liquidity event,' and most founders and CEOs will stay in their companies beyond such an event. Unicorns also tend to raise a lot of capital over time—way beyond the series A. So these founding teams had the ability to share a compelling company vision over many years and rounds of fundraising, plus scale themselves and recruit teams, despite economic ups and downs.

Missionaries survive this process far more often than mercenaries since mercenaries tend to find it overly taxing and difficult and often quit.

16

Bill Gurley

Benchmark

BILL GURLEY HAS SPENT over ten years as a partner at Benchmark. Prior to joining Benchmark, Gurley was a partner with Hummer Winblad Venture Partners. Before entering the venture capital business, Bill spent four years on Wall Street as a top-ranked research analyst. His current investments and board seats include Grubhub, Nextdoor, OpenTable, Uber, Ubiquiti Networks, and Zillow. I became friends with Bill Gurley in the mid-1990s soon after Bill Gates forwarded me a copy of his wonderful blog "Above the Crowd." I immediately signed up to receive it (by fax!). I then found a way to for us to start talking by phone and the Internet. Gurley thinks deeply and has a well-developed investing philosophy. Bill and his partners like to work shoulder to shoulder with founders on building the business. He is always looking for a business with some kind of competitive advantage. He says about the venture capital business, "There aren't that many rules. One of the games you play in venture is to know which rules to break at the right time. Therefore, we constantly challenge ourselves.

'Should we maybe be dropping this rule at this moment in time because things are changing?'"

1. "All the great investors I've ever studied have felt macroeconomics is one of the silliest wastes of time possible."

There is a nonlinear relationship between the simplicity of the system you are trying to understand and your ability to make bets that can generate financial returns that outperform a benchmark (alpha). The simplest system that one can work to understand in a way that generates valuable insight is an individual business. Charlie Munger puts it this way: "Be a business analyst, not a market, macroeconomic, or security analyst." Munger has said that microeconomics "is what we do," whereas macroeconomics is what we put up with.

2. "Venture Capital has long been a trailing indicator to the Nasdaq. Venture capital is a cyclical business."

The Howard Marks maxim that "most things are cyclical" definitely includes venture capital. Mr. Market's bipolar nature in the short term affects the venture capital business like any other business. When Mr. Market is depressed and pessimistic, a hardworking venture capitalist with cash available to invest (dry powder) can find opportunities, which do not exist when Mr. Market is euphoric. Being "long-term greedy" often means investing despite the pessimism of others. Nothing good or bad goes on forever. Yet people often extrapolate as if a phenomenon will go on indefinitely. "If something cannot go on forever it will eventually stop," Herbert Stein once famously said.

The mean reversion assumption is the rational investor's consistent friend. The best time to fund or start a business is often during a recession.

3. "There's a lot of luck involved in venture capital."

Luck is easier to describe than skill. Luck is the driver of outcomes in a game like roulette. With roulette, you know all the potential future states and the probability distribution. Because the house takes a rake in roulette, there are no professional roulette players. Michael Mauboussin writes that luck has three core elements: (1) It operates on an individual or organizational basis; (2) it can be positive or negative; and (3) it is reasonable to expect that a different outcome could have occurred. Sometimes you will hear people say things like, "The harder I work, the luckier I become." Mauboussin has easily demonstrated such a statement to be a non sequitur with a few well-chosen words: "There is no way to improve your luck, because anything you do to improve a result can reasonably be considered skill." People who acknowledge the role of luck in life are, as a rule, far more humble and less susceptible to mistakes caused by hubris.

4. "If you can't sell, venture capital is not a good industry to be in."

The idea that the venture capital business is about sitting in boardrooms thinking about strategy is false and, at most, is maybe 5 percent of what a venture capitalist does in any event. Venture capital is a service business, and the best venture capitalists hustle on behalf of their companies and to grow their personal networks. The best venture capitalists sell "early and often."

5. "Venture capital is not even a home-run business.
It's a grand-slam business. If your idea is not something
that can generate $100 million in revenue, you may not
want to take venture capital."

The size of a venture capital fund and the need for a market-beating financial return determine how much a partner in a venture capital firm should invest in a given company. For example, a $500 million fund must return at least $1.5 billion from its investments. An additional constraint on the firm is that its venture capitalists can help only so many companies at one time. This means that a business that will not generate at least the $100 million in revenue Gurley is talking about is not something that will be attractive to most venture capitalists. It is simply not a big enough return to impact the investing outcome of the firm in the desired manner. The entrepreneur in this situation is better dealing with financiers like banks, or even bootstrapping the business with internally generated cash and some investment support from friends and family. In the right circumstances, a micro VC may be a source of needed capital if a larger venture capital firm is uninterested owing to the small revenue potential of the business.

6. "Good judgment comes from experience,
which comes from bad judgment."

Warren Buffett has said that there is nothing like walking on land for a day if you are a fish to learn about life on the land. We all make mistakes, and personal mistakes can be the best learning experiences. When you listen to Gurley speak, he always takes time to thank the people who helped him along the way and to point out the good fortune he has experienced in his career. In a Quora "Ask Me Anything" interview, Gurley gave a great answer to this question: "What are the top pieces of advice you would give to your younger self?" Gurley responded,

1. Read even more than you did.
2. Thank the people (more) who helped you along the way.
3. When Larry and Sergey ask for $110 pre-money, say, "Yes, we would be very excited about that."

7. "We like to say that 'more startups die of indigestion than starvation.'"

Gurley is saying that running out of cash is often caused by a business losing focus and diverting resources unnecessarily, straying from the critical path toward success. Too much money is often the root cause of that inability to focus. Failure is often a symptom of mistakes such as premature scaling and wild goose chases. Sometimes when a business tries to do everything, it ends up doing nothing.

8. "Consumers buy from great companies because the product is so good. They aren't spending tens of millions on marketing."

Jeff Bezos might just as easily have said these words. Gurley thinks like Bezos (which is not surprising since Amazon was one of the companies he covered as a young Wall Street analyst). Too often, a lifetime-value financial analysis ends up being a justification for too much spending on nonorganic marketing. One essential task for any business is to acquire customers in a cost-effective way. Gurley says, "Organic users typically have a higher NPV [net present value], a higher conversion rate, a lower churn, and are more satisfied than customers acquired through marketing spend."

9. "High-price/revenue multiple companies have wide moats or strong barriers to entry."

If the supply of what your competitors offer is not limited in some way, the price of that offering will drop to your cost of capital. Sometimes you do not figure out your business model until after you have broad adoption, but thinking about how to generate networks effects is wise even before your business model is fully formed. Gurley has also said, "Strong-form network effect companies are far and few between. Fortunately, when they do exist, they are typically leading candidates for the 10x+ price/revenue multiple clubs." Revenue alone is not enough to sustain a business given the inevitable competitive response. A sustained return on invested capital is a prerequisite for the long-term survival of a business. In other words, "For what shall it profit a business, if it shall discover solutions to the value hypothesis and growth hypothesis, but fail anyway because it does not have a moat?" At worst, a business without a moat is never profitable. At best, a business without a moat is profitable for a while, but over time is gradually overtaken. The test of whether a moat exists is quantitative, even though the factors that create moats are qualitative. If a business has not earned returns on capital that substantially exceed the opportunity cost of capital for three to five years, it does not have a moat. Can great management or better business execution create a moat? Warren Buffett's famous quip on that point is "When a management with a reputation for brilliance tackles a business with a reputation for bad economics, it is the reputation of the business that remains intact."

10. "DCF is an unruly valuation tool for young companies. It is not because it is a bad theoretical framework; it is because we don't have valid inputs. Garbage in, garbage out."

What is sometimes called "spreadsheet disease" is a byproduct of people not thinking hard about the assumptions that go into a model. Valuing the convexity of an investment in a business is not easy, and anyone who thinks they can do it with a spreadsheet is an example of hope over experience. Establishing a valuation for a startup business will always be hard. The investor Howard Marks once said to Charlie Munger, "It's not supposed to be easy to make a profit by investing. Anyone who finds it easy is stupid."

11. "If a disruptive competitor can offer a product or service similar to yours for 'free,' and if they can make enough money to keep the lights on, then you likely have a problem."

Digital offerings have very strange economics in that multisided markets (platforms) are often involved, and offerings in such a market can have a near-zero marginal cost once they have been created. Freemium is a natural business model in many businesses when the offering is digital and has a zero or low marginal cost. By spending a relatively limited amount of money on the free items, the customer acquisition cost can drop dramatically. Because software has a marginal cost of almost zero (it costs almost no additional money to create more copies), there is a natural tendency for the price of software to drop to zero if there are no barriers to entry. Of course, some free services have real storage or egress costs, but the point remains true. Solving the "chicken-and-egg" problem inherent in any platform business usually involves either a free egg or free chicken on one "side" of the market, which is another reason why the price of any given product may drop to zero. It is easy to wake up in a digital world and have whatever you were once selling now being offered "for free."

12. "Being 'right' doesn't lead to superior performance if the consensus forecast is also right."

Being a contrarian for its sake is suicidal. Without being a contrarian on certain occasions, you cannot outperform the market. Being genuinely contrarian means you are going to be uncomfortable sometimes. Howard Marks puts it this way: "To achieve superior investment results, your insight into value has to be superior. Thus you must learn things others don't, see things differently or do a better job of analyzing them—ideally all three." It is a bit strange that most people don't realize this truth since it is common sense: You simply cannot be part of the crowd and at the same time beat the crowd, especially after fees and costs are imposed. The Nobel Laureate William Sharpe famously provided the mathematical proof for this in a paper entitled "The Arithmetic of Active Management." As restated by John Bogle the conclusion is as follows: "In many areas of the market, there will be a loser for every winner so, on average, investors will get the return of that market less fees." Of course, the part about the investors collectively getting the return of the market is key. Being a long-term investor in the progress of the economy is a very good thing. As life runs its course, some investors get more of that financial return of the market than others.

17

Reid Hoffman

Greylock Partners

REID HOFFMAN IS AN entrepreneur and a partner at the venture capital firm Greylock Partners. A *New Yorker* profile describes his early career:

> His first job was at a short-lived online service at Apple called eWorld. Then he worked at WorldsAway, a "virtual chat" community, owned by Fujitsu, where users interacted through fictionalized graphic representations of themselves. In 1997, Hoffman started his own company, called SocialNet, which created a way for people to connect with each other for various purposes, mainly dating, using pseudonyms.

Hoffman joined the payments provider PayPal in 1999, after selling SocialNet. He was a cofounder and executive chair of LinkedIn before its sale to Microsoft. He serves on the boards of Airbnb, Edmodo, Microsoft, Mozilla, Shopkick, and Wrapp. Hoffman is a coauthor of *The Start-Up of You* and *The Alliance*. His passion about issues such as the economic and social impacts of automation, the skills gap, shifting educational and career patterns, and socioeconomic stratification make his views on business and venture capital particularly interesting. The increasing importance of data and networks to competitive advantage is a topic that few know more about than Hoffman.

> 1. "The top investment is worth the total amount
> of all the other projects and more. You're looking
> for the one high-water mark, not the average.
> People don't come to you looking for singles."

In an excellent essay on venture capital economics, Andy Rachleff notes,

> The industry rule of thumb has been to look for deals that have the chance to return 10X your money in five years. . . . If 20 percent of a fund is invested in deals that return 10X in five years and everything else results in no value, then the fund would have an annual return of approximately 15 percent.

Due to the attention lavished on a few massive startup successes some people fail to understand that there are many businesses one can start that do not require venture capital. On this point, Bill Gurley has said, "If you want to get to fifty to one hundred employees, unless you've discovered the next Google AdWords, you're going to need outside funding, but that doesn't mean that venture capital investment is right for everyone." Non-venture capital–backed companies can generate attractive financial returns and can, when selected correctly, have a substantially lower probability of failure. This should not be a surprise since you simply cannot have the failure rate of venture capital–backed businesses and have the winners return only two to five times the capital invested over a similar period.

2. "At a startup or early-stage project, the only massive early-stage projects are where you're contrarian and right. The projects where everyone agrees often end up having less overall success than the projects where there was some disagreement amongst the board. Where's the contrarian thinking that, if they turn out to be right, could be really, really big? Consensus indicates it's probably not a total breakout project. If your thinking isn't truly contrarian, there's a dog pile of competitors thinking the same thing, and that will limit your total success."

Being contrarian is essential to outperforming a market. It is impossible to beat the crowd if you *are* the crowd. The crowd is usually right, so the tricky part is being able to predict when it is wrong. Just being contrarian for its own sake is a losing strategy. Moreover, of course, the bet must be convex. If you are contrarian, you do not want the upside to be a small return relative to what you put at risk. The best opportunities for a convex bet tend to be in places where other people are not looking. Michael Mauboussin explains this tendency with a simple example:

> Being a contrarian for the sake of being a contrarian is not a good idea. In other words, when the movie theater is on fire, run out the door, right? Don't run in the door. . . . Successful contrarian investing is not about going against the grain per se; it is about exploiting expectations gaps. If this assertion is true, it leads to an obvious question: How do these expectations gaps arise? Or, more basically, how and why are markets inefficient?

3. "A great founding strategy is contrarian and right.
That ensures that, at least for an important initial time,
no one is coming after you. Eventually, people will come
after you if you're on to something good."

It's so important for early-stage companies to avoid competition
because you can't isolate it to one front. Competition affects you
on the customer front, hiring front, and financing and business
development fronts—on all of them. When you're one of *n*,
your job becomes much harder, and it's hard enough already.
Difficult competition with no edge makes for a war of attrition.
People may be sucked into ruthlessly competitive situations by
the allure of the pot of gold to be had. It's like rushing the
Cornucopia in *The Hunger Games* instead of running away
into the forest.

Having a barrier to entry against competitors (a moat) is essential. Hoffman is saying here that avoiding competition during a startup's formation period greatly enables moat creation. In other words, it is helpful to have a business operating in a portion of the market that is not a "dog-eat-dog" competition from the beginning. In this sense, being contrarian as an investor has a double benefit: It allows for greater market-beating returns to be found, and it allows the business to grow in a less competitive environment.

4. "People also underestimate how much of an edge you need.
It really should be a compounding competitive edge. If your
technology is a little better or you execute a little better, you're
screwed. Marginal improvements are rarely decisive."

Unless your product is 100X better, usually your average
consumer will use what they encounter. If others are much more
successful at distribution, they have much better viral spread,
and they have a better index and SEO, it doesn't matter if your
product is 10X better; the folks don't encounter it.

Going up against an entrenched competitor with loads of cash, experience, and sales, marketing, and distribution channels is so difficult that you need a significant edge to win. Convincing a customer to move to a new product or service is hard work if the new offering is only slightly better. In other words, the cost of customer acquisition drops as the value premium over the competitor's product or service rises. When thinking about whether a product or service has core product value, Andy Johns suggests that it's important to ask two key questions: Is the problem your product is solving painful to and important for your customers, and is there a sizable market behind this problem? He adds, "Some firms create new, meaningful experiences, rather than solving an existing, painful problem. One could count Facebook, Twitter, Snapchat, Instagram, and others in this group."

5. "You want to start building a company one to four years, maybe five years, in advance. This means that when the technology converges with the world you see coming you're positioned to capitalize. You have to be right about a set of things, including what your competitors are going to do."

The great hockey player Wayne Gretzky is famous for saying "I skate to where the puck is going to be, not where it has been." One way to find "where the puck is going to be" is to profit from the inability of people to understand the exponential phenomenon. Bill Gates said once, "When things are improving so rapidly, how do you create a model in your head? Computers are doubling in power, relative to the price, about every eighteen months. Most humans don't have a situation where something doubles in its power every two years." The difficulty that most people have in understanding some phenomena creates mispriced opportunities for investors.

Being genuinely contrarian as an investor means being uncomfortable sometimes. Some people are good at being uncomfortable, and some are not. Peter Lynch has said, "To make money, you must find something that nobody else knows, or do something that others won't do because they have rigid mindsets." Successful investing is the search for the mistakes of other people that may create a mispriced asset, says Howard Marks. In other words, one person's mistake about the value of an asset is what can create an opportunity for another investor to outperform the market. People who are curious and hardworking are best at doing this kind of searching. Great investors hustle, have a huge scuttlebutt network, and read constantly. They are constantly trying to learn more about more things, and they know that the more they know, the more they will know that there is even more they do not know. If you are not getting more humble over time, you have a flawed system.

Mr. Market's irrationality creates opportunity for investors. Markets are often wise but not always. The best returns accrue to investors who are patient yet aggressive when they are offered an attractive price for an asset. Seth Klarman says, "Successful investing is the marriage of a calculator and a contrarian streak."

6. "Silicon Valley . . . should now be called Software Valley."

Software delivered over networks drives financial returns in the venture capital business because the hardware is relatively ubiquitous. You can purchase it on demand and in many cases is already in place—most notably in smartphones. Advances in silicon drive the exponential phenomenon, but the companies that surf this wave are primarily software driven. Yes, there are important and successful hardware startups and, yes, 3D printers and such. In most cases, when you look at a company that has achieved a grand-slam financial return, it is software or software-enabled cloud-based services driving the innovation and new customer value. There are also inevitably many vitally important software engineers working in what some people would call a hardware business.

> 7. "Having a great product is important, but having great
> product distribution is more important. I meet many
> entrepreneurs who think the best product is the most important
> thing and that the best product should always win. What many
> people fail to realize is that without great distribution,
> the product dies. How will you get your product in the hands
> of millions or hundreds of millions of people?"

Excellent product distribution is not optional. Customers do not magically appear at a company's doorway holding stacks of hundred-dollar bills ready to buy whatever a business is selling. An entrepreneur must either learn how to create great product distribution or find someone who knows how to do so.

> 8. "In tech, if you're not continually thinking about catching the
> next curve, one of the next curves will get you. Yahoo owned
> the front end of the Internet in 2000. It had the perfect strategy.
> However, it did not adapt; it failed at social and other trends; and
> that didn't go so perfectly. Just over a decade later, having missed
> some very key tech curves, it's in a very different position."

Because significant phenomena can emerge from complex adaptive systems with essentially no warning, you can find yourself in deep trouble for a mistake you made several years before. Looking back at the cause of what is killing a business now, the outcome may seem obvious, but that is the nature of complex adaptive systems. What is understandable retroactively is not predictable prospectively. "Missing a curve" can send a business flying over a precipice. The inverse is also true: If you can catch the next curve, it can propel your business in a nonlinear manner.

9. "If you are not embarrassed by the first version of your product, you've launched too late."

Product and market fit requires you to figure out the earliest tells. How do you bring in as much networked intelligence into that process as possible? In Silicon Valley, you bring in new advisers, employees, customers. What you are trying to figure out is, is the path I'm trying to build the company around accurate? Most people begin with the financing process as a series of hoops to get a degree of money in the bank. Nevertheless, the most interesting thing about the investment process is getting network intelligence on the critical questions of, "Is this a good plan?" "What is the piece of common intelligence about my project?" "What are the risks in their investment?"

When you have an idea for a startup, consult your network. Ask people what they think. Don't look for flattery. If most people get it right away and call you a genius, you're probably screwed; it likely means your idea is obvious and won't work. What you're looking for is a genuinely thoughtful response.

An idea that is not exposed to feedback from a robust and diverse network of trustworthy, smart individuals is not going to get better or attract the people needed to translate it into a success. Your competitors will be doing this if you do not. The winners in today's economy are the businesses that adapt best to change, and you cannot change effectively without great sources of feedback.

10. "So many entrepreneurs are worried about protecting their precious ideas, but the truly valuable thing is that you're in motion, you have momentum, and you are gathering all the necessary resources to make it happen."

We're moving from an information age to a network age. Part of that is how do you increase the possibility of a positive outcome from serendipity? There's still luck, but you can increase the probability of the right decisions made. When you have a problem

connecting challenges and solutions, that involves connections in
a human network.

An idea without execution is not going to get anyone very far
in business. Everyone has ideas for businesses and may think,
"I thought of that first," when they see success. Winning in the
market requires doing things, not just generating new ideas. Scott
Belsky agrees with Hoffman:

> Ideas are worthless if you can't make them happen. Generating
> new ideas is easy. Executing is hard. Whether it's an everyday
> problem or a bold new concept, you must transform vision into
> reality for an idea to have value. . . . All great inventions emerge
> from a long sequence of small sparks; the first idea often isn't
> all that good, but thanks to collaboration it later sparks another
> idea, or it's reinterpreted in an unexpected way. Collaboration
> brings small sparks together to generate breakthrough innova-
> tion. . . . The hyperconnectivity made possible by the Internet
> has acted as a massive accelerator for the 'small sparks' that fuel
> the refinement of ideas.

11. "Entrepreneurs are often given two pieces of contradictory
advice: persistence and flexibility. Have a vision and pursue it
through years of people telling you you're out of your mind.
Alternatively, be flexible: Look at data, iterate, and change based
on the signals you're getting. There isn't an actual algorithm.
You have an investment thesis about why this project is likely to
work and have some outside result, and usually, that's expressed
in a set of statements and hypotheses, that if you're right about,
adds up like a logical proof and gives you the output you're
looking for. Moreover, you can have varying levels of confidence
in how these pieces are adding up and supporting your theses.
The challenge is to follow them both, but know which advice is

most appropriate for which situation. You must know
how to maintain flexible persistence."

This is an example of a contradiction that Scott Belsky describes in the foreword to this book. There is no substitute for good judgment in determining the right mix of flexibility and persistence. Good judgment comes from making bad judgments but learning from the experience. Some people learn from mistakes better than others and make mostly new mistakes rather than repeating old ones. If you learn from mistakes, you will have a better life. Being a learning machine pays big dividends. It is wise to be a learn it-all-rather than a know-it-all.

12. "It's not that everyone should start a company, it's the fact
that a career ladder is no longer a strong model for how you
do your work and pursue your career. The good grades to good
university to good career path model has been broken for years,
by globalization and technology's disruption of the industry.
The model for how to think about your life, career, and work
is different. How entrepreneurs think about product–market fit,
product differentiation, creative risks, all apply to how you,
as an individual, live your life."

> The network of people around you is what extends your ability
> to be effective regarding expertise and reaching your goals.
> Put yourself out there and get feedback. Don't be afraid to take
> a risk.

> The notion of a career has changed. Whereas we used to have
> a career ladder, now we have a career jungle gym. Success in
> a career is no longer a simple ascension on a path of steps.
> You need to climb sideways and sometimes down; sometimes
> you need to swing and jump from one set of bars to the next.
> In addition, to extend the metaphor, sometimes you need to
> spring from the jungle gym and establish your turf somewhere
> else on the playground. In addition, if we want the playground

metaphor to describe the modern world, neither the playground nor the jungle gym is fixed. They are always changing—new structures emerge, old structures are in constant change and sometimes collapse, and the playground constantly moves the structure around.

Another huge thing to emphasize is the importance of your network. Get to know smart people. Talk to them. Stay current on what's happening. People see things that other people don't. If you try to analyze it all yourself, you miss things. Talk with people about what's going on. Theoretically, startups should be distributed evenly throughout all countries and all states. They're not. Silicon Valley is the heart of it all. Why? The network. People are talking to each other.

Networks of all kinds are of increasing importance. However, many of these modern networks are different from the networks people had in mind when they repeated the adage "It's not what you know, but who you know that matters." Old-school networks were about webs of "influence," and while that still exists, the types of networks that are important now are more varied. Many systems today involve being able to generate the information and feedback needed to be agile and better informed. As an example, why do some venture capitalists create so much more of the financial returns in the venture capital industry? Simply put, they have the best networks, defined in the broadest possible sense, and the quality of their networks is feeding back on itself to generate even more quality. This is the Matthew effect at work in just one dimension: Better networks get even better as success feeds back on itself.

18

Ben Horowitz

Andreessen Horowitz

BEN HOROWITZ IS A cofounder and general partner of the venture capital firm Andreessen Horowitz. Prior to a16z, Ben was cofounder and CEO of Opsware (formerly Loudcloud), which was acquired by Hewlett-Packard in 2007 for $1.6 billion, and was appointed vice president and general manager of Business Technology Optimization for Software at HP. Earlier, he was vice president and general manager of America Online's E-commerce Platform division, where he oversaw development of the company's flagship Shop@AOL service. Previously, Ben ran several product divisions at Netscape Communications. He also served as vice president of Netscape's widely acclaimed Directory and Security product line. Before joining Netscape in July 1995, he held various senior product marketing positions at Lotus Development Corporation. He is the author of *The Hard Thing About Hard Things: Building a Business When There Are No Easy Answers*, in which he candidly reveals how hard it is to start and run a company. He was born in London and raised in Berkeley,

California. Horowitz has a BA in computer science from Columbia University and an MS in computer science from the University of California, Los Angeles.

1. "You read these management books that say, 'These are the hard things about running a company.' But those aren't the hard things."

My old boss Jim Barksdale said that most management consultants have never managed a hot dog stand.

Wartime CEO is too busy fighting the enemy to read management books written by consultants who have never managed a fruit stand.

When I was a CEO, the books on management that I read weren't very much help after the first few months on the job. They were all designed to give you directions on how not to screw up your company. Nevertheless, it doesn't take long before you get beyond that and you're like, "Okay, I've screwed up my company; now what do I do?" Most books on management are written by management consultants, and they study successful companies after they've succeeded, so they only hear winning stories.

People who write about management tend to follow a formula that Michael Mauboussin has described:

The most common method for teaching business management is to find successful businesses, identify their common practices, and recommend that managers imitate them. This formula is intuitive and it includes some compelling narrative, and has sold millions of books. The reality is that attributing a firm's success to a particular strategy may be wrong if you sample only the winners. When luck plays a part in determining the consequences of your actions—as is often the case in business—you don't want to study success to identify good strategy but rather study strategy to see whether it consistently led to success.

Horowitz, like Mauboussin, believes in reality-based decision-making. Horowitz has written about what he calls "the Struggle," which is "basically what you feel like when your world is caving in." Running a business is not the equivalent of hosting a well-planned garden party. A friend told me many years ago, "Once a business gets beyond the planning stage, stuff breaks." Things will go haywire at unexpected times and places. When that happens, having great managers who have the ability and willingness to adapt and make wise decisions pays big dividends.

> 2. "Management turns out to be dynamic and situational
> and personal and emotional. So it's pretty hard to
> write a formula or instruction book on it."

There isn't one lesson that solves everything.

Nobody is born knowing how to be a CEO. It's a learned skill, and unfortunately, you learn it on the job.

The only thing that prepares you to run a company is running a company.

When a CEO is engaged in what Horowitz calls "the Struggle," there are no formulas to follow. Being a CEO is like being an investor in that you cannot simulate the experience. In both cases, you learn by doing, just like everyone who has come before you. Having said that, just because the skills required to be a successful CEO must be learned on the job does not mean that you cannot learn something by observing another CEO or manager. For example, Horowitz had the opportunity while working at Netscape to watch Jim Barksdale, who many feel is one of the best CEOs of all time. Horowitz has also identified Bill Campbell and Ken Coleman as having been among his mentors.

3. "In reality, companies are what they are, and nobody has ever worked anywhere where everything is perfect. And so pretending that things are perfect isn't very effective."

> I don't know that I'm drawn to conflict; you don't necessarily in these businesses want to conflict with other companies, though you get it a fair amount. But, and this is one of the best management pieces of advice I ever got from Marc Andreessen: He was quoting Lenin, who was quoting Karl Marx, who said, "Sharpen the contradictions." Marx was talking about labor and capital, which is not generally what you're talking about when you're running a company. However, the conflict is where the truth is. Therefore, when there's a conflict in the organization, you do not want to smooth it over. You want to sharpen the contradictions, heat up both opinions, and resolve it. Good CEOs are excellent at doing that. And it's miserable to work for someone who tries to smooth things over.

The key phrase in these quotes from Horowitz is "conflict is where the truth is." As with almost everything in life, all businesses are imperfect. The ability to successfully identify what needs to change to improve a business is based on the ability to recognize and resolve conflict. Hiding conflict causes problems to fester and grow. Horowitz believes, "You do not want to smooth over conflicts. You want the conflicts to surface, and you want to resolve them. If you don't, you have got problems. If you do surface and resolve them, you will be a pretty good manager."

4. "When a company goes astray, you talk to employees, and they say, 'We have no strategy. We don't know where we're going.' The strategy is the story. They're not different. The strategy is the story you tell. It's the why. If you can't tell that in a massively compelling way, who's going to follow you? That's what makes people get up in the morning and do stuff."

> The story must explain at a fundamental level why you exist. Why does the world need your company? Why do we need to be doing what we're doing, and why is it important?

> You can have a great product, but a compelling story puts the company into motion. If you don't have a great story, it's hard to get people motivated to join you, to work on the product, and to get people to invest in the product.

> The mistake people make is thinking the story is just about marketing. No, the story is the strategy. If you make your story better, you make the strategy better.

> Storytelling is the most underrated skill.

The CEO and founders must own the story of their business. It is their responsibility to keep it up to date and compelling. The fact that humans love a good story makes the CEO and founders' task easier. Because people often have trouble understanding or remembering ideas and instructions, stories help them stay on track and motivated. When talking about the importance of storytelling, Horowitz makes a point about strategy: What a company does differently from its competitors drives the company. The story must convey what the business does that is uniquely valuable and how that will create a sustainable competitive advantage (a moat). Why does the business exist?

As an example of the importance of a compelling story, I once had a conversation with a venture capitalist who owns a winery. We agreed that when talking about his industry, one in which the story is key to the product, wine should be front and center. The terrain, the grapes, the winemaker, and so on are all part of a compelling story. Many people seem to enjoy the story of the wine more than the wine itself.

5. "Think for yourself. That is the distinguishing characteristic of the great entrepreneurs."

> The trouble with innovation is that truly innovative ideas often look like bad ideas at the time.

> Innovation is almost insane by definition: Most people view
> any truly innovative idea as stupid because if it were a good
> idea, somebody would have already done it. So, the innovator is
> guaranteed to have more natural initial detractors than followers.

Founders who deliver new value to the world think differently.
That value comes from believing in or recognizing something as
true that other people do not see. Such founders are inevitably
breaking at least one critical assumption that others have made.

Great founders and CEOs do not outperform the market by
following the crowd. Not only must founders and CEOs occasionally be contrarian, but they must be sufficiently right about a
contrarian view that will drive outperformance. The best way to
be a successful contrarian is, as Horowitz points out, to think for
yourself. Being a contrarian by definition means that you must be
prepared to sometimes be lonely in some of your views. Thinking
differently separates you from the warmth of the crowd.

6. "People say that the CEO should be 'the best salesman
at the company' or the 'product visionary' or all these things.
No. The CEO is the CEO. They've got to deliver very quality
decisions at a very high rate of speed. And if they don't make
a decision, the company freezes up. To do that, you need to be
talking to everybody. You need to figure out what's going on
with your finance people, and your engineering people. Because
by the time this shit comes to you, you won't have time to do
that. You won't have time to make your decision."

The ability to make timely and wise decisions is the mark of great
CEOs. They make decisions look easier than they actually are by
being prepared. As an analogy, the best defensive baseball players
are standing in just the right spot waiting for the ball when it arrives.
They are in position before the ball is pitched. Similarly, great business

decision-makers are ready to make decisions when the time comes because they have done the necessary preparation. That preparation allows them to make timely and more valuable decisions.

7. "Sometimes an organization doesn't need a solution; it just needs clarity."

Often any decision, even the wrong decision, is better than no decision.

Not making decisions is making a decision, as is not making decisions quickly and decisively. Too often the answer to a request for decisions is like the old joke about the psychiatrist who asks his patient if he has trouble making decisions. The patient responds, "Well, doctor, yes and no." A common problem is that sometimes when we are presented with several options, they may blind us to other choices—including the simplest and most sensible one.

8. "The primary thing that any technology startup must do is build a product that's at least ten times better at doing something than the current prevailing way of doing that thing. Two or three times better will not be good enough to get people to switch to the new thing fast enough or in large enough volume to matter."

If you don't have a winning product, it doesn't matter how well your company is managed; you are done.

One essential element of any successful business is cost-effectively acquiring customers. If you pay too much for sales and marketing to acquire new customers, you can quickly (or slowly) go broke. Sam Altman puts it simply: "Be suspect about buying users." The better approach is to have customers who are attracted organically by a better product or service. Word of mouth alone is unlikely to grow a business, but it should be an essential part of the customer acquisition process. What drives word on mouth is a product that genuinely delights customers by delivering solutions with the increased value Horowitz describes.

> 9. "Figuring out the right product is the innovator's job, not the customer's job. The customer only knows what she thinks she wants based on her experience with the current product. The innovator can take into account everything that's possible, often going against what she knows to be true. This requires a combination of knowledge, skill, and courage."

Steve Jobs famously said, "It's hard to design products by focus groups. A lot of times, people don't know what they want until you show it to them." If something is going to be more than ten times better than what competitors are offering, the product or service needs to be vastly different than what customers have seen before. A "me-too" product or service is not going to move the needle in a sufficiently positive way for a venture-backed startup to be financially successful.

> 10. "There are only two priorities for a startup: winning the market and not running out of cash. Running lean is not an end."
>
> The only mistake you cannot make is running out of cash.

The only unforgivable sin in business is to run out of cash. Earnings are an opinion. Cash is a fact. Should a business spend every penny wisely? Absolutely. But do not run of out of cash. Is equity dilution something to be avoided? Sure. But do not run out of cash. Can too much cash allow a business to solve problems with money rather than culture? Yep, but do not run out of cash. Can innovation be greater when a company has less capital? Yes, but do not run out of cash.

11. "What do you get when you cross a herd of sheep with a herd of lemmings? A herd of venture capitalists."

> The most important rule of raising money privately: Look for a market of one. You only need one investor to say yes, so it's best to ignore the other thirty who say no.

The best founders and venture capitalists think for themselves, just as the best CEOs think for themselves. Anyone who has been paying attention over the last few decades knows that venture capital is a cyclical business. This cyclicality occurs for the same reason that economic cycles occur in other sectors: People do not make decisions independently. Information cascades sometimes cause markets to swing in a bipolar fashion. Venture capitalists who think independently and ignore the swings generate better financial returns. You find bargains where others are not looking, particularly when it comes to convex opportunities.

12. "Every time you make the hard, correct decision you become a bit more courageous, and every time you make the easy, wrong decision you become a bit more cowardly. If you are CEO, these choices will lead to a courageous or cowardly company."

It may seem odd to think about a business leader needing to be courageous. The reality is that there are few easy decisions for a business leader trying to navigate "the Struggle." People's lives will be significantly affected by the success or failure of a business. For example, whether employees and other stakeholders can pay their bills, send their children to college, or retire comfortably can all be affected by a single decision. Horowitz is saying that there are feedback loops impacting executive courage and cowardice, just like the other feedback loops that are impacting the business world today. Courage begets courage.

19

Vinod Khosla

Khosla Ventures

VINOD KHOSLA IS AN entrepreneur, investor, and technologist. He graduated with a bachelor's degree in electrical engineering from the Indian Institute of Technology in New Delhi. After graduating, he moved to the United States and obtained a master's degree in biomedical engineering from Carnegie Mellon University and a master's degree in business administration from the Stanford Graduate School of Business. Khosla cofounded Daisy Systems, the first significant computer-aided design system for electrical engineers. In 1982, he cofounded and became CEO of Sun Microsystems, which was funded by John Doerr of Kleiner Perkins Caufield & Byers. In 1986, Khosla joined Kleiner Perkins as a general partner. Among his investments at Kleiner Perkins were Cerent, Excite, Juniper Networks, and Nexgen. In 2004, he formed Khosla Ventures to focus on both for-profit and social-impact investments.

1. "I don't mind failing, but if I succeed it better be worth succeeding for."

Most technology startups fail. There's a winner, and there are seven out of ten that lose.

> I have seen too many startups where they have reduced risk to a
> point where they have a higher probability of succeeding, but if
> they succeed it is inconsequential.

People are accustomed to encountering situations that reflect a
simple proportional relationship between cause and effect. When
life is linear, we are usually able to predict the future with some
degree of accuracy. When we do X, Y happens. This type of linear change is comforting since people tend not to like risk and
uncertainty. We particularly hate anything that would cause us to
experience a loss (loss aversion). Whether we like it or not, however, the economy is currently changing in ways that are nonlinear.
When nonlinear change happens, the aggregate behavior of systems can be much more complicated than would be predicted by
summing the inputs into the system. It is this nonlinear change that
allows for sufficiently convex investing opportunities to appear,
those with the potential to produce grand-slam financial returns
for founders and venture capitalists. Making investment choices
particularly complex is the fact some future states of the world
are unknown, and probability is not even computable. Richard
Zeckhauser calls this situation the domain of ignorance. A matrix
depicting one set of meaningful relationships that impact venture
capital, based on my interpretation of Nassim Taleb's ideas of
Nassim Taleb is presented in table 19.1.

Table 19.1

	Binary Outcomes	Complex Outcomes
Thin-tailed probability distribution	Coin flip	Outcome of a horse race—statistics are helpful
Fat-tailed probability distribution	Whether a specific book will become a bestseller—statistics are helpful	Venture capital—statistics are potentially misleading and even dangerous

Because success in the venture capital industry is driven by actions that occur in the fourth quadrant, successful venture capitalists understand that their objective is not to predict outcomes with certainty since that is impossible. The task of a venture capitalist is instead to experiment on a *trial-and-error* basis to discover success from within a portfolio of thirty to forty bets that have convexity. Which bets will pay off will become apparent only after the fact since success emerges only as the years pass.

2. "We are in the company-building business, not in the 'deal' or 'capital' business."

I don't think of myself as being in the investing business. I think private equity investors are very much in the business of doing deals, putting money in, getting money out. To me, that is a very, very different business, and all that they are doing is spreadsheets. I think of myself in an entirely different business of building companies. I have not made IRR [internal rate of return] calculations on a spreadsheet ever since 2004. I either believe, or I don't. If I believe, then my goal is to get involved and make things much bigger and help them be successful. It's a different kind of business.

The venture capitalists I admire most like to spend their time and effort building real businesses. They almost always understand finance deeply, but for them, finance is an enabler of what they most love to do. One of the ironies of venture capital is that the best way to be financially successful is to pay less attention to finance and more attention to building a business. The right financial structure does not mean anything if all it does is guarantee you a high percentage of nothing. Great venture capitalists are focused on building businesses and relationships rather than "doing deals." Building a real business means creating new value through genuine innovation. What Khosla is saying is that the potential outcome is so far into the domains of uncertainty and ignorance that using spreadsheets is useless since the inputs cannot be quantified. Venture capitalists with the skill and contacts to source the best opportunities and provide entrepreneurs with the right networks of contacts and assistance experience superior returns. Founders, venture capitalists, employees, and customers will be attracted to the success, and it is a success that compounds.

3. "If you're doing what everybody else is doing, you're not doing anything interesting, and we won't want to invest."

> Doing things at the edge is what venture is about. I don't even invest in businesses where six other people have the same technology.
>
> The idea is how you can turn a technology advantage into a business advantage. It's much more like playing a chess game than it is investing. It is strategic; it depends on how much you can help the company. Therefore, it is much more fun.

You cannot outperform a market (which reflects the consensus view) by adopting a consensus view. By definition, beating a market means having a different viewpoint and being right about that viewpoint. Khosla's impressive track record illustrates the high value of intelligent contrarian thinking in a profession like venture capital.

4. "We seek out unfair advantages: proprietary and protected technological advances, business-model innovations, unique partnerships and top-notch teams."

What Khosla is talking about here is what Warren Buffett calls a moat and Michael Porter calls sustainable competitive advantage. Without a moat, competition will inevitably drop prices to a point where there is no economic profit (return on investment will not exceed the opportunity cost of capital).

"Someone, somewhere, is making a product that will make your product obsolete." This is perhaps Georges Doriot's most famous quote. What Joseph Schumpeter called creative destruction is a constant process in the business world. Schumpeter said, "The process of industrial mutation—if I may use that biological term—incessantly revolutionizes the economic structure from within, incessantly destroying the old one, incessantly creating a new one." The paradox is that in order for productivity and standards of living to grow, some aspects of the economy must be destroyed. Capitalism requires failure so that new productivity and wealth can be created. Every business is in its own way constantly fighting this phenomenon. Warren Buffett once wrote, "Capitalism is all about somebody coming and trying to take the castle. Now what you need is a castle that has some durable competitive advantage—some castle that has a moat around it." The moat of any business is always under attack by competitors even if you cannot see it. And because moats are constantly under attack, Charlie Munger points out that it is a rare company whose future will not be worse than its present.

5. "We invest more in people than in a specific plan, because plans often change."

Quickly failing is a good way to plan. Often failing makes failures small and successes large. In small failures, you accumulate learnings about what works and what doesn't. Try many experiments, but don't bet your company on just one: keep trying, keep failing small.

There are probably three or four things you can control out of ten that matter for the success of your company. Competitors control another three or four. The rest is just luck. I've never seen [a business plan] that's accurate.

The business you build is the people you hire. Entrepreneurs who can adapt are far more likely to achieve great success than entrepreneurs who expect to be able to follow a rigid plan. No plan survives first contact with competitors and customers in a real market. Investing in great teams generates optionality since great teams can adapt. The real world is dynamic and unpredictable. People who think they can predict the future with sufficient accuracy to create something like a detailed five-year plan have a lousy understanding of how business works and have not been paying attention to life. A spreadsheet is only as good as your assumptions, and when you put garbage into a spreadsheet, garbage comes out.

6. "Bad times come for every startup—I haven't seen a single startup that hasn't gone through a bad time. Entrepreneurship can be very depressing. If you believe in your product, you stick with it."

A real business operating in the real world is never about perfect execution. While great founders, CEOs, and venture capitalists have a tremendous will to succeed, many successes were at one point millimeters away from failure. Many failures were also millimeters away from success. Scott Belsky describes the stage between the glamorous moments when people just start something in the garage and a glorious event like an IPO or an acquisition as "the messy middle." It is in the messy middle where the bulk of the work gets done and the entrepreneur proves his or her mettle by solving hard problems, day in and day out. The early Microsoft executive and investor Mike Maples Sr. said once, "There's something about the struggle, adversity, the trial and error and worrying at night about things that makes the entrepreneur better and stronger."

7. "Seeking an acquisition from the start is more than just bad advice for an entrepreneur. For the entrepreneur, it leads to short-term tactical decisions rather than company-building decisions and in my view often reduces the probability of success."

I see this far too often. If money is all that makes your world go around, venture capital or starting a company is probably not the business for you. You are unlikely to make the right decisions, and you are unlikely to be happy. Missionaries are best suited to building a business and succeed more often in doing so than mercenaries. The odds of a huge financial success are not good at the start of a business. Being a founder of a startup that is backable by a major venture capital firm is not a rational act. Instead, being a founder is optimally driven by passion.

8. "We prefer technology risk to market risk."

There are many different types of risk. One type of risk is market risk, and another is technology risk. Khosla is saying that technology risk is easier to retire than market risk, especially if you are a skilled technologist. Because of his background and training, Khosla brings a unique technical skill to a startup, which impacts his preference for technology risk. There are also financial, regulatory, and people risks that must be retired to create a successful business.

9. "How would you compete against yourself?"

Every business should be thinking about what could threaten them since their competitors are almost certainly doing so. The mental exercise I am suggesting here is essentially a stress test: Ask yourself, "What would we do if we were our competitors?"

In a larger company, the process might be accomplished by using a "red-team" approach in which an independent group challenges an organization to improve its effectiveness. The founders of a startup do not have the same resources as a large company but still have the ability to think through their competitive strategy with their team or advisers.

10. "I generally disagree with most of the very high-margin opportunities. Why? Because it's a business strategy tradeoff: the lower the margin you take, the faster you grow."

This is the sort of statement Jeff Bezos makes. Your competitor's high margins are your opportunity to grow. For example, absolute-dollar free cash flow can be better with lower margins since you can sell more products and services and increase inventory turns. No one does this more effectively than Amazon and Costco. In a technology business, there is often only one dominant company, so market share matters in a huge way.

11. "Where most entrepreneurs fail is on the things they don't know they don't know."

Things go wrong. There is lots of uncertainty, and there are times when you're unsure of yourself. I've found that the less people know, the surer they are.

The best venture capitalists and founders are "learning machines" because they realize that there is no end to what one can learn. They also know that they will inevitably encounter unknown unknowns (what Zeckhauser calls ignorance). There are some things you cannot know in advance but which you will see clearly after the fact.

12. "The single most important thing an entrepreneur needs to learn is whom to take advice from and on what topic."

> Entrepreneurs could get such great help, but instead they think they need money. It's this sort of schizophrenic divide between worrying that you're going out of business and dreaming big that's needed. Sophisticated entrepreneurs know this. Less sophisticated entrepreneurs don't even know whom to ask for advice. They'll ask a marketing and a technology question to the same person. Ask different questions of different people, both those who have been successful and those who haven't.

The concept of a "circle of competence" applies not only to your skills but to the people from whom you seek advice. Warren Buffett likes to say that risk comes from not knowing what you are doing. It is wise to find people to advise you who do know what they are doing. You can learn from both success and failure. It's that simple.

Josh Kopelman

First Round Capital

JOSH KOPELMAN IS A partner at First Round Capital, a seed-stage venture firm. Before becoming a venture capitalist, he was an entrepreneur, founding three companies in succession. He formed his first company, Infonautics, when he was still attending college at the Wharton School of the University of Pennsylvania. The company went public on the Nasdaq in 1996. In July 1999, Kopelman formed Half.com, which allowed people to buy and sell used books, music, and DVDs online. eBay acquired Half.com in July 2000. Kopelman then founded TurnTide, an anti-spam business that was later acquired by Symantec. Kopelman's "three-for-three" record of accomplishment is rarely seen in the startup business world. First Round focuses on helping seed-stage startups as its name implies. Kopelman is unusual in that he is primarily based out of Philadelphia, rather than Silicon Valley. He has also been an early investor in firms like LinkedIn and Uber.

1. "We're seed-stage investors—and like to invest
in the 'first round'—so we'd rather meet with

> an entrepreneur earlier than later. (Caveat being
> that an entrepreneur should have selected an idea
> they want to pursue—and be willing to pursue
> it full time)."

First Round has adopted what has become known as a platform approach to investing, which involves providing more resources and operational support to businesses in the portfolio than was traditionally the case. Kopelman is saying that when a venture capitalist is trying to add platform value, it is easier to work with someone who does not already make problematic business decisions. In other words, it is easier to train people in the right approach than to change patterns that have already been established. The cynic might say this is because valuations are lower for the "first-dollar-in" venture capitalist. The noncynic would reply that the probability of success goes up when a business has a great start since a strong start helps retire risk and uncertainty. What is a cynic? A cynic is a person who, when they smell flowers, starts looking for a coffin.

On the last point made by Kopelman in the parentheses, it is surprising how often I talk to people who think they can get professional venture capital backing while working only part time. The best venture capitalists want the entrepreneurs they back to be "all in," pursuing the business opportunity full time. In this regard, missionaries are easier to spot since they are obsessed with the business and the customer's problem and want to go at it all the time. Mercenaries are more inclined to hedge their commitments.

2. "The typical founder spends their time either picking an idea, starting a company (hunting for product-market fit), or scaling a company (growing). Most founders spend less than 5 percent of their time on idea selection, yet I believe that 'the pick' accounts for more than 50 percent

of startup success/failure. Observation 1: Many founders rush the pick. If you're spending the next five to ten years of your life doing something, pick your idea wisely. Observation 2: In my experience, serial entrepreneurs are more likely to rush the pick due to high self- confidence and easy access to money."

Kopelman sets out a clear taxonomy with "pick," "start," and "scale" categories. Each stage has its challenges. Many venture investors believe the best ideas seem half-crazy since that degree of "craziness" increases the probability that there is sufficient undiscovered convexity to generate a grand-slam financial outcome. Financially backing ideas that are fully crazy, however, is unwise. Some things that seem nuts are nuts. As with the final bed selected by Goldilocks, "half-nuts" is most often "just right" in terms of the convexity a venture capitalist desires.

3. "Starting a company is lonely. Every day you wake up, and there are more unanswered questions and more decisions to make. Find a community of like-minded people because together, you're able to answer these questions far more effectively than individually."

> You'll benefit from having a confidant to work through doubts with and together determine the 90 percent of advice from investors and customers you should ignore.

There is nothing quite like having a conversation with someone you trust to help you think things through. That process is a lot like writing down your ideas in that you can discover things you had not yet thought through and also generate new ideas. Having trustworthy and wise colleagues around you is particularly valuable since there are no formulas for success. If there were recipes for success, everyone would be rich.

4. "We see a ton of consumer companies who say,
'We'll just make it viral.' It's hard to achieve virality.
If there were a virality button, if there were virality dust, then
no one would spend a dollar on advertising. Viral is not easy.
It's hard, and it has to be built into your product. The best viral
apps are built around viral mechanisms. The same thing applies
to the community. Building a community isn't easy.
You can't sprinkle community dust on it."

Selling anything is hard. The importance of actually asking for the order and generating cash from a sale is something best appreciated by successfully doing so. Salespeople are highly compensated for a good reason. Selling is not only a real skill but a scarce skill. A business with an offering that has a low cost of sale has usually created a process that enables the customer to self-educate and communicate the value of the products to others. The best way to get people to talk to their friends is to have a treasured product that naturally creates incentives to invite others to try it. In other words, the fastest growing and most profitable businesses acquire many of their customers "organically," without advertising. Great products, positive word of mouth, and a natural inclination for customers to invite others to use the product drive sales at such businesses. In contrast, businesses that must sell their wares with huge advertising budgets are losing their edge.

5. "Every business plan is wrong. The moment an entrepreneur
hits 'save' or 'print' the plan is out of date. Things change."

I've always said that I'd much rather bet on an entrepreneur who can adapt to change rather than an entrepreneur who is convinced that they have the ability to predict the future. But adapting to change is hard. How do you maintain flexibility yet still preserve a goal-oriented culture?

The old saying that "planning is essential, but plans are not" is attributed to a range of famous people. The quote has many variations, but the central point is always identical. Mike Tyson's version is "Everybody has a plan until they get punched in the mouth." The Jeff Bezos version is "Any business plan won't survive its first encounter with reality. Reality will always be different. It will never be the plan." The ability of a company to adapt is essential.

> 6. "You should target eighteen to twenty-four months of runway post-series seed. The best time to raise follow-on capital is when you don't need it, and two years of runway gives you the best chance to land in that situation."

Never run out of cash. Ever. A business can recover from lots of bad situations, but an absence of capital is nearly always fatal for equity holders and at least very painful for debtors. Having a margin of safety on cash is a wise idea for that reason. Raising money before you need it is also wise since at that point you still have leverage in negotiating with investors. Having the option to dial down spending to deal with the inability to generate new cash does not mean a business should not be aggressive. Instead, it means that the firm has an option if things turn sour. A business should always be careful in managing its cash, but this is more important at some times than others since venture capital is a cyclical business. For example, in February 2016, First Round put out a memo to its portfolio businesses that said,

> During the meeting, there was a conversation about the rapidly changing funding landscape. And one of the company's (bullish) later-stage investors warned the founder that the company should no longer rely on raising additional follow-on

184

financing, saying, "We need to act like we're Mark Watney in *The Martian*. We can't assume we will get a shipment of new potatoes to save us."

7. "I don't think a lot of people have been entrepreneurial about venture capital."

Venture capital is itself a business, and it is only natural that new approaches will be developed as more entrepreneurs like Kopelman get involved. There are aspects of the venture business that are unlikely to change (e.g., buying underpriced convexity) and some aspects that are likely to change (e.g., how venture capitalists interact with entrepreneurs). We have already seen different approaches to governance, investing-stage focus, and entrepreneur support. More experiments and modifications to venture capital are likely.

8. "Get to know entrepreneurs and who's best equipped to 'fill in cells,' seeking out the market and customer data they need to de-risk their business. Look for the 'heat-seeking missiles' that aim at a target, but continuously scan the environment and adjust course as they separate signal from noise."

Many things must be figured out and invented as a new business is created and grown to significant scale. In accomplishing these tasks, there is no manual for success. There are no formulas. Kopelman is saying that there is a premium on inventiveness, good judgment, and knowing what is important. The best entrepreneurs know when and how to adapt in an ever-changing world.

Retiring risk is something a great entrepreneur does every day.

9. "Start off with smaller checks than you expect to write and view them as tuition."

The venture capital business takes time to learn. Any new venture capitalist will make mistakes, especially at first. While those mistakes will have a monetary cost, Kopelman believes that making them is a necessary and valuable way to learn (i.e., it is like tuition). There is no way to learn to be a good venture capitalist without making mistakes. Good judgment comes from experience, which often comes from bad judgment. If you are not aware of your mistakes, you will not learn.

10. "Your business may not fit venture return profiles, and yet it still may be big for you! Or perhaps venture capitalists are just not into the team (which they'll never tell you!)."

> Choose bigger ideas. Ideas that, in the success case, have massive scale and the impact can be significant. Chances are you won't succeed but, if you do, the prize is worth playing for.

Not every business should raise venture capital. Sometimes it is far better for an entrepreneur to bootstrap a business. It's perfectly fine and in fact normal not to have venture capital backing when starting a business. Most businesses do not need and should not raise venture capital since not every business has the potential to generate a grand-slam financial return.

11. "We bust our ass to try to get lucky."

What Kopelman is saying humorously is that hustle, skill, and hard work can pay big dividends. Some people will call that luck, but the reality is that success is the outcome of hard work. If you can hustle, work hard, and apply skills to alter the probability of success, the change being created by those actions is not luck, but rather skill.

12. "A company's outcome should drive VC returns. When VCs' required returns drive company's outcomes, it's a recipe for trouble."

Take a $400 million venture fund. To get a 20 percent return in six years, they need to triple the fund—or return $1.2 billion. Add in fees/carry, and you now have to return $1.5 billion. Assuming that the fund owns 20 percent of their portfolio companies on exit, they need to create $7.5 billion of market value. So assume that one VC invested in Skype, Myspace, and YouTube in the same fund—they would be just halfway to their goal. Seriously? A decade ago, any one of those deals would have been (and should have been) a fund maker! As a result of this new math, VCs end up super-focused on the long bets (or moonshots) and frequently remove optionality for midtier exits. It is because of the challenges of "VC math" that First Round Capital chose to raise a relatively small fund—allowing us to continue to make initial investments that average $600,000. I understand the importance of aligning one's time and capital to the upside opportunity and recognize that there is some minimum threshold of ownership that is required for a VC to commit the time and attention to an opportunity. Does it make sense for an investor to spend the time and join the board of a company in which they only own a 2 percent stake? Probably not. However, the difference between 25 percent and 20 percent ownership—or even the difference between 20 percent and 10 percent—should not prevent a VC from investing in a promising opportunity.

The interests of a startup business and its investors are not always fully aligned. The best venture capitalists put the interests of the business first, and they do not get involved in businesses where they cannot do that. This is easy to say but sometimes tricky to do in practice. On this issue and others, an entrepreneur's best source of information is other entrepreneurs. Entrepreneurs should do due diligence on their potential investors since the relationship will last for many years.

21

Jenny Lee

GGV Capital

JENNY LEE JOINED GGV Capital in 2005 as a managing partner and was instrumental in setting up GGV's presence in China.
Her previous operation and finance work experience with Singapore Technologies Aerospace, Morgan Stanley, and JAFCO Asia
enhanced her role as a preferred board mentor and investor to
many entrepreneurs in China.

1. "Startups aren't an object. They're successful because of the people behind them."

Great people, attractive markets, and significant innovation are
the three key elements in any successful business. What a venture
capitalist wants for a founder is a certain sort of person. Founders
are inevitably unique but do tend to share certain attributes. One
of the desired attributes is a missionary attitude toward the business. Others include persistence, curiosity, energy, communication
skills, sales skills, focus, determination, intelligence, and the ability

to adapt to change. These attributes should be sought not just in founders but in the teams they assemble to build and run the business. Having a diverse team—in every sense—is important.

> 2. "Founders must have the hunger to learn about new things and have the tenacity to persist in one's judgment despite naysayers—and there will be a lot of them—and, finally, that firm belief that a single person or a single company can create products or business models that can change the world."
>
> You need to believe that you can clear everything in your path.

Some may think it an odd combination, but founders who are both confident and humble are mostly likely to succeed. A founder can be confident about what they know and at the same time humble about what they do not. Part of the reason why Charlie Munger is so wise is that he believes that "knowing what you don't know is more useful than being brilliant. Real knowledge is knowing the extent of one's ignorance." Successful founders tend to have strong views, loosely held. If you do not have strong views, you have very likely not done enough research and probably do not know both sides of an issue. And if you have strong views, but they are not loosely held, it is unlikely you will be able to adapt as new information and ideas emerge.

> 3. "We are looking for the 2 percent who are going to change the world."

To find a grand slam, a venture capitalist must discover founders who want to significantly change the world with their product or service. The best venture capitalists are constantly searching for outliers. This must be the case given how high the bar has been set by the venture capital business model.

4. "I'm a very 'gut-feel' type of investor."

There are no formulas that will always generate success in venture capital. If there were simple success formulas that could be applied mechanically, nearly everyone would be rich. However, there are some general principles that can be applied to increase the probability of success. Finding undiscovered convexity offered at a substantial bargain requires the venture capitalist to be continually looking for it in new places. Once a potential investment starts appearing regularly in newspapers and tech blogs, it is often too late to find the greatest opportunities. A new approach must be new in an important way. The business must have one key element that is fundamentally different from what has been done before. That different something is always different than what was different the last time.

5. "It's a tough market and more of a challenge to find the gems. But it's a great time to start; the quality of entrepreneurs has increased. I love the winter."

Often the best time to start a business is during an economic downturn. The competition for the best employees is lower during a financial correction, as is the competition in markets generally. During an economic downturn, there is also less noise to distract a business, which enables a greater focus on business fundamentals. In a tough market, there is often less time to think about distractions like pivoting and greater focus on getting things done.

6. "If you're a late-stage company, a growth-stage company, and you're looking to be a public company, the market fluctuation does affect you. If you are further down the chain on the early-stage side, then I would say that the capital markets have less

of an impact, but it does affect how those companies now think about the quality of that capital, the stability of the capital, and the investor behind the capital."

An early stage can be a relatively good place for a startup to be during a downturn. On the other hand, needing loads of capital during a lousy funding environment is not a great place to be. It is inevitably shocking for people going through their first business cycle when the cash spigot from investors runs dry; in other words, it becomes hard or just plain impossible to raise new cash. Always having a backup plan in the event the business can raise no new cash is wise.

7. "Founders should understand the fit between the company, their sector, the VC firm, and the partner in charge."

Every founder and startup has different skills, resources, talents, and needs. Every venture capitalist is also unique, as is every venture firm. "Founder–venture capitalist fit" is enough of a success factor in building a business that extensive due diligence by founders to find the right investors is wise, and vice versa. Founders should talk to other founders about their experiences with any given venture capitalist before making a choice. Selecting a venture capitalist is like deciding to marry someone. Unfortunately, sometimes there is only one person who will have you. But that is not your ideal situation.

8. "For work, if the product is good, there is a paying tendency."

Enterprise customers are more likely to be willing to pay cash for services than consumers who have been conditioned to expect services "for free." During the free period in the freemium model, the hope is that the customers learn the benefits of the product in a very low-cost way through self-education and become paying consumers. Freemium at its core is about lowering customer acquisition cost. If your competitor is using this "land-and-expand" approach, it can often undercut your price if you do not also adopt the approach.

9. "The monetization technique in China cannot just be advertising supported. The China population is actually a paying population. They pay for games, things that they don't even need. They pay for virtual items so they can look like a duke. They drive a virtual BMW to a concert that's all online. They can pay. This is the young generation. For them, do I line up, get stuck in traffic, buy a 300 renminbi ticket and get stuck in an auditorium? Or can I do that for 100 bucks and look like a king online? So the time has changed, and therefore, if you have users, any company should try to monetize through various ways. That's how we push our CEOs when they say, 'Well, this is how the West does it.' We say, 'Let's see if the East can do it better.' "

> The lack of . . . fully built-out offline retail and services in second- and third-tier cities in China means that many services and products are not available offline. Variety and convenience factors are lacking. Hence mobile commerce is a very natural transaction-based value for users. Thanks to Alipay and Tencent's further efforts to tie users' phones to payment providers, the ease of payment has greatly enhanced e-commerce and anytime-anywhere transactions via the mobile devices.

China is not only a huge market but a key part of the global supply chain. As a market and supply base for most companies, it cannot be ignored. So for a business, the right question is how to deal with China, rather than whether you deal with China. I spent four years of my life working in Seoul, South Korea, and even wrote a book about doing business there. What I took away from my experience living in Korea, and later Australia, was how little I knew about the countries despite living there and that even if I spent a lifetime working there, I would still have much more to learn. When dealing with a county and culture where you are not a native, it is wise to know as much as you can about what you do not know. To help deal with cross-cultural differences, it is best to have a relationship mentality rather than a deal mentality.

10. "One of the most common questions we hear today is, 'How can I take my model to the other side?' U.S. companies always come to us and say, 'I am doing this in the U.S. Should I be doing it in China first?' If you're an entrepreneur, you're no longer just thinking 'my hometown.' Some of them come from the point of 'If I don't do this on a global basis first, someone is going to copy me.' I'm sitting in China; somebody is going to copy me in the U.S. I'm sitting in the U.S.; somebody is going to copy me in China."

Once upon a time people thought of innovation as originating in the West and then moving to China. Now the flow is moving in both directions. This is a very good thing since the world benefits from more innovation.

11. "If you can do without China, and you have this fear of setting up there, then don't go. But if you are in the maker community, 90 percent of your supply chain is in China. So in not going, you will fail."

Maybe you can find that 10 percent in Vietnam, but the price is not going to be the same (and you will encounter the same problems anyway). If your business requires you to be in China, then my advice as an entrepreneur is figure out how to get smart about it. It is as simple as that. There's no perfect answer.

193

Lee is saying that dealing with China is not something that should be done lightly. Success will require a big commitment. She is also saying that China is not only a huge market but a key part of the global supply chain if you are a maker. China a great opportunity for any business, and in some industries it simply cannot be ignored. There is no substitute for having experienced local help from people who understand the current business environment in China, which can change quickly and dramatically. I lived and worked in Asia for five years and yet would not do business in or with China without the assistance of people who are aware of the situation in China right now.

12. "My friends told me I was crazy to leave the iron rice bowl that ST Engineering provided. But I had to take the risk.
To get what you want, you must get it yourself."

After graduating from Cornell, Lee started her career in Singapore as an aerospace engineer. She could have stayed in that job and been very secure financially. Instead, she did what she needed to do to achieve her goals. Startups are not a great place for people who value security highly. The reality is that most startups fail. The struggle to build a business from scratch is inevitably hard.

Elon Musk describes the process in a colorful way: "A friend of mine said running a startup is like chewing glass and staring into the abyss. After a while, you stop staring, but the glass chewing never ends." If you are not a missionary, the odds that you will endure the many rejections and hardships of the venture world are significantly lower. Venture capitalists know from experience that people who are working on someone else's idea or dream are less likely to stay the course than those attempting to realize their own dreams. Many startups have been inches from failure before eventually finding success. Getting through all the glass chewing is a job best suited for missionaries.

22

Doug Leone

Sequoia Capital

DOUG LEONE IS THE managing partner of Sequoia Capital, where he has been a partner since 1993. Prior to joining Sequoia in 1988, he worked at Sun Microsystems, Hewlett-Packard, and Prime Computer in sales and sales management positions. Leone was responsible for investments including Guardent, ServiceNow, Aruba, Meraki, Rackspace, Netezza, Arbor/Hyperion, RingCentral and MedExpress. He received an MS in management from the Massachusetts Institute of Technology, an MS in industrial engineering from Columbia University and a BS in mechanical engineering from Cornell University. He is responsible for Sequoia Capital's investments in Rackspace and Vina Technology.

1. "We want to be partners with entrepreneurs from day one . . .
We know after many, many years that your DNA is set
in the first sixty to ninety days."

Leone makes a reference to genetics in his quote here. What is the DNA of a business? In my view, it consists of culture and values, plus a range of best practices. Best practices cannot be reduced to a formula since every business is different, but there are ways to learn from others. I learned most of what I know about optimal company culture and best practices during one magical period in my life when I would sit in on meetings as Craig McCaw met various captains of industry when they visited him. A parade of executives, including Charlie Ergen of Dish Network, Alan Mulally of Boeing, and Jeff Hawkins of Palm, came into my life during that time, and what I learned in those meetings was astounding. I tried to be a sponge for knowledge and best practices and to make the best parts of their DNA part of my DNA.

> 2. "In venture, big is completely the enemy of great.
> You want very small, tight teams, the same thing
> with running an engineering department."

Leone believes that small teams of people making decisions make *better* decisions (i.e., too many cooks spoil the broth). Leone wants to find founders who understand the importance of a strong team and a teamwork mentality. As an example, he looks for founders who use the word "we" instead of "I." He advises founders to "raise as little as you can to get you to something that you can show—plus maybe a quarter or two so you have a little bit of cushion—and then raise some more money. Raise as little—not as much—as you can because that's the most expensive equity you're going to sell." He also says, "Be very generous with the early engineers that you hire. Those are the ones that you should invest in, because the first two or three engineers, if you get those wrong, you are done."

> 3. "We're happy to help recruit the first three, four, five
> engineers, but we firmly do believe that recruiting is a core
> competency that companies should learn."

Team composition and chemistry determine the success of a business. Since great people attract other great people in a nonlinear way, getting a strong early start with recruiting is essential. Leone believes that if a company cannot recruit its own people after getting assistance from the venture capitalist, it is in trouble. If great people are not being attracted to the startup, something is wrong. By contrast, a startup that punches above its weight in attracting great employees is on the right track. If you think, "How did they hire someone of her or his caliber?" that's a good indicator that the startup will be successful.

4. "There are three types of startups: (1) ones that
are so young that it's difficult to tell if the dogs are going
to eat the dog food; (2) ones where there's clear evidence of
market pull; and (3) ones that are unfortunately stuck in a push
market or have a very difficult product to sell. The trick is to say
away from (3). You only go to (1) if you are a domain expert
and you have an informed opinion on a product or market,
but this is a rare trait. The real trick is to end up in (2)."

When he made this statement, Leone was giving advice to salespeople about factors to consider when deciding whether to join a startup. The best case for a salesperson without domain expertise exists when product–market fit has been found and there is existing sales traction (type 2). In other words, the dogs are eating the dog food and want more. Leone is also pointing out that if a business has not yet established product–market fit (i.e., it's still difficult to tell if the dogs are going to eat the dog food), it's best for an ordinary salesperson to leave the opportunity to others who have domain expertise, special skills, and aptitude (type 1). When offered a type 3 job, the salesperson should decline.

5. "Little companies have really two advantages: stealth
and speed. The best thing for little companies to do is
to stay away from the cocktail circuit."

Startups need feedback when developing a product or service.
Having said that, a startup need not spend a lot of time promoting its offerings until the time is right. There are so many things
to do to prove the value hypothesis by discovering core product
value that unessential activities like attending cocktail parties are
an unwise use of time.

6. "Don't confuse the cost to start a company
with the cost of building a company."

Creating a product or service and finding product–market fit are
only small steps toward success. Unless a business finds sales, and
its marketing and distribution approach a larger scale, a startup
will not find success. There is a huge gap between finding product–
market fit and scaling a company.

There are many attractive business opportunities that do not
require and should not involve venture capital. Ben Horowitz writes,

Building modern companies is not low risk or low cost: Facebook, for example, faced plenty of competitive and market
risks, and has raised hundreds of millions of dollars to build
their business. But building the initial Facebook *product* cost
well under $1 million and did not entail hiring a head of manufacturing or building a factory.

7. "Hire the guy who has something to prove."

We want people who come from humble backgrounds and have
a need to win.

198

Leone is a big fan of hiring people hungry for success. The best venture capitalists prefer missionaries to mercenaries, and people who have something to prove tend to be missionaries. I certainly have met people who were driven by the fact that they started with literally nothing before building a business. On the other hand, I have found in my own life that many people who come from more than comfortable financial backgrounds are also driven to find success. Bill Gates and Craig McCaw are just two examples.

8. "Be incredibly, ruthlessly selfish with your equity."

Entrepreneurs who are not careful about dilution often learn a hard lesson about selling equity too cheaply. Founders need shares to compensate key people and to remain motivated to stay "all in." Bill Gurley has said that he's "seen companies take one or two angel rounds and wind up giving away half their company." There is an old saying in the venture capital business: "There are three phenomena that can wreck even the best of investments: dilution, dilution, dilution."

There are many tradeoffs involved, as the venture capital firm Andreessen Horowitz points out in advice it gives to founders:

> The easiest way to think about valuation is the tradeoff it provides relative to dilution: As valuation goes up, dilution goes down. This is obviously a good thing for founders and other existing investors. However, for some startups there's an added wrinkle; they may face an additional tradeoff, of valuation versus "structure." Which reminds us of the old adage that "you set the price, I'll set the terms."

9. "What differentiated knowledge does the angel bring? Don't just do an angel round with people whose money is thrown your way."

199

Given a choice between angel investors who add both money and other contributions, or angels with only money to contribute, founders should choose the former. Raising money is not a problem if you have a great team and an attractive offering under development with significant convexity. However, founders are increasingly realizing they need more than money from their investors. For this reason, you see more and more venture capitalists blogging and using social media to convey to founders that they have more to contribute to a business than money.

When is raising money from angel investors a good idea? Ben Horowitz writes, "If you are a small team building a product with the hope of 'seeing if it takes' (with the implication being that you'll try something else if it doesn't), then you don't need a board or a lot of money, and an angel round is likely the best option."

10. "There are venture firms that have never generated a positive return or have not even returned capital in ten years that are raising money successfully. And that surprises the heck out of me. People talk about the top quartile—it's not about the top quartile, it's barely about the top decile, or even a smaller subset than that."

Many pension funds and universities have financial return assumptions of about 8 percent for their investments. No one associated with an endowment or pension fund likes to deliver a message that requires his or her organization to cut spending or raise contributions. To achieve the desired financial return, fund managers may convince themselves that they can achieve high returns via the venture capital asset class even though this means investing in firms that have been in the bottom quartiles of performance. Such decisions can result in far more money coming into the venture capital asset class than would otherwise be the case when times are good.

11. "Just keep in mind that we are in a venture capital business. It's called venture capital because nothing is certain. But if you look at our portfolio, it doesn't include Twitter. It doesn't include Pinterest. We have made many, many errors over the last forty, fifty years. But I'll also tell you we've got many, many right."

Venture capital is a business in which you are guaranteed to make mistakes since it is all about buying mispriced convexity. Just like Babe Ruth, the greatest venture capitalists strike out a lot, but they sometimes hit massive grand slams. It is worth emphasizing that Leone is talking about uncertainty rather than risk. Uncertainty is actually the investor's friend since it is the primary cause of mispriced assets. Without mispriced assets (i.e., the mistakes of other people), you cannot outperform the market, and it is when there is uncertainty that assets are most often attractively mispriced.

12. "If you're in Cleveland, we cannot help you."

Physical location still matters, which is why there are cities that benefit from agglomeration effects. If the venture capital firm is too far away from the startup, it is hard for the venture capitalists to provide much more than money. Without more than money, Leone feels that companies do not have the same probability of success as those with investors who provide more than financial backing. Since Leone has helped established Sequoia branches overseas, he must believe that the Sequoia venture capitalists in overseas cities can help startups in those cities. Don Valentine (a Sequoia founder) agrees with Leone:

> In thirty years we haven't convinced ourselves to set up a presence in Boston. It's a very difficult business to be good at consistently over a long period of time, and it requires a lot of thoughtful and integrated decision-making. We make enough mistakes on

investments we make in Silicon Valley that we're not comfortable we can be successful three thousand miles away, never mind eight thousand miles away.

If a city is just a couple of hours away from a venture capitalist, I would argue that the rule does not apply. For example, many venture capitalists from San Francisco successfully invest in Seattle and vice versa. This does not mean that others cities cannot have their own local sources of venture capital and find success. There are people who are trying to make that happen. Whether this can be done successfully at scale raises a different and complex set of issues that would be worthy of another book.

23

Dan Levitan

Maveron

DAN LEVITAN COFOUNDED THE venture capital firm Maveron in 1998 with Howard Schultz, the Starbucks CEO. Levitan is a thoughtful advocate for specialization in the venture capital business and for the importance of finding the right mentors in life. Levitan has led many of the firm's successful investments, including Capella Education Company, Quellos Group, Potbelly, and Zuilily. He is a graduate of Duke University and Harvard Business School. After school, Levitan spent 15 years in investment banking focused primarily on consumer businesses. During his banking career, Levitan helped more than 100 companies go public. As a Managing Director at Schroders he led the firm's consumer group and founded its West Coast investment banking division. Levitan met Schultz in 1991, when Starbucks began planning for its IPO.

1. "Get the team right. Startups to me are about people, people, people."

We can find a great sector or business, but we're investing so early that unless there's this tenacious grit, determination, resourcefulness, and ability to evolve, it won't work.

The earlier a venture capitalist invests in a business, the greater the level of uncertainty and the more the investment is about buying mispriced convexity. The future of truly disruptive startups is so uncertain that founders and team members who can quickly respond to unanticipated changes have tremendous value, referred to as optionality. The ability of a startup to adapt to an unpredictably evolving world is essential. Successful venture capitalists also know that team chemistry is critical. When you are working with people you know and trust, tremendous efficiencies are created. The more you know about a group of people, the more likely an environment characterized by a seamless web of trust will be created. Successful venture capitalists and founders are obsessively focused on finding great people to work with. They spend far more of their time recruiting than most would imagine since they realize how critical a strong team is to success.

2. "We're looking for extraordinary entrepreneurs
who can create very large businesses. After eighteen years
and backing over one hundred entrepreneurs, I've learned
it's a rare person who has the combination of attributes
to get through the challenges of a startup and create
a large company that changes our lives."

The world does not need to be a zero-sum game with founders.
By contrast, there are so few great entrepreneurs and great ideas,
it is somewhat of a zero-sum game among VCs.

The venture capitalist Fred Wilson once wrote a rather famous blog post about factors that limit the scalability of the venture capital model and, by implication, the number of innovative startups that help create growth, productivity, and jobs. Levitan and many others believe that the primary bottleneck shortage in the venture industry is a limited supply of great startup founders.

What does it take to be a great founder? Levitan's firm Maveron has compiled a list:

1. Works ridiculously fast
2. Has superior communications skills with the team, investors, and partners
3. Is self-aware and can evolve
4. Balances being aware with being detail oriented
5. Is an all-star recruiter who prioritizes team and company building
6. Prioritizes value creation for company investors
7. Can sell both the product and the vision and knows the customers inside out
8. Has category advantage from past experiences and relationships
9. Is a data-driven decision maker
10. Has contagious passion and relentless perseverance

Finding someone with every attribute on this list is a tall order, but it can be done. When venture capitalists see these characteristics, they nearly always rush to invest in the founder's startup.

3. "How is the CEO recruiting? If we are two years in [after seed round] and we think this is a big idea and there's been no impact players hired, that tells you something about the space or the CEO. The best biggest companies always seem to be able to hire people they shouldn't be able to hire."

One characteristic on Maveron's list of ideal qualities for a founder is that he or she be an "all-star recruiter." Great founders know how to sell, and one key "tell" of sales skill is recruiting. If a founder cannot sell employees on the vision and prospects of the business, he or she will probably have trouble selling to potential customers. Early hires at a startup are particularly important. On the importance of hiring the right people, Levitan has quoted Maveron's cofounder Howard Schultz: "If you are going to build a one hundred–story skyscraper, make sure the corners are perfect." What Schultz means is that early hires are especially important since they set the foundation for what will become the culture of a growing business.

4. "We always talk about how you have to build a brand from the inside out, not the outside in. Brands are not wrappers. Brands are based on the values of the founders, and then they spread to the people who work for the company, and then that psychological contract is spread to the customer."

Get the people right and it flows to the customers.

When it comes to building a brand, Levitan believes that the process starts with people. What do founders value? How do they transmit those values to customers? Another great Schultz quote sums it up: "You have to stand for something important. What are your core purpose and reason for being? Those should be the guardrails within which you create the enterprise's meaning to your customers."

5. "Early-stage money is not fungible. It comes with an attitude. Make sure that the people on your bus are the people you want on your bus."

Early-stage investing in particular is all about the people.

At this point, if you have not figured out that Levitan believes people are more important than any other variable in just about everything, you are clearly not paying attention. Founders must be great people. The team must be composed of great people. Brands start with great people. Venture capitalists must be great people, too. The qualities of a great person include being trust-worthy, loyal, helpful, friendly, courteous, kind, cheerful, thrifty, enthusiastic, and brave. That's true for just about anything. But there are specific qualities that are desirable in a venture capital-ist, such as a missionary attitude and a love of building valuable products and solving customer problems. What Levitan is saying is that money received from an investor can come with a big price tag attached—so it's important to choose well. There's expensive money and value-added money. Knowing the difference is impor-tant. Life is a lot better when you get to work with great people.

6. "I spent a lot of my thirties and forties creating mentors. As I've gotten older, it's become more fun turning that around and finding someone who wants to be mentored."

One of my mentors is Bill Campbell. He's "product, product, product." Yet Howard Schultz says the first person you should hire is a human resources person.

Levitan has said he has four primary mentors: (1) Howard Schultz; (2) Bill Campbell; (3) Mike "Coach K" Krzyzewski of Duke Uni-versity; and (4) Joel Peterson. These mentors are each different and bring different skills and attributes to the relationship. As Levitan points out, they will disagree on some points. That's okay and, in fact, desirable. As you go through life, you can say, "I really like how person X does Y." But you do not need to adopt everything that person X does to benefit from a relationship with him or her. Having a number of mentors is like being at a supermarket and buying ingredients. Of course, wanting to "be like X when they are doing Y" is a lot easier said than done sometimes, but at least you know what you want. Listening to Levitan talk about his mentors is infectious. For example, it was Coach Krzyzewski who taught Levitan the central lesson of Maveron's consumer-focused success: Always ask, "Do you *love* your team?"

7. "There are lots of ways to make money in venture capital, and there are even more ways to be mediocre. We believed the world didn't need another commoditized venture capital firm. Our theory was that the operating characteristics of technology companies would be incorporated into consumer businesses in an unprecedented way. Technology-driven consumer-facing brands."

> We decided to focus on consumer very narrowly and invest only in end-user consumer brands. It's worked much better, including because we're presented with more of these types of startups; we have a greater pool of companies facing similar problems, which helps our entrepreneurs; and our LPs are getting more consistent returns.

Levitan believes that venture capital firms will increasingly specialize as competition increases. Maveron's decision to be "consumer only" in its approach to venture capital is walking the talk of that viewpoint. When you focus on something, you tend to get better at it. When you get better at it, people come to you for that skill, which makes you better yet. This feedback loop is powerful and financially rewarding if you pick skills that scale well.

8. "We dabbled in enterprise, and we sucked at it. This is a humbling business. It's really hard to be good. We asked ourselves, and every startup should ask itself, 'What do you do better than others, and how does that concentration work in your favor? What do you do well?'"

A value investor would refer to what Levitan is talking about here as implementing a "circle-of-competence" approach. A good example of someone implementing a circle of competence involves Tom Watson Sr., the founder of IBM, who once said, "I'm no genius. I'm smart in spots—but I stay around those spots." By finding, and then focusing on, what you are truly great at as an investor, you can create an investing edge. Every investor has strengths and weaknesses, and the sooner you recognize what yours are, the faster you will achieve success.

9. "I think there is a lot of temptation to go big, particularly when the press asks, 'How big is the fund?' What's more important is what's in the fund. What we've learned over the years is that one of our formulas for success is a smaller fund, where one or two significant wins can really have a positive impact. The challenge for successful venture capitalists is having the discipline to stay small and keep the fundraising within the same parameters as they originally achieved success in."

After a certain scale is reached in terms of "assets under management," size can work against performance. Sometimes $500 million is not much more effort to manage than $50 million. But once you reach a certain size, it is impossible to put more money into a single business, so you must find a new business and have the necessary time to devote to that new business. As there are a limited number of great founders with the right businesses attacking huge markets, some venture capital firms stretch too far and fund startups that will drag down returns. As with Goldilocks, what you are looking for is something that is "just right" in terms of fund size and the amount invested in each company.

10. "Capital is not the barrier for the best businesses. There's plenty of money out there for great consumer entrepreneurs with great consumer products attacking really big markets."

It is not easy to raise money for a new business, but if you have a great team of people attacking a big market with an innovative solution to a real problem, raising money is not your biggest problem. Levitan's focus is on consumer entrepreneurs, but the point applies to many sectors of the economy right now. If the idea for the business is sound, there is a big market and a great team, money is not the input that will be in short supply to a business.

11. "Some of the best ideas that we've invested in have made no sense to conventional sources."

There have been a few times in the last sixteen years when we've funded something that was a no-brainer and it worked well for us. But most of the time, it's not a no-brainer.

Levitan and his firm have chosen to specialize, and with that comes an opportunity to "think different." Being a contrarian can be uncomfortable for some people. Too many people would rather fail conventionally than succeed unconventionally. Great venture capitalists are comfortable standing apart from the crowd.

12. "We get over one thousand inquiries a year and will make four to seven core investments and fifteen to twenty-five seed investments. If businesses are not referred to us in some way or another, it is hard for us to really focus on it."

If we put $100,000 into a seed round, we want to earn the right to do the A round.

Levitan views it as Maveron's job to pick well early and then do the work to be the best partner possible. He views venture capital as a service business, and it's on Maveron to outperform once it's on your team.

Sorting through more than one thousand inquiries a year is not easy. The process inevitably means that you must deliver a lot of "no" messages and only a few "yes" messages. Delivering thoughtful "no" messages is one of the hardest jobs for any venture capitalist.

By requiring a referral before you consider an inquiry, three objectives are achieved:

1. You get a filter operating to make decisions easier.
2. You reduce the number of pitches you need to consider.
3. You put entrepreneurs to the test. (If they cannot somehow get a referral, they are not resourceful enough and may not have strong sales skills).

The biggest fear of any venture capitalist at this stage is mistakes of omission. There are no venture capitalists who have been in the business who have not passed on a big success. It's a necessary part of the process. As long as you hit your share of grand slams, errors of omission will be overshadowed.

24

Jessica Livingston

Y *Combinator*

JESSICA LIVINGSTON COFOUNDED THE world's largest and most successful startup accelerator, Y Combinator in March 2005. She is a partner of this startup accelerator and a driving force in its operation. Her cofounder and husband Paul Graham has said, "Everything we did as an organization went through her first— who to fund, what to say to the public, how to deal with other companies, who to hire, everything." Livingston has written a book entitled *Founders at Work*, based on interviews with startup founders. Jessica has said, "Writing that book inspired me to help early-stage startups—and ultimately to want to start Y Combinator. Prior to cofounding Y Combinator, Livingston was vice-president of marketing at Adams Harkness Financial Group.

1. "I definitely think of Y Combinator as a startup in many ways. There are origin stories very similar to the way a startup would get started. We were kind of thinking about a problem, and thinking we could do some cool things to solve it."

We started talking about the brokenness of the funding world in 2004 . . . and it was.

There are many ways that the venture capital business has evolved and innovated, and it will continue to do so. Livingston is saying that Y Combinator's evolution is an example of what a startup must go through to be successful. At the core of sustainable success for a business is always a real solution to a real customer problem. Livingston and her other Y Combinator cofounders found (1) core product value; (2) a way to successfully deliver it to customers; and (3) a significant barrier to entry against competitors from network effects and cumulative advantage. Firms like Andreessen Horowitz, Baseline Ventures, Benchmark, and Sequoia have similarities in terms of how they operate in the venture capital business, but they also vary in significant ways.

2. "Originally we were targeting programmers and wanted to teach them the business side of running a startup."

What Livingston describes is a noble calling. Huge value is locked up and lost to society when engineers with great ideas cannot bring them successfully to market. I have spent most of my professional life working with engineers who are sometimes challenged when it comes to business. I have seen the full spectrum: from engineers who know next to nothing and have no desire to learn to those who are business savants.

The best business mind I have ever seen up close is that of Bill Gates, who incidentally furnishes a good example of Livingston's goal of cultivating engineers for business. Gates ran the business side of the house at Microsoft from the time the business was first established in Albuquerque. He was the CFO and the CEO for many years. Contracts with customers were his responsibility. Gates was able to make intelligent decisions because he grew up with a lawyer as a dad and a mom who served on many business and nonprofit boards and had excellent business sense.

That someone with programming skills like Bill Gates also knew a lot about the law, business, and contracts was incredibly fortunate. He learned these things at the dinner table with his family; because of the many conversations that occurred there and elsewhere, Bill Gates understood the difference between a license and an outright sale in the early IBM negotiations that changed business history. Gates also sufficiently understood business, economics, and science such that he was able to recognize the value of positive feedback and the likely rise of a new industry based on software, resulting in a young man with the right mix of skills and knowledge taking IBM to the cleaners when it was in its prime. The mix of business, legal, and technical acumen characteristic of Gates is what engineers learn at a place like Y Combinator.

3. "What we wanted to do was create a standardized branded form of funding. Y Combinator wanted to be the 'first gear' for startups."

> We're not expecting the money we invest to be the last a startup ever raises. It's just to get them going. And we want to get as many startups going as we can.

Livingston is describing decisions that illustrate the power of focus in creating a valuable business. The founders of Y Combinator decided to focus on the unique problems that early-stage startups face. Because of this focus and specialization, other later-stage venture capital firms view Y Combinator as a partner, which creates a self-reinforcing positive feedback loop.

4. "Our motto is to make something that people want. If you create something and no one uses it, you're dead. Nothing else you do is going to matter if people don't like your product."

What guided the founders through this process was their empathy
for the users. They never lost sight of making things that people
would want.

The point Livingston is making here is obvious and yet so often
forgotten. If the customer is not having an "aha" moment in relation to the positive core value of a product, the business will not
be successful. Creating such value in new ways with a barrier to
entry is a rare thing. This idea also applies to Y Combinator itself.

5. "At the time we were realizing, 'Hey, it's a lot cheaper to start
a software company. I mean, all you need is a computer and to
pay some of your server costs.' So we thought, 'Why don't VCs
write smaller checks?' And finally we said, 'Let's do something.
Let's create an investment company that does standardized
branded funding. We'll have an application process, and this
will be a new thing.' But we always had thought that we'd do
asynchronous investing just like every other investor. But then we
said, 'Neither of us knows anything about angel investing. Let's
learn quickly by funding a bunch of startups at once.' "

Creating a system that runs startups through a synchronous process
to create a valuable business is efficient and logical. This reminds
me of the many years I spent in school, especially in college and
graduate school. There is no question that I learned more from my
classmates than I did from my professors. In my involvement with
accelerators, I see just this same thing going on, with founders teaching each other in addition to learning from the program itself. Micro
VCs are proliferating to a point where there are now more than 350
in the United States alone. This means that more people are getting
funded and that these people are more diverse in every sense. Founders today are able to maintain greater ownership stakes in their businesses. Founders who must sell 60 percent of their business at seed
stage do not have the same incentive to persevere in tough times.

6. "Even Y Combinator got rejected at first. Nowadays there are a lot of groups that do the kind of investing we do, but when we started, no one was. Even our own lawyers tried to talk us out of it."

> It's really important for people to remember how often startup founders, who are hugely successful now, get rejected early on. They will hear, "This is a dumb idea. You shouldn't be working on that. No investor will invest in them." I mean, there are countless examples of people trying to raise funding, and they just got turned down by investors because they thought it was a bad idea or didn't think the person was formidable enough. That's important because it's hard to start a startup. If you're a first-time founder, you're going to get rejected a lot in a lot of different ways, and it's really hard.

Livingston is arguing that the nonconsensus, contrarian view is powerful and significant. Howard Marks has also argued that to earn more than the market return, you must adopt a nonconsensus view and that view must be correct in a significant way. This is all provable with mathematics. If your idea is not a little crazier than other people's, there are very likely to be competitors already working on the idea.

7. "Perseverance is important because in a startup nothing goes according to plan. Founders live day to day with a sense of uncertainty, isolation, and sometimes lack of progress. Plus startups, by their nature, are doing new things, and when you do new things, people often reject you."

> In general, your best weapon is determination. Even though we usually use one word for it, it's actually two: resilience and drive. One reason you need resilience is that you'll get rejected a lot. Everyone you encounter will have doubts about what you're doing.

Missionaries are far more likely to successfully survive the process of creating a business than mercenaries. Steve Jobs said in 1995,

"I'm convinced that about half of what separates successful entrepreneurs from the unsuccessful ones is pure perseverance." Bill Gates has similarly said, "Perseverance has been characteristic of our great success." There is an inherent tension between the need to sing for the fences and the reality that so few startups will be a grand slam. This tension means that being a founder is not a fully rational act. The sort of people who step up and swing early for the fence tend to be maniacally driven people who are on a mission. They are less tentative and less likely to sell the business early in the process. Missionaries are builders rather than sellers.

8. "The media often glamorizes successful founders and makes their paths seem easier than they actually were."

Just be determined, and have a little luck.

There is way more luck involved in life than people imagine. You will sometimes hear people say that they worked hard to get lucky. The reality is that there is no way to increase your luck because anything you do to improve the probability of a positive outcome is skill.

9. "Starting a startup is a process of trial and error. A lot of the startups in my book *Founders at Work*, and I see this again in Y Combinator startups, they start out saying, 'We're going to do this.' They try to do it, and it doesn't really stick, and so they think, 'Oh, gosh. The users are actually more interested in this aspect of our site,' and they work on that. So there's a lot of trial and error, and it gets glamorized, I think, in the press with these successful startups. They say, 'Oh, he had this brilliant idea. We knew this was going to be big, and it was great.' That's not the way it usually is. It's usually a lot of testing one thing out, it not working, and then happening upon the right thing."

> People think startups grow out of some brilliant initial idea like
> a plant from a seed. But almost all the founders I interviewed
> changed their idea as they developed it.

Mistakes are essential in venture capital since they are how information is acquired, and they enable benefits to be captured. Capitalism without mistakes and failure does not work since it is an
evolutionary system. Similarly, creating a successful startup or running any business is impossible without mistakes since both startups and established businesses are evolutionary systems interacting
with other evolutionary systems. As in nature, the startups that
survive are the ones that are best able to find a successful place
for themselves in the ecosystem and adapt as conditions change.
The best way to discover that place is by testing value and growth
hypotheses using the scientific method. Part of what Y Combinator
has done so successfully is systematize this discovery process in a
way that scales well. By running these experiments simultaneously
for a class of startups and making coaching and other resources
available, the success rate of the startups increases, particularly for
founders who have never been through the process before.

10. "Innovations seem inevitable in retrospect, but at the time it's an uphill battle."

Michael Mauboussin points out, "Increasingly, professionals are
forced to confront decisions related to complex systems, which are
by their very nature nonlinear. Complex adaptive systems effectively obscure cause and effect. You can't make predictions in any
but the broadest and vaguest terms." After the fact, people tend to
think they knew what was going to happen all along, but that is
often an illusion. Wikipedia describes hindsight bias well: "Sometimes called the 'I-knew-it-all-along' effect, hindsight bias is the

tendency to see past events as being predictable at the time those events happened." Most people say to themselves at one time or another as they go through life encountering new products, "Hey, I thought of that idea a long time ago." Okay, but what did you do actually about it then?

11. "People like the idea of innovation in the abstract, but when you present them with any specific innovation, they tend to reject it because it doesn't fit with what they already know."

Livingston is describing how powerful the "person-with-a-hammer-syndrome" can be (to the person with a hammer everything looks like a nail). The most interesting example of this I have ever seen comes from how AT&T saw mobile in the early days of mobile phones. The mobile phone was definitely an innovation, but no one at AT&T really knew how big it would be. So the company hired consultants to find an answer. McKinsey in its famously botched study vastly underestimated demand for mobile-phone service by assuming that no one would use mobile phones when they had access to a land line. Mobile phones did not fit with what McKinsey and AT&T already knew. Even when AT&T bought McCaw Cellular in 1995, it thought it was doing so to save the long-distance business. I remember Craig McCaw laughing out loud at this and lamenting that he had to sell AT&T the entire business since you cannot partner with a firm that does not understand core product value or even its own industry. AT&T had the cash from its legacy business to pay off the debt used to build the industry, so it was decided that the deal needed to be done. AT&T bought McCaw Cellular for the wrong reasons, but it was the right decision anyway. It is sometimes better to be lucky than good.

12. "Investors, most of them, have a herd mentality.
They want to invest only if other people are investing.
It's like a catch-22, like not being able to get a job
because you don't have enough experience."

The best and most experienced founders and the best venture capitalists know how to profit from this aspect of human nature by being contrarians. They know that most people like to do what other people are doing since, when facing uncertainty, it is efficient from an informational standpoint. The opportunity for a venture capitalist is to find assets or opportunities that are mispriced owing to the herding instinct. In his book *Extraordinary Popular Delusions and the Madness of Crowds*, Charles Mackay wrote, "People think in herds; it will be seen that they go mad in herds, while they only recover their senses slowly, and one by one."

25

Mary Meeker

Kleiner Perkins Caufield & Byers

MARY MEEKER IS A partner at the venture capital firm Kleiner
Perkins Caufield & Byers. Every spring, Meeker issues her impressive and insightful "Internet Trends" report consisting of hundreds
of slides identifying what Meeker believes are the most important developments and trends in the technology. These presentations are widely read and discussed. Meeker's investments include
Houzz, Instacart, LegalZoom, Slack, and Twitter. Before becoming
a venture capitalist, she was a managing director, research analyst,
and technology analyst at Morgan Stanley from 1991 to 2010,
before which she worked at Salomon Brothers. Meeker serves on
the boards of DocuSign, Lending Club, and Square. Meeker is a
prolific writer and the coauthor of the industry-defining books
The Internet Report (1996) and *The Internet Advertising Report*
(1997). Meeker received a BA from DePauw University and an
MBA from Cornell University.

1. "In a typical year, there are generally two technology
   companies that go public and become ten-baggers,

which means they deliver a ten-times return on investment.
We were trying to find those two companies."

This statement of Meeker's reflects a fundamental truth about the venture capital business. There are firms that follow a different venture capital model but what Meeker is describing here is the dominant model. The traditional venture business is all about the Babe Ruth effect; that is, that it is magnitude of success and not frequency of success that matters. As just one an example, the venture capitalist Fred Wilson has said that his firm loses all its money in over 40 percent of its venture investments. This is a normal and essential part of the traditional venture capital business. The number of times something like Facebook can happen in the global economy is constrained top down by a number of factors, including addressable market. It is simply impossible to have even a tiny number of Facebook-style financial outcomes every few months or even every few years.

2. "The race is won by those that build platforms
and drive free cash flow over the long term (a decade or more).
That was my view in 1990, 1995, 2000, 2005, 2010,
and it remains the same today."

The key word in this quotation is "platforms." Platforms are increasingly dominating the world economy. While the platform value has been the same over the period Meeker notes, the pay-off from owning shares in a successful platform has never been bigger. The grand-slam financial returns venture capitalists like Meeker seek are most often found in businesses that operate software platforms. To generate big returns, you need a business that scales amazingly well, and nothing scales better than software. A software business, like any other business, also needs a moat, and that can sometimes, with a lot of effort and luck, be created through network effects. When a platform is created in the right way, there is almost zero marginal cost to deliver the service and therefore very attractive margins.

3. "I read an article in the *New York Times* written by John Markoff about Jim Clark going to the University of Illinois at Urbana–Champaign to invest in a company selling a Web browser called Mosaic Communications run by Marc Andreessen. It was one of those moments. I picked up the paper and said, 'That's it.' This was 1994. Morgan Stanley then raised money for Mosaic— I actually have that business plan somewhere. The company promised to 'change the way the publishing world works.'"

Here Meeker is pointing to a major turning point in business history. The ability to spot a change as big as this one is a very valuable thing. What many people miss is that sometimes a change like this is mostly going to benefit consumers. The assumption that such a change will produce new gushers of profit is often mistaken, or at least the profit imagined is far more than is reasonable.

At the time Meeker describes, I was working for Craig McCaw, who is a good friend of Jim Clark. Jim Barksdale, who was running McCaw Cellular at the time, left McCaw to become CEO of Netscape in 1995. We were naturally very curious about what was going on at Netscape. McCaw sent a colleague and me from Seattle to visit Netscape. We were impressed by the products. Meeker is right that at that time, it seemed like something extraordinary was imminent. Each year after that visit in 1995, the startup launch parties grew bigger, and the spending on just about everything grew more lavish. Capital was flooding into the technology sector in ways that we had never seen before. In one sense, we were all frogs in a pot of water that was steadily getting hotter. Something that cannot go on forever will eventually stop, the economist Herbert Stein once famously stated.

4. "It is one thing to be wrong about the valuation and the timing. It's another thing to be wrong about the business model."

In evaluating a potential investment, it is possible to make a range of mistakes, including on valuation and timing. If an investor's mistake involves missing that the business model is unsound, the mistake is usually fatal. Sometimes a business can correct that problem before they run out of cash, but it is not an easy task. A venture capitalist like Meeker will closely examine the unit economics of a business to determine whether it has a sound business model. Key in this analysis are the assumptions since most models can be made to work well financially if pretend assumptions are used. If you are looking at a spreadsheet model, the first thing to examine is the assumptions.

5. "In general, a good rule of thumb is that for an attacker to beat an incumbent, the attacker's product typically needs to be 50 percent better, and 50 percent cheaper, and the attacker needs to sustain that competitive advantage for a year or two, to be able to gain material market share."

There is a lot of inertia in human behavior. Consumers do not always rationally address decisions like which products to use. In the mass market, people generally want a margin of safety when asked to move to a new product. The greater the value differential between the new and existing product, the lower the cost required to move the customer to a new product with sales and marketing. This challenge ratchets up the value that a challenger must deliver to generate customers at a reasonable cost. The greater the value differential between the new product and the incumbent's product, the lower the customer acquisition cost and the less cash that will be burned in getting the business to critical mass.

6. "Technology stocks are volatile."

J. P. Morgan once said the same thing about stocks generally: "The stock market will fluctuate." Technology stocks can be especially volatile. Or not. The best way to deal with volatility is to remember that you can make it your friend. If stock prices were not volatile, there would not be as many bargains. Remembering that risk is not the same thing as volatility is very important. Why are technology stocks more volatile? When conditions impacting a business change more often owing to changes in technology, prices are going to be more volatile. If technology falls within your circle of competence, the sector can be a great place to invest.

7. "You never want to catch a falling knife."

The metaphor of a falling knife is used to describe a situation in which the price of an asset has fallen significantly over a short period and in which there is significant uncertainty about how much further it will fall. Because momentum and emotion are involved when a knife is falling, the risk of mistiming the bottom is significant. Making accurate predictions about human behavior is difficult, especially after transactional costs are deducted. It would be great if someone could ring a bell when a knife hits bottom, but that never happens. Knives can continue to fall further longer that you can remain solvent. However, if you stay focused on valuation relative to a benchmark like intrinsic value, you are far better off than you would be trying to time markets. One way to reduce the risk of catching a falling knife is to have a margin of safety when buying assets. The idea is simple: With a margin of safety, you can make mistakes or have bad luck and still do fairly well. Having a margin of safety when buying assets is like keeping a safe driving distance between you and a car ahead of you when driving at 70 miles an hour.

8. "One of the greatest investments of our lifetime has been New York City real estate, and investors made the highest returns when they bought stuff during the 1970s and 1980s when people were getting mugged. The lesson is that you make the most money when you buy stuff that's out of consensus."

It is mathematically provable that to outperform a market-average result, an investment must be contrarian in a way that is correct. Buying when other people are fearful can produce great bargains. It can also produce great losses as well. You must buy assets that are out of consensus, and you must be right to outperform the market average. This reality is true in both venture and value investing, and in fact true in all investing.

9. "Buy technology stocks when no one is interested in them. Sell when everyone is interested in technology (or when attendance at technology conferences reaches record levels or when your grandmother wants to buy a hot technology IPO)."

This is a restatement of the Mr. Market metaphor. Be greedy when others are fearful and fearful when others are greedy. Meeker makes the additional point of the folly of following a crowd into hot sectors when valuations get too high. When the shoe shine operator at the airport or your Uber driver tells you what stocks you should buy or what "hot" sectors are best for venture capital investments, that is a "tell" that the market is overheated.

10. "Don't fall in love with technology companies. Remember to view them as investments."

This statement is a bedrock tenet of value investing. A share of stock is not a piece of paper to be traded but instead a partial interest in a real business that must be understood fundamentally to be properly valued. The business should be evaluated dispassionately based on sound data and analysis, and only once it is within your circle of competence. There is a significant danger in getting swept up in the madness of the crowd by an interesting story.

11. "I've made my best personal investments when I've been a user of the product."

The famous investor Peter Lynch takes pains to keep people from misrepresenting his views, most notably by saying, "I've never said, 'If you go to a mall, see a Starbucks and say it is good coffee, you should buy the stock.' " What he actually said was, "People seem more comfortable investing in something about which they are entirely ignorant." Meeker is saying that this idea also applies to venture investing: People seeking a solution to a real problem that a startup is trying to create will make better investments. Actually using a product that can be improved is one very important source of research. Lynch also said,

> Investing without research is like playing stud poker and never looking at the cards. You can't understand a business and its place in an industry without doing some research. And the objective in doing the research is to find something that the market does not properly discount into the price of the stock or bond.

As an example, a venture capitalist who uses databases in his or her work is more likely to make better decisions about a startup trying to improve databases. This is circle-of-competence thinking. Risk comes from not knowing what you are doing.

12. "I love data. I think it's very important to get it right,
and I think it's good to question it."

The amount of data in Meeker's massive slide decks is legendary. Some of that data are from companies making self-serving statements (e.g., talking about their books), and some are not. Meeker believes that you need to think carefully about all data to make sure they do not lead you to make a false conclusion. For example, it is easy to confuse correlation with causation. In thinking about data, it is best to avoid acting like the drunk who uses lampposts for support rather that illumination. Sometimes the data you need are in a dark corner of the parking lot where there is no light. In that case, you may need to put your decision in the "too hard" pile.

26

Michael Moritz

Sequoia Capital

MICHAEL MORITZ IS THE chairman of the venture capital firm Sequoia Capital. Before his venture career, he was a journalist and once worked at *Time*, where he was the San Francisco bureau chief. Moritz wrote an influential biography of Steve Jobs in 1984 and cowrote *Going for Broke: The Chrysler Story*. Of Moritz, *Vanity Fair* has said, "Michael Moritz is one of the only journalists to become a billionaire." Moritz's investments have included businesses such as Apple, Cisco, Flex, Google, Kayak, PayPal, Yahoo!, YouTube, and Zappos. In a *Forbes* interview, he once noted,

> Every time we invest in a little company, it's a battle against the odds. We're always outgunned by companies that are far larger than we are who have threatened founders and us with extinction. It's incredibly thrilling to prove everyone wrong. You can't get a bigger rush than that.

His investing style is eclectic, covering a range of different types of businesses. Born in the United Kingdom, Moritz was knighted for his business and philanthropic contributions. He received a BA and MA in history from Christ Church, University of Oxford, and an MBA from the Wharton School of the University of Pennsylvania.

1. "When we help organize one of these companies at
the beginning, it never looks like the world's greatest idea.
I think it's the marketing and PR department that rewrites
history and tells you that it was always the world's greatest idea.
What they don't say is that at the very beginning there was
great uncertainty and a great lack of clarity."

We just love people who perhaps to others look unbackable.
That has always been our leitmotif of doing business.

The best venture capitalists understand that success in the venture capital business is about buying mispriced convexity. Something "not looking like the world's greatest idea" is actually helpful in finding convexity since uncertainty is the friend of the wise venture capitalist. In other words, it is uncertainty that causes others to misprice convexity. Without some elements that make the start-up's ambition seem a little crazy, the potential financial return is unlikely to be the type of grand slam needed to make the venture capitalist's fund a success.

2. "Every single time you write a check,
you expect, or pray depending on your inclination,
for that investment to succeed."

In order to harvest convexity, a venture capitalist must believe that each swing of the bat may potentially produce a grand slam— even though statistically about 30 percent of startups fail outright with no return of capital, and even more will survive but with poor outcomes. And many successful startups nearly crash into the ground before they soar. Of course, others just crash into the ground. But in the beginning, the venture capitalist must believe that all startups have the potential to succeed. As time passes, however, the venture capitalist must decide which startups deserve more attention and funds. These choices are neither simple nor easy. Deciding not to support a startup further is one of the most painful aspects of being a venture capitalist. Real people whom you get to know are impacted in a significant way by these decisions.

3. "While there is danger in the venture business in getting too far away from the crowd, it can often pay to be unconventional. Don Valentine, the founder of Sequoia Capital, told me to trust my instincts, which lets you avoid getting dragged into conventional thinking and trying to please others."

In order to outperform any given market, it is mathematically true that you must not essentially be that market. This may seem like common sense, but you would be surprised how much herding happens since many people would rather fail conventionally than succeed unconventionally.

4. "If you have been around the start of success, it is far easier to recognize it again."

The venture capitalist Bruce Dunlevie of Benchmark once said to me, "Pattern recognition is an essential skill in venture capital." While the elements of success in the venture business do not repeat themselves precisely, they often "rhyme." In evaluating companies, the successful venture capitalist will often see something that reminds them of patterns they have seen before. It might be the style, chemistry, or composition of the team or the nature of the business plan. Some things will be fundamentally different, but other things may be familiar. And while the pattern will be similar, something in what the team is doing will seem to break a rule in a significant way. Part of the pattern being recognized is a rule-breaking innovation of some kind that will drive new value. One of the best ways for a venture capitalist to become more skilled at pattern recognition is to actually be a founder or an early employee in a startup.

5. "There's nothing more invigorating than being deeply involved with a small company and everybody's betting against us."

Great venture capitalists love the process of creating companies and more importantly creating customer value. Venture capital is a service business. Making others successful is the driving activity in the work. Finding vicarious joy in the success of others is essential.

6. "The very best companies are the ones where founders build the companies and stay with the companies for a very long time."

The most successful founders have a passion for building a business. This passion is highly correlated with a desire not to flip the business for a quick financial profit. A venture capitalist can help convince founders to stay the course by allowing them to generate some reasonable liquidity to lower their risk and making efforts to increase their confidence.

7. "The venture capital partnership that invests small amounts of money judiciously is almost always going to outperform the venture capital partnership that tries, to use an ugly phrase in the business, 'to put a lot of money to work.'"

At a certain point, the size of a fund works against performance. Emotional errors kick in when people have more to spend than they need or than their ideas require. Even worse, people can end up investing too many times, which can lead to a lack of focus. A top venture capital firm may hear thousands of pitches and invest in only eight to ten new companies a year (depending on the firm). A few outlier venture capital firms may make investments in twenty new startups a year, but that is not the norm.

8. "Five-year plans aren't worth the ink cartridge they're printed with."

Great teams are able to respond to a world that changes in ways that cannot be foreseen. This is why venture capitalists spend so much on the people employed by the startup. A strong team of people means the startup itself has convexity. The ability to "steer" as conditions change is more valuable than the ability to create medium- and long-term plans.

9. "It takes a tremendously long time to build a company of value. In many cases, the best venture returns don't happen in the private phase of the company; they happen in the time that the company is public. It takes a long time for sales to grow, and it takes a long time for true value to be achieved."

> People would be staggered at the length of time that we hold investments. It's not uncommon for us to hold investments for ten years or more. It's certainly not uncommon for the partners at Sequoia to own stock for fifteen or twenty years.

Most outsiders underestimate the importance of patience in venture capital. Building great companies takes time. Unfortunately, a few stories about relatively short-term payoffs from someone selling out for a big return have warped the views of many people about the time required to find success in the venture business. An overnight success can take many years to make happen.

10. "A downturn can be a very good time to build a company. The parvenus and the pretenders are gone. The only people who want to start a company in a time like this are the ones with the greatest conviction. It gets rid of all the riffraff. There isn't as much chaff in the air. There is more time to be thoughtful. You don't spend your day reacting to all sorts of fruitless entreaties. So to some extent it is easier. It is easier to hire and find places to locate companies, and in some respects also it is easier to get customers. Oddly enough in recessionary times, customers are prepared to take more risk with a young company if they believe that that company offers them a tremendous advantage that will help them become more efficient or lower their costs."

Howard Marks likes to say that business cycles are inevitable. The best time to be planting seeds is often when others are in a panic and depressed. Thinking countercyclically pays big dividends in business and not just in venture capital. People too often see the recent past and then extrapolate it into the future in positive and negative ways. Volatility is actually the friend of the investor with control over their emotions.

11. "My wife calls me the Imelda Marcos of books. As soon as a book enters our home it is guaranteed a permanent place in our lives. Because I have never been able to part with even one, they have gradually accumulated like sediment."

The most effective way to learn is by making personal mistakes, since the experience is so direct and vivid. Because some mistakes are quite painful to make yourself and so you can learn faster, learning from the mistakes of others through observation and reading is also a good idea. Charlie Munger has been described as a book with legs sticking out. He believes that it is far better to learn vicariously when it comes to many of the more painful mistakes one can make in life. At one shareholder meeting, when describing Berkshire's mistakes in the shoe business, Munger quoted Will Rogers: "There are three kinds of men. Some learn by reading. Some learn by observation. The rest of them must pee on the electric fence for themselves."

12. "A chimpanzee could have been a successful Silicon Valley venture capitalist in 1986."

I know there are millions of people around the world who have worked as hard and diligently as I have, and weirdly enough, like [former U.S. president] Jimmy Carter said years and years ago, "Life's unfair." I just happen to have been very fortunate.

Luck has way more to do with outcomes in life than most people care to admit. The benefits of luck compound as successful people attract other successful people. Adding to the bounty that luck can provide is the fact that being around other successful and skilled people makes you more skillful. If you happened to be lucky enough to be working as a venture capitalist in 1986 somewhere near Stanford, you very likely were the beneficiary of a massive tailwind that not only made people richer but more skilled. If you were that lucky but are not humble, you have not been paying attention. Are these people more skilled? Yes, because being lucky puts you in situations in which you acquire new skills. Luck feeds back on itself not only to create more luck, but also more skill.

27

Chamath Palihapitiya

Social Capital

CHAMATH PALIHAPITIYA IS THE outspoken and insightful founder of the venture capital firm Social Capital. He looks at the world very differently from most others, which is part of what makes what he says so interesting. He is not afraid to break eggs in order to make a successful omelet. His wealth is self-made, and his goals to improve society are admirable. Palihapitiya was an early member of the Facebook senior management team, and he was Facebook's vice-president of growth, mobile, and international. Prior to joining Facebook in 2007, he held senior positions at AOL, Mayfield Fund, Spinner.com, and Winamp. He graduated from the University of Waterloo with a degree in electrical engineering in 1999.

1. "Most people when they think about growth they think it's this convoluted thing where you're trying to generate these extra-normal behaviors in people. That's not what it's about. What it's about is a very simple, elegant understanding of product value and consumer behavior."

Core product value means creating a real connection with someone. I think now we all euphemistically call it the "aha" moment with the consumer. But also the power of how these communication networks, when they develop, create real entrenched usage and scale, and how these things can just dramatically accelerate adoption and engagement.

After all the testing, all the iterating, all of this stuff, you know the single biggest thing we realized [at Facebook]? Get any individual to seven friends in ten days. That was it. You want a keystone? That was our keystone. There's not much more complexity than that.

It's not just top-line growth. It's acquisition, engagement, ongoing product value. It's understanding the core value and convincing people who may not want to use it.

What we did at that company was we talked about nothing else. Every Q&A, every all-hands, nothing was spoken about other than this. Monetization didn't really come up. Platform came up but again in a secondary or tertiary context. But it was the single sole focus. But because we had defined it in this very elegant way that expressed it as a function of product value, it was something that everyone could intrinsically wrap their arms around.

Knowing true product value allows you to design the experiments necessary so that you can really isolate cause and effect. As an example, at Facebook, one thing we were able to determine early on was a key link between the number of friends you had in a given time and likelihood to churn. Knowing this allowed us to do a lot to get new users to their "aha" moment quickly. Obviously, however, this required us to know what the "aha" moment was with a fair amount of certainty in the first place.

There is no substitute for delivering core product value to the customer, which Chamath says is far harder and occurs far more rarely than most people imagine. He is adamant that metrics measuring factors that do not relate to core product value, like the number of invitations sent to friends on Facebook, can be not only distracting but harmful. For Facebook, Chamath says the keystone was to "get any individual to seven friends in ten days." Once that keystone was achieved, Facebook customers were receiving enough core product value that they were unlikely to churn and more likely to recommend the service to others because they had experienced their "aha" moment about the value of the service. If the founders of a business do not know what the "aha" moment is for their product or service in the first place, they are highly unlikely to succeed. Getting distracted by theories about monetization, virality, or other factors can be an impediment to creating the scalable connections with customers that create operating leverage.

2. "At Facebook, to generate growth we actually just looked at a lot of data, we measured a lot of stuff, we tested a lot of stuff, and we tried a lot of stuff. Now that masks over a lot of more nuanced understanding, but at an extremely high level that's really what we did. What's shocking to me is when I see a lot of products out there, it's unbelievable to me that people are trying to shroud products in this veneer of complexity. Measure some shit. Try some shit. Test some more shit. Throw out the stuff that doesn't work. It's not that complicated."

Chamath is saying that a business must measure the right things if the process is going to be useful. What a business measures as a keystone must capture its core product value. For example, measuring daily active users is not the right keystone since this measure does not capture core product value. The Internet entrepreneur Justin Kan once tweeted, "Startups mostly don't compete against each other, they compete against no one giving a shit." If a business does not deliver core product value, no one will care, and notifications or invites will be viewed as spam.

3. "Most people and most companies can barely get one thing right. We all kid ourselves about doing so many different things,

but there is a value to focus, which is that it constrains optionality and it forces you to have clarity of thinking. Because otherwise what happens is you have all these outcroppings of people within a company who can have their own anecdotal point of view about any kind of random thing. If they practice that rhetoric enough, they sound like they know what they're talking about. Then what happens is you invariably try a bunch of different things, and then you end up nowhere. But if you constrain the problem to say there's one thing, it forces everyone to be an expert or know that one thing, then speak intelligently and most importantly factually about that one thing."

Anyone who has worked at an actual business knows there are challenges inside every company. Nothing is ever perfect. Maintaining focus is essential. Clarity of thinking and action is powerful when done right. The famous CEO Jim Barksdale likes to say, "The main thing is to keep the main thing, the main thing." Every business has a profit engine that lies at its core. And that engine is invariably simple if you strip away everything extraneous. Two former Barksdale colleagues have written about the "main thing" principle:

We loved that expression when we first heard it from Barksdale, who was then the COO of FedEx. That single sentence captures the greatest challenge that executives and managers face today: keeping their people and their organizations centered on what matters most. Every organization needs a Main Thing—a single, powerful expression of what it hopes to accomplish. Without it, it's not possible to align the four elements that produce organizational efficiency and effectiveness: strategy, people, customers, and processes.

Founders today typically discover their main thing through data science. They look at their business and search for the core product value that Chamath is talking about. One example comes from Pinterest, which the venture capitalist Sarah Tavel describes on her blog as follows:

> The growth team then created and executed on a product road map that poured new users into the top of our sign-up funnel. The problem was that while monthly average users (MAUs) did increase, we had a leaky bucket. While the growth team was pouring people into the top of the funnel and the product teams were focused on increasing engagement of existing users, no one was responsible for making sure those new users became engaged, productive users. Realizing this, the team shifted their focus from MAUs to increasing the number of new weekly active pinners (the people who use Pinterest to pin or repin something new on the site that week — Pinterest's core action).

4. "Users are only ever in three states: they've never heard about it; they've tried it; and they use it. What you're managing is state change. So the framework is, what causes these changes? The answer should be rooted more in preference, choice, and psychology than in some quantitative thing."

> What I want to hear about are the three most difficult and hard problems that any consumer product has to deal with. How to get people in the front door? How to get them to an "aha" moment as quickly as possible? And then how do you deliver core product value as often as possible? After all of that is said and done, only then can you propose to me how you are going to get people to get more people. That single decision about not even allowing the conversation to revolve around this last thing in my opinion was the most important thing that we did.

> I hate the term "growth hacker." There are a lot of snake-oil salesmen in this field. Let's not create some wizard-behind-the-curtains thing about this concept called growth hacking. It existed well before me. It's called product and marketing.

One of the more interesting things happening today is how businesses generate these three phase changes Chamath describes (they've never heard about it, they've tried it, and they use it). Slack CEO Stewart Butterfield has said,

> I think we can get away with not having a sales team in any kind of traditional way probably forever. This is how we have grown so far, and we'd like to continue this forever, which is that people really like it and so they tell other people about it, and then other people start using it. And that's by far the best because when someone you trust tells you that this thing is good, then you're much more likely to be inclined to use it.

5. "(1) Approach with humility; (2) have strong opinions but weakly held; (3) change your mind a lot; and (4) experiment and iterate."

Encountering high levels of risk, uncertainty, and ignorance is inevitable, especially when it comes to anything related to technology. Being humble is a great way to stay within your circle of competence and avoid dysfunctional heuristics like "person-with-a-hammer syndrome" and overconfidence. Having strong opinions is important since they tend to mean you have developed strong arguments to your views. But at the same time, those strong views should be weakly held, because otherwise you may become a victim of dysfunctional thinking approaches like confirmation bias. The justification for changing your mind a lot has to do with being able to profit from convexity.

6. "Success begets more success."

Cumulative advantage is everywhere in the world today if you know how and where to look for it. This "success-begets-success" phenomenon has always existed, but not in terms of the magnitude of its impact. Once the world went digital and was increasingly connected by networks, the impact of cumulative advantage accelerated. Chamath's life is particularly interesting in no small part because he was involved in one of the most striking versions of cumulative advantage in business history (i.e., Facebook) and is funding many other firms through Social Capital that benefit from the phenomenon. Even the Golden State Warriors benefit from cumulative advantage since the more success the basketball team has, the more great players (particularly great team players who want to win) want to play there. Additionally, the more success a team has, the more revenues rise, which enables more success (the cycle of which repeats). A business can generate benefits from cumulative advantage in just the same way as a basketball team.

7. "How to pick a VC: (1) Must be a good picker; (2) must create interest from others for follow-on; (3) can help you grow; and (4) is morally aligned."

> A founder can't afford to be in a situation where, in the absence of operational help, you could run out of oxygen.

> You want to have a situation where your venture investors have the benefit of the doubt with other investors.

The reputation of a venture capitalist has significant signaling effects for other venture capitalists and potential employees. When uncertainty and fear are high, humans have a tendency to form herds and follow pack leaders. The signaling power of a great venture capitalist can get a business through a rough patch. If a business has raised money from a motley crew of investors and there are no leaders, or if times for that business get tough or uncertain, there may be no leader to step up and inspire confidence among the other existing investors or potential new investors. Founders essentially enter into partnerships with the venture capitalists investing in their businesses, so it is important to choose well. Chamath has said many times that if a founder is not morally aligned with his or her venture capitalist, big problems can result.

8. "The business model of the future is to serve individuals, because individuals are now relatively smarter. That's not correlated with education, by the way—they are smarter because they have access to tons more information. And so we are all more connected, we are all more engaged, and as a result we are all more cynical. And we all see that the emperor has no clothes. That's true of banking, that is true of people who run educational institutions, and it's true of health care. So the model of the future is to basically deconstruct all of that and empower the edges. That is the way you build a multi-gajillion-dollar company. Give people individual power."

Providing consumers with information that was formerly locked up in proprietary information systems means that consumers are at less and less of a disadvantage when purchasing goods and services since they no longer have less information than the provider. Quality goes up. Service levels go up. The bar is set higher. A big enabler of all of this is the mobile phone. Nearly everyone now has access to high-quality product information at all times, and the result is phenomena like showrooming (looking at the prices of other vendors online while you are in a brick-and-mortar store). Chamath is saying that the platform businesses that empower individuals are businesses with the potential to create huge value for investors and improve societal welfare.

9. "This is the time when people should be building really big, crazy things."

It really comes down to a very simple thing, which is the principle of *n* of 1 versus 1 of *n*.

Chamath has a strong view that neither the venture capital industry nor founders are swinging for the fences enough with their investments of time and capital. In short, he thinks they are not being ambitious enough. He believes this so strongly that it is part of the investing thesis of his firm. He tries to find businesses that will become "foundational layers in society that can develop something discontinuous. When you put those things together, that allows a company to separate themselves from the pack, and eventually, everything falls away, and they're an *n*-of-1 company."

10. "We're trying to coach our CEOs that the window dressing is both expensive from a cash perspective and tremendously expensive from a culture perspective. It distracts the team from building what they need to build. Don't waste money on things that get away from your mission, which confuse employees about why they're actually there. Meaning, the quality of the office and the quality of the food are all part and parcel of a lack of discipline, which speaks to the fact that the mission isn't compelling enough."

It's fine to fail. But if you fail because you didn't have the courage to move to Oakland and instead you burned thirty percent of your cash on Kind bars and exposed brick walls in the office, you're a fucking moron.

The company builders are just cheap, they're just grimy, and just, shitty office space, and they've got to keep it under 8 or 9 percent of their total burn, and they find people who really, really believe in the thing they're making, and they decide to just live in Oakland and pay for Lyft, and it's still cheaper. They do all kinds of creative things that deserve capital so they can build. So it forces us to ask those questions like "How are you really company building?" And that's how we get the truth on who's going to stand the test of time.

Every penny not spent on achieving a business's objectives is not only wasted, but a potential contributor to a cash deficit that can kill the business. The only unforgivable sin in business is to run out of cash. People driven to build a business (i.e., missionaries) do not spend on fluff like free Kind bars since those expenses increase the risk that they will not achieve their goals.

11. "Poker is a microcosm of my own life."

Michael Mauboussin likes to refer to the cigar-chomping gambling legend Puggy Pearson to illustrate a point about how there are similarities between playing poker and investing:

> Born dirt poor and with only an eighth-grade education ("That's about equivalent to a third-grade education today," he quipped), Pearson amassed an impressive record: He won the World Series of Poker in 1973, was once one of the top ten pool players in the world, and managed to take a golf pro for $7,000—on the links. How did he do it? Puggy explained, "Ain't only three things to gambling: knowin' the 60–40 end of a proposition, money management, and knowin' yourself." For good measure, he added, "Any donkey knows that."

Charlie Munger attributes no small amount of his financial success in investing to the time he has spent playing poker and bridge. Munger has said, "The right way to think is the way Harvard professor Zeckhauser plays bridge. It's just that simple." At a fundamental level, investing is just one form of making a bet. It's essential, however, that the bet be made in a way that is investing (where net present value is positive) rather than gambling (where net present value is negative).

Investing is inherently a probabilistic exercise, and experience with other games of chance can be helpful. Richard Zeckhauser, who is a great bridge player, points out:

Bridge requires a continual effort to assess probabilities in at best marginally knowable situations, and players need to make hundreds of decisions in a single session, often balancing expected gains and losses. But players must also continually make peace with good decisions that lead to bad outcomes, both one's own decisions and those of a partner. Just this peacemaking skill is required if one is to invest wisely in an unknowable world.

Warren Buffett also believes that bridge shares many characteristics with investing:

> Every hand is different and yet what has happened in the past is meaningful. In investing you must make inferences about every bid or card and cards that are not played. Also, as in bridge, you can benefit from having a great partner and having strong interpersonal skills. Understating probability and statistics is essential in card playing, business and investing.

12. "The qualities to look for in a founder include very high IQ; strong sense of purpose; relentless focus on success; aggressive and competitive; high-quality bar bordering on perfectionism; likes changing and disrupting things; new ideas on how to do things better; high integrity; surrounds themselves with good people; cares about building real value (over perception)."

> We try to find businesses that are technologically ambiguous, that are difficult, that will require tremendous intellectual horsepower, but can basically solve these huge human needs in ways that advance humanity forward. Those things don't necessarily take lots of money, but they generally do take lots of time. And they require really mission-driven people.

Chamath's list of attractive founder qualities speaks for itself. On the last point, this book repeatedly makes the point that mercenary founders are not as likely to care about building real value as missionary founders. Why repeat the point? Because it is so important and universal. You do not hear any venture capitalists say, "Wow, I really like to invest in mercenary founders who are starting a business to get rich." People like Chamath believe that missionary founders are naturally aligned with the interests of their investors and customers. Creating a startup is such a challenging endeavor that having missionary founders significantly increases the probability that the company will prosper, and that is because of this alignment. Chamath puts it this way: "What you value is what you achieve."

28

Keith Rabois

Khosla Ventures

KEITH RABOIS HAS BEEN a partner at the venture capital firm Khosla Ventures since March 2013. Rabois was a senior executive at PayPal and subsequently served in influential roles at LinkedIn and as chief operating officer of Square. He joined PayPal when the monthly burn rate was $6 million and LinkedIn, Slide, and Square when they had no revenue. His investments include Airbnb, Counsyl, Eventbrite, Lyft, Mixpanel, Palantir Technologies, Quora, Skybox, Weebly, Wish, Yammer, and YouTube. He is an active and outspoken participant on social media and lectures on industry topics often. He received a BA from Stanford and a JD from Harvard Law School.

1. "The only way to learn how to invest is to invest.
You can't simulate it."

Getting feedback is fundamental to the learning process. Reading and learning from others are helpful, but at some point the only way to refine your skill is to invest real money. As an example, many people have taken a class in which they make trades that simulate investing in a stock market. Unfortunately for people who do this, a simulation is no substitute for investing, since most mistakes in investing are psychologically based. Without actually testing your emotions and learning from genuine feedback, you really have not put yourself in a place where you can test your ability to control your emotions.

One of the most useful papers I have read on investing is "Investing in the Unknown and Unknowable," written by the Richard Zeckhauser. In it, Zeckhauser states,

> The wisest investors have earned extraordinary returns by investing in the unknown and the unknowable (UU). But they have done so on a reasoned, sensible basis. This essay explains some of the central principles that such investors employ. It starts by discussing "ignorance," a widespread situation in the real world of investing, where even the possible states of the world are not known. Traditional finance theory does not apply in UU situations. . . . Most big investment payouts come when money is combined with complementary skills, such as knowing how to develop new technologies.

Who has these complementary skills? Zeckhauser writes,

> Venture capitalists can secure extraordinary returns . . . because early-stage companies need their skills and their connections. In short, the return on these investments comes from the combination of scarce skills and wise selection of companies for investment.

Table 28.1 presents the chart Zeckhauser uses to clarify that risk, uncertainty, and ignorance are very different things.

Table 28.1 Escalating Challenges to Effective Investing

	Knowledge of states of the world	Investment environment	Skills needed
Risk	Probabilities known	Distributions of returns known	Portfolio optimization
Uncertainty (U)	Probabilities unknown	Distributions of returns conjectured	Portfolio optimization; decision theory
Ignorance (UU)	States of the world unknown	Distributions of returns conjectured, often from deductions about others' behavior; complementary skills often rewarded alongside investment	Portfolio optimization; decision theory; complementary skills (ideal); strategic inference

Venture capitalists with complementary skills have developed them over a period of years through experience in real-world investing and involvement in the startup world as founders or early employees. Simulations of bets involving risk do not enable the investor to profit in the uncertainty and ignorance domains. The best way to become a venture investor is to make venture investments. There is no substitute for real-world experience.

2. "Early stage, almost every successful entrepreneur I know doesn't care as much about the economic terms as much as who they are going to work with."

If you have the option, raise money from one lead investor who has the right skill set, background, and temperament to help you.

Khosla Ventures believes that the quality of the advice and mentoring given to founders by venture investors is so important that they present the firm as "venture assistance" rather than venture capital. Using Zeckhauser's taxonomy, it is the complementary skill and not the money that creates the extraordinary investing result. Founders who pay attention have figured out that it is the same venture capitalists consistently generating the grand slams year after year.

An important aspect of any person's skill set is early luck. People who get lucky early in life end up with more skill through a process called cumulative advantage. What entrepreneurs should take from this is that while money is fungible, the skill of the venture capitalists is not. Money is money (assuming deal terms are equal), but not all venture capitalists are the same. Skill should drive an entrepreneur's choice of venture capitalist.

In addition to the importance of complementary skills, it is hard to deny that there are signaling benefits from having a top venture firm as an investor. The world is filled with uncertainty, and people look for signals when making decisions. Employees and others are attracted to startups that others are attracted to. Success create more success with a nonlinear impact.

3. "You are looking for outliers as founders."

Convexity is everywhere if you know where to look, but the best types of positive convexity are found in places where no one else is looking. If a founder is an outlier, it is much more likely that he or she will find something that others are not looking at or can see. An investor will not find mispriced convexity by following the crowd. The critical point here is that when you are a highly skilled venture capitalist, uncertainty and ignorance are your friends. This is where you find the outliers that Rabois is talking about.

4. "The best founders can relay incredibly complex ideas in simple terms, can see things you don't see, are relentlessly resourceful and are often contrarian."

Rabois identifies four important qualities of a great founder in this statement. First, they can convey their ideas in ways that are easy for people to understand. Second, they have a unique way of looking at problems. Great founders do not think like other people in at least one important way, and they are fearless about at least one important thing. Third, successful founders almost always have the quality that Jeff Bezos said he looked for in a wife; Bezos said that he wanted someone "who would be resourceful enough to get me out of a Third World prison." And finally, they understand that to deliver an outsized result from their startups (financially and otherwise), they must be contrarian about something important, and they must be right in their contrarian view. There are also many other attributes in addition to these four that make for a great founder, including the ability to recruit talented people and to hire others who complement their skills.

The ability to find outlier founders (especially in new categories) is an especially valuable skill for a venture capitalist. I believe there is no question that the skills involved in finding the best founders are based on pattern recognition. The more founders a venture capitalist sees in action, the better their ability to "know it when they see it."

5. "There are fundamental differences between an angel, what I call an amateur investor, and being a professional investor, a venture capitalist."

Once a person is investing other people's money, he or she is no longer an angel but rather a professional investor. Great professional seed-stage investors like Ron Conway and Mike Maples Jr.

should, in my view, be referred to not as angels but as professional seed-stage investors. Professional investors provide much more than money and are far less likely to distract the founders with requests that do not add value.

6. "We want to be doing what used to be called venture capital, not growth capital."

Venture capitalists who excel in the early stage of a business provide much more than money to the business. Late-stage financing is often more about finance than receiving significant help from a venture capitalist to build a business. The move of large mutual funds and others into the growth capital business has naturally pushed some venture capitalists to focus on earlier financing rounds where they can add more value.

7. "Many entrepreneurs are raising more money than they need, and it can cause derivative consequences down the road that are not healthy."

Stories have been written about venture capitalists pushing a startup to raise too much money. Experienced venture capitalists often spend time with entrepreneurs counseling them to raise less money, not more. The experienced investor know that if a business raises too much money, there can be a tendency to use suboptimal approaches to solving the inevitable problems that arise early in the existence of a startup. Trying to solve those problems with money rather than strategy tends to cause dysfunction in one form or another. In other words, solving hard problems with just money does not scale. The better approach is to solve problems with innovation and a sound business culture. For example, it may be possible to use money to retain a talented but divisive software developer who is threatening to quit, but a better approach may be providing coaching or inviting the person to leave the business for another opportunity.

8. "First principle: The team you build is the company you build."

Rabois said that he first heard this phrase from Vinod Khosla when he joined the board of Square. Some investors believe that everything in a business starts with people. Other people would argue that product is more important, but it is clear that both are foundational elements in building a business. Still other venture capitalists believe that a massive addressable market is most important. One could argue that the process of ranking which element is most important is a bit like asking a parent which of their children is their favorite. Most parents would answer, "I like them all the same."

9. "There are two categories of good people: there is ammunition and there are barrels. You can add all the ammunition you want, but if you only have five barrels in your company, you can literally only do five things simultaneously. If you add one barrel, you can suddenly do a sixth; if you add another, you can do seven. So finding those barrels that you can shoot through is key."

I once met with one of the top executives at Boeing with Craig McCaw, and the executive said that of the tens of thousands of engineers in the company, only seven were capable of designing an entire airplane. And he said he could name each of those seven engineers. These engineers are the equivalent of what Rabois calls barrels. Barrels are the unique employees who give other employees direction toward a goal. Finding and hiring barrels is difficult and occurs rarely. Barrels are scarce in the real world—hiring too many barrels is not a phenomenon often encountered.

10. "Silicon Valley . . . tends to fragment talent across too many companies, so you get a suboptimal number of successful companies."

Generally speaking you want to hire people who share first principles, which involve strategy, people, and culture.

As you get into the uncharted territory where you don't actually have any intellectual background, you need perspectives from people who are very different from you. At that point, it's actually quite valuable to have people who are diverse.

There are only so many great founders with audacious ideas possessing convexity, as well as talented engineers and other team members who can create a great business. This scarcity tends to create strong rivalries in the venture industry since the competition for the best talent is intense.

11. "Matching your priorities against your time is really important."

The scarcest resource of any venture capitalist is his or her own time. A venture capitalist can sit on only so many company boards or help so many businesses with recruiting. Firms or partners can invest in only so many startups before they dilute themselves and begin to underperform.

12. "Your job as an executive is to edit—not to write. Every time you do something, you should think through and ask yourself, 'Am I writing or am I editing?' And you should immediately be able to tell the difference."

What came to mind when I read this quote is Eric Schmidt's advice to Marissa Mayer:

> "It's your job as leadership to be defense, not offense. The team decides we're running in this direction, and it's your job to clear the path, get things out of the way, get the obstacles out of the way, make it fast to make decisions, and let them run as far and fast as you possibly can.

The executive must decide what is important. Editing should be reserved for matters that are important. More supervision is needed in certain cases, as Rabois points out: "There are people who just know what they don't know, and there are people who don't. Until someone shows the propensity to distinguish between those things you can't let them run amok."

29

Andy Rachleff

Wealthfront

ANDY RACHLEFF COFOUNDED AND was a general partner of Benchmark from 1995 until 2004. Rachleff is one of the deepest thinkers in the venture capital business. The way he has created and articulated a cohesive philosophy of venture capital is unmatched. The more closely you examine his ideas, the more you realize how fundamentally sound and deep they are. His willingness to teach others both by example and in academic settings such as the Stanford Graduate School of Business is an inspiration. Prior to cofounding Benchmark, Rachleff was a general partner with Merrill, Pickard, Anderson & Eyre. He is a cofounder and the executive chair of Wealthfront. He earned a BS from the University of Pennsylvania in 1980 and an MBA from the Stanford Graduate School of Business in 1984.

1. "When a great team meets a lousy market, market wins. When a lousy team meets a great market, market wins. When a great team meets a great market, something special happens."

> If you address a market that really wants your product, if the dogs are eating the dog food, you can screw up everything in the company and you will succeed. Conversely, if you're really good at execution but the dogs don't want to eat the dog food, you have no chance of winning.

A great product in a great market can make an executive look great, regardless of his or her skill. Similarly, when a talented executive tries to achieve success with a lousy offering or a lousy market, the result is inevitably lousy. Warren Buffett has expressed a similar thought: "When a management with a reputation for brilliance tackles a business with a reputation for bad economics, it is the reputation of the business that remains intact." Rachleff wants great management and a great market when he invests.

2. "A disruptive product addresses a market that previously couldn't be served—a new-market disruption—or it offers a simpler, cheaper, or more convenient alternative to an existing product—a low-end disruption. Silicon Valley was built on a culture of designing products that are 'better, cheaper, faster,' but that does not mean they are disruptive."

Anyone involved in a business, or a profession like medicine, can see the pace of innovation is increasing rather than decreasing. That people are no longer buying as much capital equipment (such as machine tools) is not evidence that innovation has slowed. That software is replacing capital goods is obvious to anyone paying attention to the real economy. Innovation is racing ahead, but not all innovation is profitable. A simple way to think about disruption is to say that it happens when one business creates an innovation that is able to harm or eliminate the competitive advantage of another business. Innovation both creates and destroys competitive advantage, and therefore also profit. Consumers always benefit from innovation. Producers only sometimes benefit from innovation, depending on whether the innovation creates or harms a moat.

3. "Instead of starting with the market and then finding the product, the really big winners start with a product and find a market."

Discovering really big new markets can be especially profitable. This is more likely to happen if the product is improved by a non-linear phenomenon, like Moore's law. Google and eBay are often cited as examples of businesses that started with a product and then found a new market. Convincing customers, distributors, and other partners to see the world differently to create this new market is not easy, but it is often the source of a great business.

4. "It's very difficult to manufacture innovation."

Great entrepreneurs are far more missionaries than mercenaries. The missionaries are true to their insight, and the money is secondary to it. Mercenaries, whose primary goal is money, fall somewhere on the middle of the entrepreneur bell curve. They seldom have the desire to change the world that is required for a really big outcome, or the patience to see their idea through. I don't begrudge them their early payouts. They're just not the best entrepreneurs.

Since only a very small number of new grand slams created each year are what drive the bulk of venture capital returns, the odds are low that the same founder will get lighting in a bottle at that level multiple times. It is possible for a given person to hit more than one of those grand slams, but there is a top-down constraint on the total number of people who succeed at that level. People who flip the business early or midstream usually do not last long enough to do this. Experience has shown that it is very likely to be genuine passion and domain knowledge, and not what Rachleff calls "manufacturing innovation," that produces grand slams.

5. "We never meet with companies that aren't referred or where we don't know the entrepreneurs."

It's sort of a test, if you can't get an introduction to the venture capitalist you are unlikely to succeed in selling the other constituencies.

Being an entrepreneur requires effective selling in the broadest sense of the word. Entrepreneurs must sell ideas, products and services, partners, investors, prospective employees, the media, and so on. Above all, they must sell the idea behind the company to investors.

6. "Venture capital is a very cyclical business. So there was a cycle from 1980 to 1983 that looked a lot like 1996 to 1999. Only an order of magnitude smaller on every dimension."

I don't think a bubble is an environment where things are valued highly; I think it's an environment where crappy companies are valued highly.

Rachleff and many other investors are fans of the famous investor Howard Marks. Marks is fond of pointing out that business cycles will always exist and that the best approach is to expect their inevitable and unpredictable changes. Marks cautions that you can prepare but not predict. Venture capital is more cyclical than many other markets. The timing of business cycles in different industries and sectors is often not synchronized, which makes life both interesting and challenging. Venture capitalists prepare for this by having committed capital so they have liquidity at all times but, more importantly, have cash during a downturn.

Some of the best investments are made during a market correction since talent is easier to hire and other resources are more widely available.

7. "All our advice on Silicon Valley careers is based on a simple idea: that your choice of company trumps everything else. It's more important than your job title, your pay, or your responsibilities."

Feedback is what drives returns in today's markets, and as Reid Hoffman has said, what company you work for and who you learn from matters more than ever. Networking "early and often" is an excellent approach to business, and life, especially in a digital world. Building a network is a skill. Learning to give to others first and to be trustworthy are invaluable life lessons. The more you give to others, the more you get, especially in a networked economy.

8. "Human beings want returns, but they don't like risk."

Most people talk a good game about risk and uncertainty but will typically back off when it comes time to actually do anything. This tendency of most people to be risk averse means that some people who are skillful and comfortable with risk can sometimes find a mispriced bet.

9. "It doesn't matter how many losers you have, all that matters is how big your winners are."

You can only lose one times your money as a venture capitalist. You make bets, and you have to be willing to be wrong a lot. It's one of the few industries I know of where you can be wrong 70 percent of the time and be brilliant.

No one has made this point more simply than Michael Mauboussin: "The frequency of correctness does not matter; it is the magnitude of correctness that matters." Much of what venture capitalists invest in are businesses that sell a product that is social in nature, and anything social will experience cumulative advantage and path dependence. That tends to produce a few huge winners and lots of startups that fail.

10. "When it comes to investing in venture capital,
I would follow the old Groucho Marx dictum about
'never joining a club that would have you as a member.'"

The very best venture capital firms do not need your money. The odds that you will get a chance to invest in a top-ten venture capital firm are low since such firms have longstanding limited partners who invest in every fund. The best venture capital firms can often raise far more money but do not since doing so would drag down financial returns. Venture capital is a business that does not scale well. For example, a venture capital firm might decide to raise $400 million even though they could raise $800 million, or in some cases far more. The more a firm takes on from limited partners, the harder it is to more than triple that money during the life of the fund.

The takeaway for founders is that they should find the very best investors they can. Obviously, not every startup can get funding from a venture firm in the top 10 percent.

11. "Investment can be explained with a two-by-two matrix.
On one axis you can be right or wrong. And on the other axis
you can be consensus or non-consensus. Now obviously if you're
wrong you don't make money. . . . What most people don't
realize is if you're right and consensus, you don't make money.
The returns get arbitraged away. The only way as an investor

262

and as an entrepreneur to make outsized returns is
by being right and nonconsensus."

You cannot outperform a crowd unless you are sometimes contrarian, and *right* enough times when you decide to be contrarian. Ideally this means making investments with convex outcomes.

12. "Other than my wife, Bruce Dunlevie is the most influential person in my life. His advice was to always put the gun in the other person's hand. In other words, if you are in negotiations with someone, you tell them to tell you what they think is fair, and then you do it. It's a much better way to live to give trust first, rather than to make someone prove he is trustworthy."

The venture capitalist Bruce Dunlevie is someone I have learned a lot from, especially about being a thoughtful, well-rounded, trustworthy human being. A colleague with these qualities is a fine thing to have in life. As a bonus, when you develop a network of high-quality people whom you can trust, you have what Charlie Munger calls a "seamless web of deserved trust"—which enables efficiency and better financial returns. But these benefits should not distract anyone from the fact that being a good person is its own reward.

30

Naval Ravikant

AngelList

NAVAL RAVIKANT IS THE CEO and cofounder of AngelList. Ravikant previously cofounded Epinions (which went public as part of Shopping.com) and Vast.com. Ravikant also worked in the strategic planning group at @Home Network and served as a consultant in the high-tech practice area of the Boston Consulting Group. He was a seed investor in many businesses including Optimizely, Postmates, Stack Overflow, Thumbtack, Twitter, Uber, and Wish. Ravikant earned degrees in computer science and economics from Dartmouth College.

1. "The cost of starting a company has collapsed."

As the cost of running a startup experiment is coming down, more experiments are being run.

Three years ago, companies could for the first time get all the way through a prototype of a service before they even raised seed money. Two years ago, they could make it through launch before raising money. Now, they can start to get traction with a user base by the time they come looking for seed money.

Entrepreneurs are engaged in "deductive tinkering" as they search for better products and services. Eric Ries describes the process this way: "Learning how to build a sustainable business is the outcome of experiments that follow a three-step process. Build, measure, learn." Why is experimentation so important in an economy? Because experimentation is the best way to deal with complex, adaptive systems, such as the economy.

An economy is a complex system in that it is networked and therefore adaptive, unlike a simple formalism, such as that used in classical physics, which is unable to accurately predict outcomes. In the case of complex, adaptive systems, such as an economy or a business, the correct approach is to discover solutions via trial and error rather than prediction. Nassim Taleb describes why the experimentation approach works well in business:

> It is in complex systems, ones in which we have little visibility of the chains of cause–consequences, that tinkering, bricolage, or similar variations of trial and error have been shown to vastly outperform the teleological—it is nature's modus operandi. But tinkering needs to be convex; it is imperative. . . . Critically what is desired is to have the option, not the obligation, to keep the result, which allows us to retain the upper bound and be unaffected by adverse outcomes.

As an example of a convex financial proposition, the most a founder or venture capitalist can lose is 100 percent of what they invest in a startup, yet they can potentially gain many multiples of that investment.

2. "Success rates are definitely coming down, but that is because the cost of running a startup experiment is coming down, so more experiments are being run. In the old days, we would have one company spend $10 million to figure out

if it has a market. Today, maybe that same company
could do it under $1 to $2 million. The capital, as a whole,
may make the same or better returns, but yeah, if the failures
don't cost half of what they used to, you are actually
saving money; it is a more efficient market."

More experiments inevitably mean more failures on an absolute basis.
As the rate of business experimentation rises, there will inevitably be
an increase in the number of poseurs trying to create new businesses,
which will increase failure rates. A lower overall success rate caused
by an increase in the number of experiments is a positive tradeoff
overall, however, since society benefits from the increased innovation. This net societal benefit occurs even though most experiments
fail and some experiments are being conducted on the margin by
poseurs who have little or no idea what they are doing. Some failure
is essential to the capitalist process since it is experimentation and
innovation that fuel success. What the vast reduction in the cost of
running business experiments has done is radically increase the pace
of the innovation discovery process. Because the creative destruction process is now operating as if it has taken steroids, the rate at
which profit is turned into consumer surplus has never been greater,
especially in the technology sector. A real economy is messy, with lots
of failure. But failure is an essential part of the process of creating
innovation and a healthy economy. Failure is literally everywhere
and is essential to making capitalism work.

3. "The funding market is so bifurcated because outcomes are so bifurcated."

Startup outcomes fall on a power-law distribution. So startup
financings look the same way. You're unfundable until you're
oversubscribed.

The nature of the markets has in many cases become more con-
sumerized. People have caught on to how network effects work.

Network effects are increasingly driving both financial success and failure. Google is an example of a company generating strong network effects. Motorola and BlackBberry are examples of businesses that lost network effects. Since venture investors increasingly understand that the network-effects phenomenon is what determines success, they are investing more money in a smaller number of firms, those deemed to have momentum since they were first to achieve product–market fit. As a result, some businesses can easily raise billions of dollars in venture capital whereas other firms cannot raise even small amounts of capital.

4. "The Internet is very efficiently arbitraged. Anything you can think of has been thought of and tried. The only way you're going to find something is if you stick to it at an irrational level and try a whole bunch of things."

The number of business experiments being conducted is increasing so quickly that the more obvious opportunity spaces for entrepreneurs are being exhausted with unprecedented efficiency and speed. There are fewer places to hide from the relentless pace of competition if a businessperson's plan is to do something conventional. This phenomenon places a premium on genuine product breakthroughs, often resulting from original research and development and rapid and frequent experimentation.

5. "You get paid for being right first, and to be first, you can't wait for consensus."

In a modern networked economy, the first business to achieve product–market fit often wins. This means that an entrepreneur who is timid because he or she is making a contrarian bet is at a tremendous disadvantage. If another business starts its flywheel first by correctly making the same contrarian bet, catching up can be impossible or prohibitively expensive. Speed and agility have never been so important in business.

6. "The market has to be huge because everyone makes mistakes. You never quite get it right the first time. Companies that don't do giant pivots are always doing micro-pivots. You need a large enough market that you can pivot in . . ."

Venture capitalists and entrepreneurs have always favored large addressable markets. But owing to the increasing levels of competition caused by advances in technology, this has never been more true than it is today. Having a huge addressable market increases the convexity of the potential financial outcome since it increases optionality. In other words, there is more room for a business to make adjustments if the addressable market is large. In contrast, small addressable markets provide entrepreneurs with fewer options and are not as convex.

7. "A $1 billion seed fund would destroy the entire market and put prices up 20 percent overnight."

> We don't think we can allocate that kind of capital without distorting the market.
>
> Even the $400 million we raised will be spread out over six to eight years. Maybe the first year, we'll deploy $20 or $30 million as we figure out the model, and then scale it out.

The market for venture capital is top-down constrained by the potential for financial exits for businesses created by entrepreneurs. This scalability problem, which Fred Wilson and others have written about, means that in a country like the United States, only about eight hundred startups raised venture capital for the first time in 2016. This constraint is driven by the fact that an economy is limited in its ability to absorb new businesses. The capacity of an economy to provide venture-backed businesses with financial exits does gradually rise over time, however. In theory, the total dollar value of exits could grow bigger faster than in the past, but in practice, the numbers do not suggest that as likely to happen.

8. "It's just as hard to build a large company as it is a small company, so founders might as well build a large company. It's roughly the same effort."

If a founder has the choice between doing one of two things that involve roughly the same amount of work and effort with equal odds of success, but the payoff of one is potentially huge whereas for the other it is relatively small, it is a simple decision to select the one with the bigger payoff. All the decision requires is a basic opportunity-cost analysis. Many important decisions should be made the same way, but unfortunately this is too rarely the case. All investment opportunities should be considered on the basis of expected value. Warren Buffett's advice is to "take the probability of loss times the amount of possible loss from the probability of gain times the amount of possible gain. That is what we're trying to do. It's imperfect, but that's what it's all about."

9. "I use Warren Buffett's criteria for assessing the team: Intelligence, Integrity and Energy. You want someone who is really smart, very hardworking, and trustworthy. A lot of people forget the integrity part, but if you don't have that, then you have a really hardworking crook, and they will find a way to cheat you."

Intelligence and energy are easier to measure. Integrity is the most important factor.

Having an honest colleague or partner increases the optionality of an investment since trust gives you more options. Decisions can get made faster and with greater confidence. The work is more fun. Life is better. Research studies show that "high-trust societies achieve higher economic growth due to lower transaction costs. Since trust protects property and contractual rights, it is not necessary to divert resources from production to protection." These ideas about the value of trust apply at both a company and personal level. One reason the innovation economy is still so concentrated in Silicon Valley is because of the Valley's highly interconnected trust network. Everyone knows everyone else, and there are lots of easy ways to check out and validate (or invalidate) new entrepreneurs and investors.

10. "Companies only fail for two reasons: The founder gives up, or they run out of money."

Don't be proud. Get the cash wherever you can. Cash is everything.

Raise twice as much, and make it last four times as long. Pretend that you don't have the money in the bank; run lean. Assuming your unit economics are at least breakeven, keep your headcount low, raise money, and stay in it for the long haul. It takes a decade to build a great company. There are no short cuts.

The only unforgivable sin in business is to run out of cash. What does cash give a business? Options. What do options create? Convexity! By now you have probably figured out that convexity is everywhere, if you know how to look. Ravikant says,

There is a whole set of companies that are not financeable by the venture community: service businesses, markets that are heavily played out. If you are fighting a war that has already been won, . . . you better have some really core differentiation and traction. Other disqualifiers include not enough technical people on the team, . . . if you are completely out of market, . . . pre-launch companies tend to not do well, . . . and teams that have no credibility. The companies that fail to raise funding are the ones that use too many words and too few actions. Your biography is a record of your past actions. Your execution on your current business is a record of your current actions. Talking about what you are going to do in the future is almost pointless. Talking about what you can become is almost pointless. People want evidence. There is a lot of talk out there.

Most startups are unable to raise venture capital, but this is not the end of the world for those businesses. There are many ways to finance a business that do not involve venture capital.

11. "When building a startup, microeconomics is fundamental; macroeconomics is entertainment."

Getting real traction is hard. Raising millions of dollars is hard. Building a sustainable, long-term company is hard. Your pre-traction company has not achieved product–market fit, and so it has a hard time hiring.

There isn't a shortage of developers and designers. There's a surplus of founders.

Understanding microeconomics is essential if you want to be successful in business. The distinction between micro- and macroeconomics was explained by Charlie Munger at the 2016 Berkshire Hathaway shareholder meeting: "Microeconomics is what we do; macro is what we have to put up with."

12. "It seems like too many people, public and private sector, are making a living slicing the pie rather than baking it."

Life is far too short to work with poseurs. If you hang out with people who do not actually do anything, there is a significant danger that you will eventually start to adopt doing nothing as your own standard practice. Those that can do, do. Find and work with them. It is that simple. Nothing is better than making a positive difference.

31

Heidi Roizen
Draper Fisher Jurvetson

HEIDI ROIZEN IS CURRENTLY an operating partner at the Silicon Valley–based venture firm DFJ. She is a pioneering entrepreneur, corporate executive, corporate director, venture capitalist, and educator. Roizen understood very early in her career how important relationships are in the technology world. She cofounded the software company T/Maker and was its CEO for over a dozen years. After a year as vice-president of worldwide developer relations at Apple, she became a venture capitalist. Between 1999 and 2007, Roizen was a managing director at Mobius Venture Capital. She has also served on the board of TiVo, Great Plains Software, and the Software Publishers Association, among other firms and organizations. She has an undergraduate degree from Stanford University and an MBA from the Stanford Graduate School of Business.

1. "Even though the numbers will likely be wrong,
the thinking behind how you arrived at those numbers is
critically important. . . . Think of each assumption as a dial.

Which ones connect to things that matter, and what impact would they have on your ultimate outcome if they turn out to be only half as effective—or then again, twice as effective? Of the ones with the biggest impact, what underlying factors determine *their* outcome? Which ones can kill your business?"

It is amazing how much credibility some people give to numbers once they are in a spreadsheet. The numbers in a spreadsheet are just numbers. Too often they are someone's wild guess or spreadsheet "goal-seek" plugin. The reality is that a spreadsheet is all about the assumptions underlying the numbers, and these are usually hidden until you go looking for them. If garbage goes into a spreadsheet, garbage comes out. What Roizen is saying here is that it is the relationship among the numbers (and in particular, their sensitivity to each other in a financial model) that can provide the greatest insight. For example, if it costs a lot to acquire a customer, you can learn from the financial model that customer churn is particularly harmful and that investing heavily in customer retention would be a very good idea. Similarly, if you are spending more than 50 percent of revenue on sales and marketing, you need to ensure your cost of goods sold is low.

2. "One of the biggest mistakes entrepreneurs made in the last couple of years is, 'Hey, I own a company, and I sold 50 percent of it for $5 million, and the day that $5 million gets in my bank, I've got $2.5 million.' No, you don't. You have $5 million of debt and usually three or four liquidity preferences and participation you must pay back before you ever see a dime. That money is very dear and very precious, and that's why I would caution everyone that terms are more important than valuation. Many of our investments will be lost, and we won't ever see that money again. But if there's any value in the company that gets created as a result of your sweat and our money, it's our money that's paid first."

Inexperienced entrepreneurs pay too little attention to deal terms. It is extremely important to understand the terms that govern issues like liquidation preferences. Money raised can be much more expensive than many founders and CEOs imagine, especially if all they pay attention to is the cash received up front and not the terms of the financing. Dilution is painful, yet some people think that the best use of money raised is a fancy office with a spectacular view.

3. "When you're the CEO, you have the least freedom, because you can't just quit."

I raised that money. I hired every one of these people. I gave those venture capitalists my commitment that I was going to bring it home for them. I'm not just going to walk out the door. I remember walking into my company every day. We had about one hundred employees. And I would count the cars in the parking lot, and I would think about the car payments and the mortgage payments.

You do not need to be the CEO to feel responsible for fellow employees when involved in a startup. When I worked for a startup, I often thought about employees not being able to make their mortgage payments or having to go home to their families without a job. Responsibility is a tremendous motivator, if you are a responsible person. Of course, some people will be there for you in a crisis or when things turn out badly, but others will not.

4. "Entrepreneurship is a team sport with very many lonely moments."

I was once an entrepreneur, and I did not live a balanced life. I think we live our lives in a serial fashion—there are periods where you won't have time to do everything you want. If you're really excited about something, you can run on that for a while.

275

In the 1990s, I spent five years of my life flying five hundred thousand (mostly international) air miles a year, almost always by myself doing business development at a startup. My life was not balanced. At the time, I felt there were three things I could do: work, family, and personal life. I decided to focus on the first two. To say you will make no tradeoffs in building a startup business is, in my view, unrealistic. You can say that you will try to balance things out later, but sometimes, or even all too often, that balancing out does not happen. Starting a business is an extreme sport. It works better if your significant other is a candidate for sainthood.

5. "If you want to be the smartest person in the room, you're going to build a crummy team. Do you really want a VP of sales who knows less about sales than you? Do you want a CFO who knows less about accounting? No, of course not. You have to take risks to find the right people and then trust in those relationships. Your job becomes empowering those people and making sure they get along. My goal is always to be the dumbest person in the room because I want to be surrounded by really bright, really amazing people. That's when exciting, world-changing things get done."

The best and most talented people want to work with the best and most talented people. The key to the success of a business is generating positive feedback loops, and hiring the very best people is arguably the most important positive feedback loop of all.

6. "The most important thing you have is time because you can't make more of it."

Time is almost always your scarcest resource. Spend it wisely. Find ways to cut off people and activities that are a time sink. As Peter Drucker once said, "There is nothing so useless as doing efficiently that which should not be done at all."

7. "Not every deal should have VCs."

There are a lot of businesses that can produce an attractive financial return that are not candidates for venture capital. These businesses can be bootstrapped or built based on sources of capital such as savings and bank loans. Lots of people build their businesses without raising a penny of venture capital. Some very successful businesses do not raise venture capital for many years after starting. They may start out as lifestyle businesses and grow more than their founders imagined. Bill Gurley points out that "it's only cheap to build two-to-three-person companies with sweat equity. The minute you start paying engineers, you will realize it is quite expensive." If founders want to create the potential for grand-slam financial outcomes, however, they will need to raise venture capital to generate the necessary growth.

8. "When you fail, and we all fail all the time, get over it. . . . Own up to it, make amends, make sure you don't let it happen again, and move on."

Mistakes are a useful part of most processes, as long as they are not too big and as long as the mistakes made are new ones. Failure is a necessary part of venture capitalism since it is an essential part of harvesting convexity. You cannot make an omelet without breaking eggs, but you can also break a lot of eggs without ever making a decent omelet.

9. "Things outside of your control will happen. You need to lean into this fact."

So much in life is determined by luck. She is saying you often have no control over what happens in life and when it does you must face the change and deal with it head on. When something unfortunate happens the worst thing you can do is deny that it is happening.

10. "The twenty-forty-sixty rule: In our twenties, we worry about what other people say about us. At forty, we realize it's not important to worry about what people say, and at sixty, we acknowledge that no one was thinking about us."

> Your boss is not thinking about you. Your peers are not thinking about you. You need to think about you.

When people feel embarrassed about a failure they have experienced in life, it is often the case that they are the only ones who actually noticed what happened. Do not worry. Reboot your personal energy and move on. In a functional culture, "failure" is just another word for "experienced." Similarly, when you think someone is looking after you, the reality is next to no one is. So it is wise to take care of yourself and treasure the few people who do care about you. If you find a supportive work environment, treasure that, too.

11. "'Networking' is a negative term that means climbing the monkey bars. It's about building relationships and connecting with people you find interesting."

> Be relationship oriented as opposed to transaction oriented.
>
> Building your network also means starting with what you can give.
>
> There is this book called *Drive*, by Daniel Pink, where he talks about the rule of reciprocity—which means if you do someone a favor, they will feel more obligated to do something for you."

I have cowritten a book about building strong relationships entitled *The Global Negotiator*, which is free to download on my blog. The book's overall message is simple: Build relationships rather than do deals. In his book *Influence*, Robert Cialdini describes the reciprocity principle simply: "People will help if they owe you for something you did in the past to advance their goals. That's the rule of reciprocity." The reverse is also true: When you do someone a disfavor, you will often find that disfavor reciprocated.

12. "Negotiation is the process of finding the maximal intersection of mutual need."

To create a durable relationship, it is best to focus on the intersection of mutual need rather than try to create a clever legal agreement. The pace of change today means that it is impossible to anticipate how the world will change in an agreement. Relying on lawyers to enforce deals should be a last resort.

32

Mark Suster

Upfront Ventures

MARK SUSTER IS AN entrepreneur, angel investor, and the managing partner of Upfront Ventures. Suster is the godfather of the rising Los Angeles startup and venture capital community. He is generous with advice and writes and speaks clearly. He is also fearless in terms of the positions he takes on issues, even if they are contrarian, which makes what he says quite interesting. Before joining Upfront Ventures, Suster was vice-president of product management at Salesforce.com following its acquisition of Koral, where Suster was the founder and CEO. Prior to Koral, Mark was the founder and CEO of BuildOnline, a European software-as-a-service (SaaS) company. Mark received a BA in economics from the University of California, San Diego, and an MBA from the University of Chicago.

1. "If it's your first time getting funding, you shouldn't over-raise. Take whatever the right amount of money is for you, whether that's $1 million, $5 million, or $10 million."

Try to raise eighteen to twenty-four months of capital.

When the hors d'oeuvres are passed, take two. . . . But, put one in your pocket.

What I like about raising less money is it allows you to move slower, and with a new company, you don't really know what the demand for your startup will be. If you realize, "Holy crap, we're on to something here," then you can always raise more money.

If you raise, say, $7 million off the bat, you're on the express train. It's either a big outcome or nothing if you assume investors are expecting four times [4X] their money. Keep in mind that companies aren't regularly bought for $100 million-plus either.

VCs want meaningful ownership . . . and the "fairway" is 25 to 33 percent of your company.

Be careful about ever dipping below six months of cash in the bank. You start fundraising when you have nine months left and begin to panic if you get down below three months.

The right amount of money to raise and to have on hand in any given case will depend on factors including the following:

- The nature of the business (e.g., how capital intensive it is, how high the customer acquisition cost is, how high the burn rate is)
- The current state of the business cycle, which is constantly in flux; venture capital is a very cyclical business

Bill Gates famously wanted enough cash in the bank to cover a full year of expenses in the early years of Microsoft, but that was a different time and place with very different business models, and the business was generating that cash internally. Microsoft raised no venture capital, except for a small amount near the initial public offering to convince a specific investor to join the board of directors.

2. "There is no 'right' amount of burn. Pay close attention to your runway."

Your value creation must be at least three times [3X] the amount of cash you're burning, or you're wasting investor value. Think: If you raise $10 million at a $30 million pre- ($40 million post-), that investor needs you to exit for at least $120 million (three times) to hit his or her *minimum* return target that his or her investors are expecting. So money spent should add equity value or create IP [Intellectual Property] that eventually will.

Raising venture capital is like adding rocket fuel to your company— which leads to a lot of bad behavior.

There is a big difference between a cash burn rate that is too high and valuations that are too high. The media has a tendency to transform information about burn rates being too high into a comment about valuations being too high. I suspect this happens because the concept of wealth is both easier to understand and a topic with which readers are fascinated. But burn rate and valuation are not the same. Businesses can be spending too much cash in an environment where valuations are reasonable. Spending too much cash is a fast ticket to painful dilution or a broken capitalization table. Having some cash in reserve can come in very handy when markets essentially stop providing new cash for a period of time.

Bill Gurley tells a great story about how OpenTable had to cut its cash burn rate severely when the ability to raise new cash dried up in the early 2000s when the Internet bubble popped. By conserving cash, the company was able to hang on for many years until growth resumed. Since market disruptions in the short term cannot be predicted with certainty, some amount of cash cushion has positive optionality.

3. "The average VC, traditional VC, does two deals per year . . . from maybe one thousand approaches."

A founder should not take it personally if a venture capitalist does not want to invest in his or her startup. There are many reasons potential investors say no. Entrepreneurs should also remember that the numbers cited by Suster here refer only to venture capitalists (individuals, not firms) in the top-one hundred; these individuals make only about two hundred investments a year. Given that about four thousand startups are looking for funding in a given year, not all will be funded by a top–one hundred venture capitalist. The scarcest asset a venture capitalist has is time, and as a result, he or she can be helpful to only so many portfolio companies and serve effectively on so many company boards. In other words, a venture capitalist is more time limited than capital limited.

4. "You have to ask for the order."

In order to sell a product successfully, you need to "ask for the order." If you do not, you will never close a sale. The best product or service does not always win if the team does not learn how to sell it. It can be awkward for some people to ask someone to buy something. Other people have no problem doing so. Why this is true is a bit of a mystery, but I have noticed over the years that people who were B and C students in school "ask for the order" more easily than A students as a general rule. People who were A students often seem to think they should not have to ask. It is a helpful life experience to spend some time selling something. It usually makes you a better buyer and certainly a better seller.

5. "Tenacity is probably the most important attribute in an entrepreneur. It's the person who never gives up— who never accepts no for an answer."

What do I look for in an entrepreneur when I want to invest? I look for a lot of things, actually: persistence (above all else), resiliency, leadership, humility, attention to detail, street smarts, transparency, and both obsession with their companies and a burning desire to win.

There are times in the life of every successful startup when it seems to be flying inches from disaster and close to death. If the founders and leadership of the company lose their nerve and persistence, the outcome is very seldom pretty.

6. "I hate losing. I really hate losing. But you need to embrace losing if you want to learn. Channel your negative energy. Revisit why you lost. Ask for real and honest feedback. Don't be defensive about it—try to really understand it. But also look beyond it to the hidden reasons you lost. And channel the lessons to your next competition."

> I think the sign of a good entrepreneur is the ability to spot your mistakes, correct quickly, and not repeat the mistakes. I made plenty of mistakes.
>
> The excuse department is now closed.
>
> There are a lot of people with big mouths and small ears. They do a lot of talking; they only stop to listen to figure out the next time they can talk.

Learning from your mistakes is such a simple idea. There is nothing like rubbing your own nose in a mistake to force yourself to confront what needs to be changed. The best founders actually make the changes necessary to adapt rather than merely talk about change. One way to better identify mistakes is to surround yourself with people you can trust to honestly tell you how they see things. If you have someone in your life who is loyal and trustworthy, listens well, has good judgment, and is willing to give you sound advice, you have something truly invaluable.

7. "It's in the down market that real entrepreneurs are formed."

The best time to form a business is often in a down market. People are easier to recruit, and there is less competition. For example, the ability of Google, founded in 1998, to hire great people was enhanced by the downturn caused by the Internet bubble popping a few years later.

8. "If you have options in life, you won't get screwed."

Getting to Yes became a bestseller owing to this simple idea. In the book, which is about negotiation, Roger Fisher and William L. Ury discuss the importance of having a BATNA (best alternative to a negotiated agreement). When you have an alternative, you can get better terms and a better price. As a simple example of this principle in operation, you should never agree to buy anything before agreeing on terms—including price. Negotiate before you agree to do something, not afterward.

9. "You can read lots of books or blogs about being an entrepreneur, but the truth is you'll really only learn when you get out there and do it. The earlier you make your mistakes, the quicker you can get on to building a great company."

If you're going to lead an early-stage business, you need to be on top of all your details. You need to know your financial model. You need to be involved in the product design. You need to have a detailed grasp of your sales pipeline. You need to be hands on.

The skill that you need to be good at to be effective as an entrepreneur is synthesis.

Don't let your PR get ahead of product quality.

Your competitors have just as much angst as you do. You read their press releases and think that it's all rainbows and lollipops at their offices. It's not. You're just reading their press bullshit.

Do not be dismissive of your competition.

Successful founders tend to have a big bag of skills that are the result of a mix of real-world experience and natural aptitude. Everyone makes mistakes, but some people have the ability to maintain a higher ratio of new mistakes to repeated mistakes. Successful founders pay attention and learn. They know how to multitask. And they surround themselves with smart people who also confront their own mistakes. One good test of whether you are looking at your mistakes is: Have you changed your mind on any significant issues over the past year? If you have not, how deep are you digging? How much are you thinking?

10. "Entrepreneurs don't 'noodle'; they 'do.' This is what separates entrepreneurs from big-company executives, consultants, and investors. Everybody else has the luxury of 'analysis' and Monday-morning quarterbacking. Entrepreneurs are faced with a deluge of daily decisions—much of it minutiae. All of it requiring decisions and action."

In the 1990s, I was once in a meeting with a group of venture capitalists on Sand Hill Road, and someone referred to a particular business executive as "Mr. Ship." This was meant as a compliment. What the person meant was that this executive shipped promised products on time. Getting things done is an underrated skill. People who can generate a few months of publicity and look swell gazing off into the distance in a tech publication cover photo are not people who create value in the long term.

11. "Don't hire people who are exactly like you."

When I see a CEO who takes 90 percent of the minutes of a meeting, I assume that as a leader, that person probably doesn't listen to others' opinions as much as they should. Either that or he or she doesn't trust his or her colleagues. Let your team introduce themselves.

Diversity in the broadest possible sense makes for a better team: different and complementary skills, different personalities, different interests, different methods, and different backgrounds. Suster also believes that a genuinely functional team does not rely on a single person to get things done.

12. "Focus on large disruptive markets."

We want the 4 Ms: management, market size, money, momentum.

In the startup world, low gross margin almost always equals death, which is why many Internet retailers have failed or are failing (many operated at 35 percent gross margins). Many software companies have greater-than–80 percent gross margins, which is why they are more valuable than, say, traditional retailers or consumer product companies. But software companies often take longer to scale top-line revenue than retailers, so it takes a while to cover your nut. It's why some journalists enthusiastically declare, "Company X is doing $20 million in revenue" (when said company might be just selling somebody else's physical product) and think that is necessarily good, while in fact that might be much worse than a company doing $5 million in sales (but who might be selling software and have sales that are extremely profitable).

There are a range of things a venture capitalist looks for when investing in a startup. Suster identifies some of these things in the quotes included here. For example: a large addressable market, significant convexity, and high gross margins. He also points to one of my biggest pet peeves about business: journalists obsessed with the top-line revenue of a business. Unfortunately, such journalists too often pass this obsession with top-line revenue on to others. Revenue is not profit. You cannot tell whether a business is creating value with just an income statement. An investor must understand unit economics to understand when value is being created.

33

Peter Thiel

Founders Fund

PETER THIEL IS AN entrepreneur, venture capital investor, and political activist. He cofounded PayPal and, famously, was Facebook's first outside investor. He is unquestionably the most controversial figure in Silicon Valley today owing to his outspoken views and outsized personality. His politics are a mix of libertarian and conservative ideas. He is the president of Clarium Capital and a managing partner of Founders Fund. He is also the coauthor of the book *Zero to One*. Thiel also helped launch and served as chair of Palantir Technologies, an analytical software company. Thiel was born in Germany but moved with his family to the United States as a child. Part of his childhood was also spent living in Africa. He received a BA in philosophy from Stanford University and a law degree from Stanford Law School.

1. "Great companies do three things. First, they create value. Second, they are lasting or permanent in a meaningful way. Finally, they capture at least some of the value they create."

More important than being the first mover is the last mover. You have to be durable.

The most critical thing for every startup is to be doing one thing uniquely well, better than anybody else in the world.

All businesses must create a moat to be sustainably profitable. Unfortunately, sometimes a business that creates new value is not able to capture any of that value in a sustainable way, and the only beneficiary of the business is the customer. One of the best explanations of this value-capture point comes from Charlie Munger's fantastic "Worldly Wisdom" essay:

> There are all kinds of wonderful new inventions that give you nothing as owners except the opportunity to spend a lot more money in a business that's still going to be lousy. The money still won't come to you. All of the advantages from great improvements are going to flow through to the customers.

2. "Maybe we focus so much on going from 1 to *n* because that's easier to do. There's little doubt that going from 0 to 1 is qualitatively different, and almost always harder, than copying something *n* times."

And even trying to achieve vertical, 0-to-1 progress presents the challenge of exceptionalism; any founder or inventor doing something new must wonder, "Am I sane? Or am I crazy?"

Doing something that has never been done before is genuinely hard enough that many people consciously or subconsciously would rather chase the tailpipes of others than genuinely innovate "from 0 to 1." Failing conventionally, rather than succeeding unconventionally, is unfortunately the path chosen by many people. Progressing from 1 to *n* will not generate a new business with a grand slam outcome.

3. "We see the power of compounding when companies
grow virally. Successful businesses tend to have
an exponential arc to them."

Maybe they grow at 50 percent a year, and it compounds for a
number of years. It could be more or less dramatic than that. But
that model—some substantial period of exponential growth—
is the core of any successful tech company. And during that
exponential period, valuations tend to go up exponentially.

It is nonlinear phenomena, the ones that drive the grand-slam
financial outcomes, that a venture capitalist needs to be successful.
Straying too far from a nonlinear phenomenon like Moore's law
can be harmful to a venture capitalist's financial health. Moore's
law is not the only phenomenon with an exponential arc, but it is
an important one. Sam Altman has explained an important reason why people tend to not understand the power of a nonlinear
phenomenon: "The hard part of standing on an exponential curve
is: when you look backward, it looks flat, and when you look forward, it looks vertical." Few things in life are exponential, so it is
relatively easy not to see or understand the impact of something
nonlinear when it happens.

4. "If you're going to start a business, you might as well
try to start one where, if it works, it will be really successful,
rather than one where you're competing like crazy with
thousands of people who are doing something
just like you all the time."

The prime territory for finding mispriced convex outcomes with
the potential to produce a grand slam is not where thousands of
other people are looking. The second point Theil is making here
is that if you are going to swing the bat, you may as well have the
potential for a very significant positive outcome. These two points
are simple but often overlooked.

5. "Consider a two-by-two matrix. On one axis, you have good, high-trust people, and then you have low-trust people. On the other axis, you have low alignment structure with poorly set rules, and then a high alignment structure where the rules are well set. Good, high-trust people with low alignment structure is basically anarchy. The closest to this that succeeded is Google from 2000 to maybe 2007. Talented people could work on all sorts of different projects and generally operate without a whole lot of constraints. Sometimes the opposite combination—low-trust people and lots of rules—can work, too. This is basically totalitarianism. Foxconn might be a representative example. Lots of people work there. People are sort of slaves. The company even installs suicide nets to catch workers when they jump off the buildings. But it's a very productive place, and it sort of works."

The low-trust, low-alignment model is a dog-eat-dog sort of world, argues Thiel. It is best to avoid this combination. Thiel believes that the ideal combination is high-trust people with a structure that provides a high degree of alignment since those people are rowing in the same direction, and not by accident. Equity incentives, properly structured, are an important way to create alignment in startups. Table 33.1 provides an illustration of Thiel's two-by-two matrix.

Table 33.1

	Low Trust	High Trust
Low alignment, poorly set rules	Worst investments (e.g., investing in an investment bank)	Example: Google from 2000 to about 2007
High alignment, well-set rules	Example: Foxconn	Ideal startup or company

6. "Angel investors may have no clue how to do valuations. Convertible notes allow you to postpone the valuation question for series A investors to tackle. Other benefits include mathematically eliminating the possibility of having a down round. This can be a problem where angels systematically overvalue companies."

> If you must have a down round, it's probably best that it be a really catastrophic one. That way, a lot of the mad people will be completely wiped out and thus won't show up to create more problems, while you start the hard task of rebuilding. You should never have a down round. If you found a company and every round you raise is an up round, you'll make at least some money. But if you have a single down round, you probably won't.

Thiel is saying that there are many angels investing today who can mess up a capitalization table via a poorly priced valuation. A down round happens when a business raises capital at a lower valuation than that of the previous round. In a down round, some investors will often get a larger number of shares based on antidilution provisions in the contracts used in the previous round. This dilution can lower the incentive of employees and founders to stay with the business.

7. "A robust company culture is one in which people have something in common that distinguishes them quite sharply from the rest of the world. If everybody likes ice cream, that probably doesn't matter . . . you also need to strike the right balance between athletes (competitive people) and nerds (creators) no matter what."

Thiel is describing some of the core elements of a winning business culture, such as a unique shared mission and the right mix of passionate people. Great leaders know how to create the right mix of these inputs, which can vary from team to team. They can spot the right mix of people via pattern recognition and good judgment. There is no reason why a diverse team cannot have a unique but shared mission.

> 8. "VCs rely on very discreet networks of people that they've become affiliated with. That is, they have access to a unique network of entrepreneurs; the network is the core value proposition."

Personal networks of all kinds matter more than ever as the world becomes more and more digital. Your personal network of individuals and organizations can grow in power and value in just the same way. More than ever, success begets success. This happens because connections create what Nassim Taleb calls optionality. Taleb has said, "Optionality can be found everywhere if you know how to look." Living in a city, going to parties, taking classes, acquiring entrepreneurial skills, having cash in your bank account, and avoiding debt are all examples of activities that increase optionality. Working purposefully to develop your network can pay big dividends.

> 9. "The founders or one or two key senior people at any multimillion-dollar company should probably spend between 25 percent and 33 percent of their time identifying and attracting talent."

The people who do this well have superior pattern recognition skills, which, as I have said previously, is an important element of good judgment. A top venture capitalist said to me once, "When I see the right team, I feel like I have seen the pattern before. The people and chemistry will not be exactly the same as other successful teams, but there is nevertheless a pattern. The pattern will not be just the same and yet will still seem familiar." The right team will be diverse and its members will have skills and other attributes that complement each other. Levels of trust will be high, and the culture will be tolerant of people who learn via experimentation. Attributes like a strong work ethic and sound judgment are essential.

10. "Hubris is an issue at every one of these Silicon Valley companies that are successful."

It can be hard to know a lot about one area, and even more so about many areas, yet still be modest enough to admit that you do not know everything. The venture capitalist and author Morgan Housel absolutely nailed it when he wrote, "There's a strong correlation between knowledge and humility." Charlie Munger has said that he seeks "intellectual humility" and has pointed out that "acknowledging what you don't know is the dawning of wisdom." The Internet bubble in particular was a period of time during which many otherwise smart people made boneheaded mistakes owing to hubris. As Warren Buffett has said,

> The line separating investment and speculation, which is never bright and clear, becomes blurred still further when most market participants have recently enjoyed triumphs. Nothing sedates rationality like large doses of effortless money. After a heady experience of that kind, normally sensible people drift into behavior akin to that of Cinderella at the ball. They know that overstaying the festivities ¾ that is, continuing to speculate in companies that have gigantic valuations relative to the cash they are likely to generate in the future ¾ will eventually bring on pumpkins and mice. But they nevertheless hate to miss a single minute of what is one helluva party. Therefore, the giddy participants all plan to leave just seconds before midnight. There's a problem, though: They are dancing in a room in which the clocks have no hands.

11. "I've always tried to be contrarian, to go against the crowd, to identify opportunities in places where people are not looking."

You cannot do better than average by being average. If you cannot be courageously contrarian, you cannot possibly beat the market average as an investor. It is the existence of a gap between expected value and market price that should drive investment decision-making. If your views reflect the consensus of the crowd, you are unlikely to outperform a market since a market by definition reflects the consensus view. However, bucking the crowd's viewpoint is not easy in practice since the investor is fighting social proof. In many cases, following the crowd makes sense. Sticking with the warmth of the crowd is a natural instinct for most people.

12. "Bad VCs tend to think that all companies are created equal, and some just fail, spin wheels, or grow. In reality, you get a power-law distribution."

Thiel believes that you can't play "small ball" (i.e., win with just singles and doubles) in venture capital and succeed financially. He advocates a swing-for-the-fences approach that seeks grand-slam outcomes.

34

Fred Wilson

Union Square Ventures

FRED WILSON IS A cofounder and managing partner of Union Square Ventures. Wilson has been a venture capital backer of businesses including Foursquare, Kickstarter, Tumblr, Twitter, and Zynga. Wilson is also the leader of the rising New York startup and venture capital community. His writing, including his blogging at avc.com, is always insightful and interesting. The topics he writes about range from technical (e.g., convertible notes) to social (e.g. health care). He was previously a general partner at Euclid Partners, and he is a cofounder of Flatiron Partners. Wilson has a bachelor's degree in mechanical engineering from the Massachusetts Institute of Technology and an MBA from the Wharton School of the University of Pennsylvania.

1. "Venture capital is a hits business. All of the returns come from the top cohort of investments."

Anything less than three times your money over a ten-year period [is a mediocre return in venture capital].

The money needs to generate 2.5 times net of fees and carry to the investors to deliver a decent return. Fees and carry bump that number to three times gross returns.

Venture capital has always been a place where high-risk ventures can get funded. I think it still is the best kind of capital for somebody who's building a company that has a lot of risk but has a lot of upside as well.

If $100 billion per year in exits is a steady-state number, then we need to work back from that and determine how much the asset class can manage.

A venture capitalist selects a portfolio of investments that have significant convexity. Over the lifetime of the fund, the venture capitalist strives to invest in a way that generates what he or she knows will be a very small number of grand slams. After a successful grand slam emerges, it will seem obvious to many that the grand-slam startup was destined to be a success. This survivor bias causes many who are not involved in the industry to forget that many of the venture capitalist's investments returned no capital. Venture capitalists, however, tend to have less survivor bias in such cases since they watch real companies fail, companies that employ real people whom they like and care about. An experienced venture capitalist knows that "the whole" of what emerges from the startup creation process is not predictable by looking at the sum of the parts.

2. "Ideas that most people derided as ridiculous have produced the best outcomes. Don't do the obvious thing."

Will Rogers made this same point in a different way: "Always drink upstream from the herd." Trying to find positive convexity in areas where others are intensely focused is what investors call a crowded trade (i.e., too many people trying to do the same thing). You cannot do better than a mob if you are part of the mob.

People who follow the crowd and expect success remind me of an old joke: Late one night, a police officer finds a drunk man crawling around on his hands and knees under a streetlight. The drunk tells the police officer that he is looking for his keys. When the police officer asks if he is sure this is where he dropped his keys, the drunk man replies that he believes he dropped them across the street. "Then why are you looking over here?" the officer asks. "Because the light's better here," explains the drunk man.

A venture capitalist who follows the crowd is like the drunk looking for his keys under the streetlight when his keys are across the street.

3. "Getting product right means finding product–market fit. It does not mean launching the product. It means getting to the point where the market accepts your product and wants more of it."

> The first step you need to climb is building a product, getting it into the market, and finding product–market fit. I think that's what seed financing should be used for. The second step you need to climb is to hire a small team that can help you operate and grow the business you have now birthed by virtue of finding product-market fit. That is what series A money is for. The third step you need to climb is to scale that team and ramp revenues and take the market. That is what series B money is for. The fourth step you need to climb is to get to profitability so that your cash flow after all expenses can sustain and grow the business. That is what series C is for. The fifth step is generating liquidity for you, your team, and your investors. That is what the IPO or the secondary is for.

There is a rhythm to raising capital that is essential to understand. No two funding processes are exactly the same, but all tend to follow a roughly similar beat. In other words, there are milestones and heuristics that investors and companies tend to use. To paraphrase Mark Twain, startup financing successes never repeat themselves exactly, but they do rhyme. At the two bookends, getting a valuation that is too high can turn into a painful down round or worse, and selling too cheap can mean painful dilution. Like Goldilocks, the entrepreneur must find something that is "just right" when it comes to financing a business.

> 4. "It is dangerous to ramp up head count and burn
> until you are certain that you have the right product
> and the right people and processes in the organization
> to support the product. And early revenue traction,
> often driven by a passionate founder,
> can be a nasty head fake."

These points remind me of the "margin-of-safety" concept from value investing. Making successful predictions about systems that can be impacted by risk, uncertainty, and ignorance is a process in which errors are inevitable. Having a margin of safety means that even if you make mistakes, you can still win since you have built in a financial safe driving distance. The only unforgivable sin in business is to run out of cash. If you have some cash on hand, you can live to fight again another day if you make a mistake. Trying to grow a business before the value hypothesis is proven to be sound is a mistake.

> 5. "Equity capital is expensive.
> Every time you do a raise, you dilute."

I like to tell the story of a young company founder who told me he was very proud of the expensive new Herman Miller Aeron chairs in his conference room. He bought them with cash that had been invested in his company by some new investors. When I explained to him how much the chairs would eventually cost via dilution if the company went public someday, the smile on his face turned into a frown. Dilution matters. Do the math. It has been said that Warren Buffett can tell you nearly exactly how much income you have forgone if you show him an expensive toy like a sports car. It is a bit unnerving actually, since he does the math so precisely in his head. When a real estate agent shows a founder some expensive potential office space with an expansive water view, the founder should immediately think "Dilution!"

6. "You need more than a lean methodology; you need a lean culture."

To me, lean is a state of mind that a founder and his or her team needs to have across all aspects of the business. The specific product and engineering approaches that are at the core of the lean startup movement are paramount for sure. But if you can apply lean to hiring, sales, marketing, customer service, finance, and everything else, you will be rewarded with a fast, nimble company.

Businesses that are more "lean" in the broadest sense of the word are more agile and can adapt far better to change as a result. Adaptability increases optionality.

Steve Blank notes that "a minimum viable product is not always a smaller [and] cheaper version of your final product." The MVP should deliver value to the customer even though it is not as complete as is could be.

7. "Putting together the initial team, creating the culture, and instilling the mission and values into the team are all like designing and building the initial product."

Most people underestimate how much value a great venture capitalist puts on the people who make up a startup team and their chemistry. Great people on a fantastic team give a startup valuable optionality since they can quickly adapt to change.

8. "You simply can't be tentative in a startup. You have to go for it at every chance you get. And if the leader of the organization is anxious, his or her fear pervades the organization."

Creating a startup, especially in a business with the potential to produce a grand-slam financial result, is an "all-in" process for a founder, employee, or investor. Both fear and fearlessness are contagious. It is particularly important that founders be fearless. Being the fourth person to join a startup that was at one point valued at $3 billion is something I am glad I experienced. But like anything valuable in life, it came with certain tradeoffs. At the time it seemed like the right choice, but it was in some ways totally irrational given my other options at the time. When I look back at the experience, it surprises me how fearless I was about what I was doing.

9. "Being an entrepreneur is hard. Having supportive and caring investors helps."

One of the hardest things to do in the venture business is to stick with a struggling investment.

Experienced venture capitalists know that a successful business is often almost dead before it begins its rise to the top of the league tables. Knowing the difference between a walking-dead business and an opportunity is part of what makes a great venture capitalist.

10. "Reputation is the magnet that brings opportunities to you time and time again. I have found that being nice builds your reputation."

Being a nice person is highly underrated, and its importance is on the rise now that the importance of personal networks is increasing.

Plus, being nice is its own reward. So is being polite. Charlie Munger puts it simply: "Avoid dealing with people of questionable character." Munger believes that by dealing only with ethical people, overhead drops significantly, because you can operate more efficiently owing to a "seamless web of deserved trust."

> 11. "Top VCs get to see the most interesting investment opportunities, but the opportunity cost of saying yes to an investment is that they take themselves out of the running for everything else in that category going forward."

The opportunity cost of investing in a particular company is that the venture capitalist will usually decide not to invest in other companies in the same category because of a conflict of interest. The greater the probability that a given company will pivot into another category, the more nervous the venture capitalist should be about potential conflict creating lost opportunities.

> 12. "All markets have boom-and-bust cycles, and I think the venture capital market has even more exaggerated boom-and-bust cycles."

Howard Marks once said, "Rule number one: Most things will prove to be cyclical. Rule number two: Some of the greatest opportunities for gain and loss come when other people forget rule number one." You cannot predict changes in the business cycle with certainty, but you can prepare for change. The cyclicality of the venture business may surprise newcomers but not an experienced investor like Wilson.

35

Ann Winblad

Hummer Winblad Venture Partners

ANN WINBLAD IS A founding partner of Hummer Winblad Venture Partners. She is a well-known and respected software industry entrepreneur and a pioneering role model and advocate for increasing the role of women in venture capital. Her firm's specialization in software investing was prescient. She is on the board of public and private firms, including MuleSoft. She began her career as a programmer at the Federal Reserve Bank. Prior to forming Hummer Winblad, she served as a strategy consultant at IBM, Microsoft, PricewaterhouseCoopers, and numerous start-ups. Winblad cofounded the accounting software company Open Systems Inc. in 1976, which was funded by an initial investment of $500 and later sold for $15 million. She has also coauthored the book *Object-Oriented Software*. Winblad is both a model for and a strong advocate of increasing the number of women involved in venture capital. She received a BA in mathematics and business administration from St. Catherine University and an MA in education and international economics from the University of Saint Thomas.

1. "We only fund software companies."

We don't fund inventions. We like inventions.

Winblad makes two important points here. The first is that she decided early in her career as a venture capitalist to invest only in software companies. She was ahead of her time in understanding the value of software and the value of specialization. The second point concerns the difference between an invention and a profitable business. Many people mistakenly think that an idea or invention is what makes for a successful startup. However, what makes a successful startup is a mutually reinforcing network of positive feedback loops that build from the core, which consists of innovation and a talented team. Talent, customer traction, partners, press, and money, all attract more of each other and, under the right conditions, can scale in nonlinear ways to become one of the very few grand slams that drive returns in the venture capital industry.

2. "We look closely at the products and technology to see if what you're going to deliver to market can at least for the foreseeable future deliver a sustainable competitive advantage."

If a business does not have a sustainable competitive advantage (a moat), what it does to create value can easily be copied or imitated, and the business will never see a profit that exceeds its opportunity cost of capital. This is such a simple idea, but it is frequently poorly understood. Having a great product or service is not enough to achieve significant profitability. Sometimes the only people who benefit from an innovative product or service are customers.

3. "We invest in markets. If the opportunity is not large, then the business, independent of the people or the technology, will fail. Because of this issue of intense competition

and capital efficiency, opportunities always get smaller
as soon as you fund the company."

Even with a moat and significant market share, if the relevant
market is small, the venture capitalist will never earn the financial returns that it takes to generate the grand-slam financial outcome he or she desires. Each venture capitalist can have only so
many startups in his or her portfolio, given that time is the venture
capitalist's scarcest asset. This means that a venture capitalist will
want to own a significant share of the equity in each startup. Only
very large opportunities justify that sort of investment since every
investment made by a venture capitalist must at the outset of the
investment potentially be capable of being a grand slam.

4. "Warren Buffett's quote, 'The market bats last,' means,
Have you figured out if there are customers out there?"

Do the dogs have their head in the dish? Are the customers
buying?

Completing the customer development process, during which a
startup tries to find product–market fit and create a minimum
viable product, is an essential step to complete before moving on
to scaling a business. If the dogs will not eat the startup's dog
food, the only alternative (that is not shutting down) is to pivot
the business or begin the customer discovery process again with a
restart. Which is when a highly adaptable team becomes particularly important.

5. "If you start a company, in order to get your engineering
team staffed, to hire your other executives, you've got
to get people to leave other jobs. So we look
at your ability to attract excellence."

The ability of any business to attract great employees is critically important, and the earliest hires are the most important hires, which is why venture capitalists often personally get involved in hiring—particularly in the earliest stages of a business.

6. "The role of venture capitalists is to be great opportunists. The visionaries are the entrepreneurs. I gave up my visionary hat when I moved to California and became a venture capitalist in the late '80s."

Venture capitalists who focus on enabling the entrepreneurs to be the visionaries rather than substituting their own vision will have far greater success. It is that simple. No one has a limitless source of ideas that will generate enough core product value to produce grand-slam results. Even the greatest entrepreneurs of our times have had a limited number of world-changing successes. Some founders have only one great success in their entire life.

7. "Startup building is hard. There is no manual for it."

You're always going to be short of people, you're always going to be short of money. . . . So you have to find leverage points versus working your way up through tiny little rungs and seeing if you get there. Think like a big dog and find leverage to get there.

Finding innovative ways to scale different aspects of a startup is a mission-critical activity. In other words, innovations are needed not only in terms of the product or service itself, but also in terms of how the company is created and how the product or service is developed and brought to market.

8. "What does separate some entrepreneurs from other entrepreneurs is they're not handwringers. They don't worry

about the unknown. They don't really worry
about the risk points ahead."

> As you get older and you get more experience, you train yourself
> to think ahead about the risk points versus just taking the next
> hill. But non-risk-takers and non-entrepreneurs would really
> have big headaches about this. They would need some level
> of comfort and safety. That's something that we look for in
> entrepreneurs—that they have the courage to do the job. That
> they'll have the ability to judge the business situation. They'll
> have the ability to lead people. They'll have the ability to interact
> with the marketplace and to really build confidence into strategy.

Uncertainty is fundamentally the friend of the rational investor.
Most founders instinctively know that uncertainty is what creates the
greatest opportunities since it causes others to misprice convexity.

9. "All we are is good pattern matchers, but we do look for a few indicators."

> One: Do they seem like they need control over everything that's
> not scalable?

> Two: Are they going to have a trusting relationship with all
> of their stakeholders, their employees, their partners, their
> customers, as well as their investors? Can we all grow together?

> And three: Do they have the intellectual and physical stamina to
> go the distance in building a company? It is very hard to build a
> company from scratch.

> The majority of companies fail by self-inflicted wounds [from]
> the leadership team.

Great founders and teams need a mix of skills, and for this reason
a diverse team is a stronger team. As Walt Kelly's comic strip character Pogo once famously said, "We have met the enemy and he is
us." Having a diverse team lowers the risk of groupthink. Diverse
teams can adapt faster and see solutions easier and more quickly.

10. "Errors of omission are to me as stupid as sins of selection."

The biggest mistakes in life are often the ones we do not make. The businesses a venture capitalist does not invest in and the people he or she does not recruit can be the biggest mistakes of all. As an analogy, Warren Buffett has said that one of the biggest mistakes he made was not investing in Walmart and that this "mistake of omission" probably cost Berkshire $10 billion. In venture capital, some of the best investors passed on or did not pursue Amazon, Facebook, and Google. Such mistakes of omission are an inevitable part of the profession.

11. "Being goal oriented and focused is a glass half full. You have to look at the positive and optimistic side. Women in particular should hold this glass in front of them all the time."

[When we] went out to raise our first fund, we had 132 meetings before we got our first commitment. Most people would have given up. But John [Hummer] and I were pretty competitive. The more noes we got, the more motivated we were. John neglected to tell me when we went out to raise the first fund that no new venture fund had been created for several years. I always pick bad economic times to start things.

These quotes remind me of a story about a boy and some horse manure. Worried that their young son was too optimistic, the boy's parents sent him to see a psychiatrist. The psychiatrist had seen this same condition in patients before. He took the child to a special room containing nothing but a huge pile of horse manure. The young boy immediately began digging into the pile of manure with his hands and gleefully cried out for everyone to hear, "With all this manure, there must be a pony in here somewhere!" This confirmed the diagnosis of "overly optimistic."

The best venture capitalists I know are optimists. Great venture capitalists power through bad news like that young boy pushed through that pile of manure. They are also tireless when doing things like helping recruit the right employees for their portfolio companies, connecting with potential limited partners, and receiving rejection after rejection. Winblad's experience is also another example of finding success in doing things at what otherwise seem to be the worst possible times.

12. "Mary Gates was an amazing person. She clearly was a great mother because she has three great children [including Bill Gates]. A great wife, she had a great and loving husband. Mary herself was active in the schools, on the board of the University of Washington, on multiple other boards.

> Whenever you would meet Mary, you got a handwritten thank-you note. And she always looked put together, she never looked tired, she always was present in the moment. I said to her, thirty years ago, "Mary, how do you find time for all this?" At this point in time, I am a relatively young venture capitalist, I'm not on that many boards, I haven't yet joined my university board, and I haven't joined a nonprofit board yet. She said, "You know, Ann, it's amazing how much time you really have, and how much time you waste, and how much time you can find for others, how much time you can find to sit down quietly and thank others, how much time you can find for kindness, let alone how much time you can find for contributing your own intellectual capital, as well as your financial capital. As you get older, you'll find that you actually get even better at that." And that was a real inspiration to me, to say, hey, it's not about how fast you pedal, it's about how clearly you focus.

Other than my own family, Mary Gates and her husband, Bill Gates Sr., have had more to do with who I am as a person than anyone else. Mary Gates was a dynamo far ahead of her time. She was whip smart and liked by everyone she met. She sat on many boards before it was common for women to do so. She helped many people, including me, at key points in their careers. For example, she was the person who convinced me to work in the mobile industry in the 1980s. She knew about the opportunity because she was on the board of one of the very first "cellular" companies. People like Ann Winblad carry on Mary Gates's tradition of being a role model for women in the venture world, and everywhere.

I like ending the book with this last quote from Winblad since the biggest opportunity that exists in the venture capital business comes from involving as diverse a group of people as possible. Great diversity makes systems more agile, resilient, and productive. Staying close to the warmth of the herd was a good strategy for most of human evolution. But great entrepreneurs and great venture capitalists are not normal people. They are oddballs in the best possible sense of the word, and no two of them are exactly alike.

Conclusion

VENTURE CAPITAL IS FUNDAMENTALLY a service business. Success in the venture business requires hustle, wisdom, judgment, hard work, and some luck. The venture capitalists I admire most love to spend their time and effort building real businesses. They always have a strong understanding of finance, but for them, finance is an enabler of what they most love to do. The right financial structure does not mean anything if all it does is guarantee a high percentage of nothing. One way to look at venture capital investing is as a stool with three legs: people, markets, and product innovation. All three legs are essential for success, but different venture capitalists put different emphasis on different legs at different times. A successful business is a result of success happening in many dimensions and feeding back on itself. Talented and hardworking people, customer traction, partners, brand value, and money all attract more of each other and, under the right conditions, can be scaled in nonlinear ways to allow a startup to become one of the small number of successes that drive the venture capital industry's financial returns each year. The venture capitalist's job is to be an important hub that helps enable this phenomenon to happen. After reading this book, I hope you now understand that implementing these ideas is more of an art than a science. Never stop learning.

Glossary

A round: *See* Series A.

Accelerator: An organization offering startups a system to accelerate the growth of their business, often in return for equity in the participating company.

Adviser: An individual able to provide founders with business advice, access to networks, and other forms of support.

Alpha: A measure of an investment's performance in relation to a benchmark such as an index.

Angel: A wealthy individual who makes direct investments in early-stage businesses. Some angel investors are professional investors in seed-stage companies, whereas others engage in this type of investing on a part-time basis.

Asset class: A group of assets that exhibit similar characteristics in markets (e.g., equities, bonds, cash equivalents).

Balance sheet: A financial statement that identifies the assets, liabilities, and shareholders' equity of a business.

Barrier to entry: *See* Moat.

Board of directors: A group of individuals who represent stockholders with regard to significant company decisions.

Bootstrap: To finance a company using personal funds and reinvesting the profits of the business itself (derives from the phrase "to pull oneself up by one's bootstraps").

315

Business model: The way that a business converts innovation into economic value.

Burn rate: A metric reflecting how quickly a business spends its capital, typically calculated over monthly or annual periods.

Capitalization table: A spreadsheet or table depicting ownership held by each investor.

Chicken and egg: A situation in which two or more factors can produce the desired result only when all are present.

Circle of competence: The perimeter of the area within which a person has knowledge and expertise which is superior to an average investor.

Complex adaptive system: Consists of three characteristics. The first is that the system consists of a number of heterogeneous agents, each of whom makes decisions about how to behave. The most important aspect of this element is that the decisions evolve over time. The second characteristic is that the agents interact with one another. That interaction leads to the third characteristic, something that scientists call *emergence*: the whole becomes greater than the sum of the parts. The key issue is that one cannot understand the whole system by simply looking at its individual parts.

Contrarian investing: Investing in businesses in ways that are contrary to the views of most other investors (i.e., not following the crowd).

Convexity: In the context of venture capital, significant asymmetry between potential for gains (large) and the losses (small or harmless).

Correlation: How asset prices move in relation to each other.

Crowdfunding: A process of funding a startup by raising relatively small amounts of capital (typically via the internet) from a larger number of people (the crowd) than is typical in raising capital from professional venture investors.

Cumulative advantage: When something happens to be slightly more popular than its competitors at just the right point, it tends to become still more popular. *See also* Matthew effect.

Customer Development Process: A systematic approach to discovering a repeatable and scalable business model.

Deal flow: A combination of the quality of and the rate at which investment proposals are generated by a venture capitalist.

Dilution: A reduction in an investor's ownership associated with a new financial investment.

Discounted cash flow (DCF): Discounting the net cash flows from an investment at an appropriate interest rate.

Distribution: Returning capital to partners following a liquidity event.

Down round: A financing round in which the valuation of a business is lower than in the previous round.

Due diligence: The process of investigating, analyzing, and assessing individuals and institutions prior to engaging in a transaction.

Early stage: investing in a startup well before it is fully formed; can include seed stage but also additional financing round.

Elevator pitch: A presentation by a founder to a potential investor to promote his or her business that lasts only a few minutes (about as long as an elevator ride).

Equity: Ownership of shares in a company.

Exit: The sale of a portfolio investment in either whole or in part, including corporate acquisitions, secondary buyouts, and initial public offerings. Also called a liquidity event.

Extrapolation: Making predictions about the future based on past trends and present data.

Founder: A person who initiates and fosters the creation of a new business.

Free cash flow: Cash available after expenses, debt service, capital expenditures, and dividends are taken into account.

Fund: A collection of capital commitments from investors that form a pool for making investments.

General partner: A person or entity in a limited partnership who manages a fund. The general partner earns a management fee and receives a percentage of the carried interest if the fund is successful.

Grand slam: In venture capital, a term that refers to an investment that produces a distributed spendable (liquid) return of one or more times the size of an entire venture capital fund.

Gross margin: The amount of revenue remaining after subtracting cost of goods sold.

Growth hypothesis: How new customers will discover and purchase a product or service.

Hedge: The purchase of an asset intended to deliver an inverse return to another asset to offset the impact of price changes.

Heuristic: A mental shortcut that enables a person to solve problems and make judgments quickly; a mental rules of thumb. These shortcuts can sometimes cause bias and result in mistakes.

Income statement: A document identifying the profit or loss of a business.

Incubator: An organization established to support the development of startups, typically by providing office and lab space and access to advisers; an incubator is more focused on generating ideas than an accelerator.

Initial public offering (IPO): The initial offering of publicly available shares of stock by a private company.

Internal rate of return: The discount rate at which the present value of all future cash flows are equal to the initial investment.

Investment thesis: The fundamental idea that is the basis for a plan to create new value.

Intrinsic value: The present value of future cash flows.

Investment: The purchase of an asset to generate a return.

Investment bank: A financial institution that provides services such as serving as an agent or underwriter when new securities are issued.

Investor: An individual or organization that commits money to investment products with the expectation of financial return and that is trying to assess the value of an asset rather than the behavior of other people (i.e., an investor is not a speculator).

Key performance indicators: Metrics used to determine the performance and state of a business.

Late stage: A period of venture capital investment that occurs later in the lifetime of a business.

Lead investor: The primary financier of the financing round; this investor performs certain functions like setting the price per share of the financing round.

Lean Startup: a scientific approach to creating and managing startups designed to get a desired product to customers' hands faster.

Limited partner: An investor who invests capital in a limited partnership.

Limited partnership: An organization in which a general partner and its various limited partners conduct business and the liability of the limited partner is bounded by a limit.

Liquidation: The process of selling assets in order to pay creditors and/or shareholders.

Liquidation preference: The right of an investor to priority in receiving proceeds from the liquidation of a business.

Liquidity: A measure of how easy it is to sell an asset for cash or a cash equivalent.

Liquidity event: Selling an asset such as equity or liquid assets such as cash or stock enabling a return of capital to investors. Also called an exit.

Lollapalooza: A term coined by Charlie Munger describing a phenomenon driven by feedback that creates an outcome that can be either positive or negative and is more than the sum of its parts.

Long: To buy something based on a prediction that its price will go up.

Macroeconomics: The study of the aggregate behavior of an economy.

Management fee: A fee charged by a venture capital fund for its management services, often 2 percent of the assets under management.

Margin of safety: In finance, the difference between the intrinsic value and the market price of the asset.

Matthew effect: A phenomenon in which "the rich get richer and the poor get poorer." *See also* Cumulative advantage.

Mental model: A working cognitive representation of phenomena with which people interact.

Micro VC: A professional venture capitalist who invests at early stages in the life of a startup, primary at seed stage or a follow-on to a series A investment.

Microeconomics: The study of the individual elements that make up an economy.

Minimum viable product (MVP): A product offering that has just enough features to allow the product to be deployed.

Moat: A barrier to market entry by competitors that enables a business's sustainable value creation. A company with a moat must sustainably be able to generate returns in excess of its cost of capital and earn an economic return higher than the average of its competitors. Factors that can create a moat against competitors include brand, regulation, supply-side economies of scale, network effects, and intellectual property.

Mr. Market: A metaphor to describe the unpredictable nature of markets in the short term.

Net present value: The present value of the cash flows from an investment less the cost of the investment.

Network effects: Demand-side economies of scale that exist when the value of a format or system depends on the number of users. These effects can be positive (e.g., a telephone network) or negative (e.g., traffic congestion). They can also be direct (e.g., increases in usage leading to direct increases in value to users, as with the telephone) or indirect (e.g., usage increasing the production of complementary goods, as with cases for mobile phones).

Nonlinear: When the aggregate behavior of a system is much more complex than would be predicted by summing the inputs into the system; output is not proportional to input.

Opportunity cost: The value of a foregone alternative.

Option: The right of a holder of a contract to purchase a specified amount of a security or other assets at a specified price at some defined point in the future.

Optionality: The potential for options. In finance, a situation where the investor has alternative opportunities in addition to the one that he or she is presently pursuing.

Path dependence: Occurs whenever there is an element of persistence or durability in a decision.

Pitch deck: A presentation created by founders to promote a potential investment.

Pivot: Occurs when a startup pursues a new direction by leveraging what it has learned from previous experience; pivots are not complete restarts.

Platform: A market with multiple sides that creates value by enabling direct interactions between two or more customer groups.

Portfolio company: A business that has received an equity investment from a venture capital firm or other investor.

Power law: A functional relationship between two quantities in which a relative change in one quantity results in a proportional relative change in the other quantity, independent of the initial size of those quantities; one quantity varies as a power of another.

Preferred stock: Shares that include terms that ensure preference over common stock with respect to factors such as dividends or payments.

Product–market fit (PMF): The state of having a product that satisfies market demand.

Present value: the current worth of a future sum of money or stream of cash flows (or payments) that will be received in the future.

Scalability: The ease with which a new business can increase a factor like growth.

Security: A debt or equity instrument issued by a private firm or government.

Seed stage: The earliest stage of venture capital investing; a period when relatively small investments are typically made in startups that typically consist of little more than the founders, an idea, some early employees, and a bit of progress toward establishing product–market fit.

Series: Financing rounds that typically occur around certain milestones that are categorized by means of a letter depending on how many rounds have occurred beyond seed stage in the past (e.g., series A, B, C, and D rounds).

Series A: A company's first post–seed stage round of venture capital funding.

Speculator: A person trying to guess the future price of an asset by guessing what the behavior of others will be in the future.

Stock: A share of ownership in a company.

Term sheet: An outline of the structure of an investment or other transaction agreed upon before the final binding agreement.

Tipping point: The moment that critical mass is achieved in some aspect of a business.

Unicorn: A startup that has been valued at $1 billion or more through either private or public investment, in many cases before terms such as liquidation preferences are considered.

Value hypothesis: whether a product or service really delivers value to customers once they are using it.

Venture capital: A type of private equity that focuses on investments in businesses with high-growth potential over the long term.

Venture capital fund: A committed pool of capital raised periodically by venture capitalists, usually in the form of a limited partnership. The fund typically has a fixed life measured in years (although extensions of several years are often possible to obtain from investors).

Venture partner: an individual engaged by a venture capital firm to source and manage investments but one who is not a general partner.

Virality: A measure of how often existing customers generate more customers via referrals.

Volatility: The fluctuation of a variable such as a market price over time.